Intellectual Property Law in Denmark

Intellectual Property Law in Denmark

Fifth Edition

Thomas Riis

This book was originally published as a monograph in the International Encyclopaedia of Laws/Intellectual Property Law.

Founding Editor: Roger Blanpain
General Editor: Frank Hendrickx
Volume Editor: Hendrik Vanhees

Wolters Kluwer

Published by:
Kluwer Law International B.V.
PO Box 316
2400 AH Alphen aan den Rijn
The Netherlands
E-mail: lrs-sales@wolterskluwer.com
Website: www.wolterskluwer.com/en/solutions/kluwerlawinternational

Sold and distributed by:
Wolters Kluwer Legal & Regulatory U.S.
920 Links Avenue
Landisville, PA 17538
United States of America
E-mail: customer.service@wolterskluwer.com

ISBN 978-94-035-1899-2

e-Book: ISBN 978-94-035-1909-8
web-PDF: ISBN 978-94-035-1919-7

The Author

Thomas Riis was born in 1966. He obtained an M.Sc. (Business Administration and Commercial Law) from Copenhagen Business School in 1991; an LLM (specializing in intellectual property law) from Queen Mary and Westfield College, University of London in 1994; a PhD from Copenhagen Business School in 1996; and an LLD (dr.jur.) from Copenhagen Business School in 2006. Since 2010, he has been employed at the Centre for Information and Innovation Law at the Law Faculty of the University of Copenhagen as a professor in innovation law. His primary research fields are intellectual property law, law & economics, information technology law and the law of marketing practice. He has published various books and articles within his research fields.

The Author

Table of Contents

List of Abbreviations

CJEU	Court of Justice of the European Union
CPC	Community Patent Convention
DKK	*Danske kroner* (the Danish Currency)
DSMD	Directive (EU) 2019/790 on copyright and related rights in the Digital Single Market
EC	European Community
EEA	European Economic Area
EEC	European Economic Community
EPC	European Patent Convention
EPO	European Patent Organization
EU	European Union
EUIPO	European Union Intellectual Property Office
FT	*Folketingstidende* (the Gazette of Folketinget [the Danish Parliament])
NATO	North Atlantic Treaty Organization
Ø	*Østre Landsret* (Eastern Court of Appeal) (when used as a suffix to *Ugeskrift for Retsvæsen* [the Danish Weekly Courts Report])
O.J.	Official Journal
PCT	Patent Cooperation Treaty
PLT	Patent Law Treaty
SCPA	US Semiconductor Chip Protection Act (1984)
SH	*Sø-og Handelsretten* (Maritime and Commercial Court) (when used as a suffix to *Ugeskrift for Retsvæsen* [the Danish Weekly Courts Report])
TRIPs	Agreement on Trade-Related Aspects of Intellectual Property
V	*Vestre Landsret* (Western Court of Appeal) (when used as a suffix to *Ugeskrift for Retsvæsen* [the Danish Weekly Courts Report])

List of Abbreviations

VAT	Value Added Tax
WIPO	World Intellectual Property Organization
WTO	World Trade Organization

General Introduction

§1. General Background

1. Denmark is a constitutional monarchy, reigned by King Frederik X since 2024. The national flag '*Dannebrog*' is a white cross on a red background.

I. Geography

2. Denmark is located in northern Europe, in the southernmost part of the Nordic countries, bordering the Baltic Sea on the east and the North Sea on the west. It is separated from Norway by the Skagerrak and from Sweden by the Kattegat and the Oresund and shares a 69 km border with Germany, which is the only Danish land frontier. The country has an area of 43,075 km^2. The three main parts of the country are the peninsula Jutland (*Jylland*), north of Germany; the islands Funen (*Fyn*); and Zealand (*Sjælland*), on which the capital Copenhagen is located. The three parts are connected by bridges. The country comprises 405 smaller islands. The many Danish islands make a total coastline of more than 7,000 km.

The terrain ranges from low and flat to gently rolling plains. The highest natural point is '*Møllehøj*', measuring 170.86 m. Denmark has 1,032 named lakes, which make a total area of 700 km^2. The largest one is Arresø, with an area of 37 km^2. The deepest lake is Furesø, with a depth of 36 m. Besides the capital, Copenhagen, the major cities are Århus, Aalborg and Odense. The Kingdom of Denmark also includes the autonomous areas of Greenland (area: 2.2 mill. km^2, population 56,699 (2024)) and the Faroe Islands (area: 1,400 km^2, population 53.664 (2024)).

A. *Climate and Vegetation*

3. Denmark has a temperate sea climate. The weather is often humid and overcast. The winters are relatively mild and windy, and the summers are cool. The temperatures in Copenhagen range normally between –2°C and 3°C in February and between 11°C and 20°C in June. The precipitation differs in various locations but amounts on average annually to 782 mm.

Denmark is part of Europe's temperate deciduous forest belt. The natural vegetation in most of the country is a mixed forest in which the beech is the most common tree. Nowadays, most parts of the country are under cultivation, and virtually all the existing forests have been planted. In 1805, Denmark had a 4% forest cover.

Since then, the forest cover has steadily been increasing and now makes up 14,6% of the land surface. Approximately 61% of the land surface is used for agricultural production.

II. Cultural Compositions

4. The Danes descend from various Germanic tribes, and the country was settled approximately 10,000 years ago.

By virtue of section 4 of the Constitutional Act, the Evangelical Lutheran Church is the established church of Denmark and as such is supported by the State. 73.2% of the population are members of the Evangelical Lutheran Church. It is estimated that 2% are other kinds of Protestants and Roman Catholics, and 15% have other religions. Immigrants and their descendants comprise 8.7% of the population. The ten most significant countries of origin of the immigrants in descending order are mentioned herewith: Turkey, Poland, Romania, Ukraine, Syria, Germany, Iraq, Lebanon, Pakistan and Iran. During the last decade, heavy restrictions on immigration have been adopted, and in recent years, right-wing political parties campaigning against the cultural influence of groups with a foreign ethnical background have gained widespread support in the population.

Danish is a Germanic language of the Nordic branch that is, to a certain extent, mutually intelligible to Norwegian and Swedish.

III. Political System

5. Similar to most other Western countries, the Danish democracy is based on the tripartition of power. Accordingly, the supreme power in Denmark is divided into three independent organs that control one another: the legislative, the executive and the judicial powers. The legislative branch consists of the unicameral Parliament called *Folketinget*. *Folketinget* has 179 seats, and its members are elected by popular vote on the basis of proportional representation to serve four-year terms. The legislative and executive powers are balanced against each other in the sense that a majority among the 179 members of *Folketinget* can overthrow a Cabinet or a Minister by presenting an order paper that contains a vote of no confidence. On the other hand, the Prime Minister can dissolve *Folketinget* at any time in the hope of gaining a more stable majority.

Any member of *Folketinget* can introduce a bill. A bill shall be read three times in *Folketinget* before it can be adopted. The thoroughness of legislation is safeguarded by the committee works that come between the first and second readings in the Chamber.

When Denmark's first democratic parliament was constituted by the Constitutional Act of 1849, no political parties existed. Individuals were elected solely on the basis of their personal qualities and points of view. The first political parties appeared around 1870. In order to stand for Parliament, the parties shall either have been elected to Parliament previously or should have collected the number of signatures corresponding to 1/175 of the votes cast in the latest election which amounts to approximately 20,000 signatures. By virtue of section 56 of the Constitutional Act, the members of *Folketinget* shall be bound solely by their own conscience and not by any directions given by their electors. Nevertheless, members of political parties are expected to follow the line that the party has agreed upon. There are different practices in the various parties as to the extent to which deviations are accepted.

After the latest general election, the following twelve political parties gained seats in *Folketinget:* Social Democrats (fifty seats); Liberals (thirty-four seats); The Moderates (sixteen seats); Socialist People's Party (fifteen seats); The Liberal Alliance (fourteen seats); The Danish Democrats (fourteen seats); Conservatives (ten seats); Unity List – Red-Green Alliance (nine seats); Social Liberals (seven seats); The Alternative (six seats); The New Conservatives (six seats); and Danish People's Party (five seats). In addition, four members of *Folketinget* are affiliated with exclusive Greenlandic and Faroese parties.

IV. Population Statistics

6. Apart from the period 1981–1984, the Danish population has been increasing. By April 2024, the population was 5,967,824, and the annual rate of population growth was 0.80%. The rate of growth includes a total fertility rate per woman of 1.49%. The sex ratio at birth is 1.07 males/females. Of the total population, 50.29% are females. The sex ratio reflects the fact that females have a higher life expectancy at birth (83.1 years) than males (79.4 years).

In 2023, the share of the population under 16 years of age was 17%; the share of the population between 16 and 66 was 64 %, and the share of the population older than 66 was 19%.

The population density is 138 per km^2. 88% of the population lives in urban areas, and 12% of the population lives in rural areas. The largest city, Copenhagen, including surrounding areas, accounts for approximately 20% of the Danish population.

§2. Historical Background

7. The Danes of the Viking Age (787–1066) successfully raided various foreign countries. The nautical skills of the Vikings and the characteristic Viking longships were probably the most important reason for the superiority of the Vikings in battles. At the height of the Viking era, the Danish king *Knud den Store* (Canute the Great) (1018–1035) ruled over a vast kingdom that included present-day Denmark, England, Norway and South Sweden. After the death of *Knud den Store*, the empire disintegrated.

The Danish king *Harald Blåtand* (Harald Black-Tooth) was baptized in 965, and during the following 100 years, Christianity became widespread. The five-year-old Crown Prince Olof of Norway was elected King of Denmark in 1375 with his mother, Queen Margaret of Norway as regent. From 1389 to 1396, Queen Margaret of Norway and Denmark united all the Nordic countries as a single kingdom, the

Kalmar Union, under the underage Eric of Pomerania. The Kalmar Union was dissolved in 1523 when the Swedes revolted as a reaction to the 'Stockholm bloodbath' performed by King Christian II of Denmark. Denmark and Norway remained united.

In 1429, duty on goods through Øresund was instituted by Eric of Pomerania. The duty created animosity among many foreign powers.

From 1534 to 1536, a civil war took place between the rivals to the throne. The primary policy issues of the war were a dispute on the Hanseatic influence and whether a national Lutheran State Church should be established. After the war, the Hanseatic influence was broken, the Reformation took place and Denmark became Lutheran in 1536.

At the end of the eighteenth century, the agricultural sector was significantly reformed. Villages were split into separate farms, so farmers came to live closer to their land, more distant from their neighbours. The detested serfdom, *Stavnsbåndet*, was abolished in 1788. *Stavnsbåndet* was introduced in 1733 and implied that male peasants under the age of 36 were disallowed to move from the manor without consent of the landowner. At that time, less than 5% of the land was owned by peasants. During the reforms at the end of the eighteenth century, most farms were sold to the peasants, and consequently, in 1815, 60% of the farmers owned their own land.

At the Battle of the Roadstead of Copenhagen (*Slaget på Reden*) in 1801, Denmark was attacked by the British fleet under Admiral Nelson and forced to retreat from the Armed Neutral Alliance with Sweden and Russia. Six years later, the British fleet under Wellington bombarded Copenhagen, and Denmark became a French ally. However, the alliance with Napoleon became a disaster for Denmark. The country went bankrupt, and in the treaty of Kiel, among other things, Denmark had to cede Norway to Sweden.

In 1849, wide-ranging social and educational reforms took place, and King Frederik VII authorized a new Constitutional Act instituting a representative form of government. The Constitutional Act with subsequent amendments is still in force. Parliamentarism was introduced in 1901, implying that no government could rule against the majority of the Parliament.

During World War I, Denmark remained neutral. At the beginning of World War II, Denmark had declared itself neutral. Nevertheless, on 9 April 1940, Germany occupied Denmark, and the Danish government gave up military resistance. The Danes retained control of their government and parliament. Most of the Danish Jews were evacuated to Sweden in 1943.

Denmark joined the North Atlantic Treaty Organization (NATO) in 1949 as one of the founding members. The country joined the European Community (EC) in 1972 after a referendum. In a referendum on the Maastricht Treaty in 1992, a small majority voted 'no' to the Treaty. A new referendum on the Maastricht Treaty was arranged the following year, allowing Denmark to opt out on issues such as the common European currency, citizenship, defence policy and police. The new referendum provided a 'yes' to the Treaty, which was strongly recommended by the government and the parliament. In an election in June 2022, a majority of the population voted to re-enter the EU's cooperation on defence policy.

Chapter 1. Copyright and Neighbouring Rights

§1. Sources – Legislation

8. Danish copyright law is statutory and based on the Copyright Act. The first Danish Copyright Act was enacted in 1741, and by that, Denmark probably became the first country on the European continent to enact a Copyright Act just thirty-two years after the world's first Copyright Act, the English Act of Anne, from 1709. The Danish Act, however, was not influenced by the Act of Anne.

A major revision of the 1961 Copyright Act was completed in 1995 after almost twenty years of preparations. Among other things, the results of the new Act were that the Act on Rights in Photographic Pictures, which provided sui generis protection of all photographs, was abolished and the relevant provisions were amended and incorporated into the new Copyright Act; the protection of works of visual arts was increased; the protection of producers of sound recordings and recordings of moving pictures was increased; the characteristic Nordic system of extended collective licences was elaborated; and the term of protection was extended. In preparation for the new Act, a Committee on a Revision of the Copyright Act was established; from 1981 to 1990, the Committee issued eight reports on various copyright-related problems.[1] The reports are important contributions to the interpretation of the Act. Since the 1995 Act was adopted, the Copyright Act has been amended several times, among other things, in order to implement the EC copyright directives.

9. The Berne Convention for the Protection of Literary and Artistic works was ratified by Denmark in 1903. Moreover, Denmark is a party to the Universal Copyright Convention as revised in 1971, the Rome Convention for the Protection of Performers, Producers of Phonograms and Broadcasting Organizations of 1961, the Geneva Convention on Phonogram Protection of 1971, the Convention Relating to the Distribution of Programme-Carrying Signals Transmitted by Satellite of 1974, the Convention for the Protection of Producers of Phonograms Against Unauthorized Duplication of Their Phonograms of 1971 and the European Agreement on the Protection of Television Broadcasts of 1960 and subsequent protocols.

Denmark has implemented the Agreement on Trade-Related Aspects of Intellectual Property (TRIPs) Agreement and is a signatory to the World Intellectual Property Organization (WIPO) Copyright Treaty and the WIPO Performances and Phonograms Treaty.

10. In the area of intellectual property law, a close cooperation has developed between the Nordic Countries. In the period after 1972, when Denmark joined the

1. Report No. 912 Copenhagen 1981 '*Licenskonstruktioner og fotokopiering*'; Report No. 944 Copenhagen 1982 '*Båndafgift, sanktioner, påtale*'; Report No. 962 Copenhagen 1982 '*Beskyttelse af kunstneriske præstationer*'; Report No. 1000 Copenhagen 1984 '*Film-og videogramspørgsmål*'; Report No. 1038 Copenhagen 1985 '*Ophavsretligt biblioteksvederlag*'; Report No. 1063 Copenhagen 1986 '*Billedret*'; Report No. 1064 Copenhagen 1986 '*Ophavsret og edb*'; Report No. 1197 Copenhagen 1990 '*Slutbetænkning*'.

EC as the only Nordic country, Nordic cooperation was less important. Still, however, many similarities between the Nordic acts on intellectual property law exist, and case law from the other Nordic countries may to a certain extent have legal effects on Danish intellectual property law. Additionally, preparatory works from Norway and Sweden have been used to interpret provisions in the Danish Copyright Act.[2] The consolidated Copyright Act is, at present, Act. No. 1093 of 20 August 2023.[3]

In addition to the Copyright Act, an Act on Collective Management of Copyright was adopted in 2016.[4] This Act implements Directive 2014/26/EU of 26 February 2014 on collective management of copyright and related rights and multi-territorial licensing of rights in musical works for online use in the internal market.

§2. Subject Matter of Protection

11. Copyright is the most wide-ranging of the different intellectual property rights as regards protectable subject matter. Historically, copyright protection was related to aesthetic phenomena; however, gradually, functional and, most recently, creations of modern information technology have been incorporated into the copyright system.

I. Different Categories of Protected Works

12. By virtue of section 1 paragraph 1 of the Act, the person creating a literary or artistic work shall have copyright therein, be it expressed in writing or in speech as a fictional or a descriptive representation or whether it be a musical or dramatic work, cinematographic or photographic work, or a work of fine art, architecture, applied art or is expressed in some other manner. Thus, literary and artistic works are the two main categories of works. Pursuant to section 1 paragraphs 2 and 3, maps and drawings and other works of a descriptive nature executed in graphic or plastic form shall be considered literary works, and works in the form of computer programs shall be considered literary works too. The different categories of works mentioned in section 1 do not constitute an exhaustive list of protectable subject matter; all kinds of literary and artistic works are protectable subject matter irrespective of the form in which the work is expressed.

2. Cf. the Supreme Court case reported in *Ugeskrift for Retsvæsen* 1978.42 H.
3. Under the provisions of the Act, various regulations have been issued: Ordinance No. 218 of 9 Mar. 2010 on the Application of the Copyright Act in Relation to other Countries; Ordinance No. 1192 of 1 Sep. 2016 on the application of s. 30(1) and 30(2) of the Copyright Act; Ordinance No. 1146 of 25 Oct. 2014 on the diligent search for and registration of orphan works; Ordinance No. 2659 of 28 Dec. 2021 on a Levy System for Reproduction for private Purpose (Blank media levy); Ordinance No. 25 of 14 Jan. 2004 on the Copyright License Tribunal; Ordinance No. 763 of 2 Oct. 1997 on Settlement of the Costs of the Working of the Mediator Mentioned in s. 52 of the Copyright Act; Ordinance No. 197 of 5 Feb. 2015 on the procedural rules applicable to the authorization of collective administration organizations according to the Copyright Act.
4. Act No. 321 of 5 Apr. 2016.

Within the two main categories of works, in particular, the specific substantive provisions of the Act distinguish between literary works, musical works and works of fine art. Literary works include, in addition to, for example, novels, short stories, professional articles, poems, letters, speeches, interviews, etc., works expressed in Morse code, Braille, shorthand writing and the like. Musical works include all kinds of compositions in the form of music sheets, etc. Works of fine art include all kinds of works of visual arts, for example, paintings, drawings, mosaics, photographs, sculptures, reliefs, architectural works and works of applied art.

13. Adaptations of existing works are protected as independent works. The author of the adaptation has a right to control his/her work, but it is without prejudice to the copyright in the original work.[5] Similarly, by virtue of section 5, compilations of existing works or parts of works are protected as independent works, but the right is without prejudice to the rights in the individual works. Compilations of data that are not considered works or parts of works are protectable subject matter under section 1 of the Act.

14. A variety of different subject matters are protected by neighbouring rights (sections 65–72 of the Act, *see infra* paragraph 115-132.

15. Subject matter protected by neighbouring rights includes performances by performing artists, sound recordings, recordings of moving pictures, broadcasts, photographic pictures, compilations and databases, and press releases. Creations protected by neighbouring rights are not considered works within the meaning of the Copyright Act.

II. Works Excluded from Protection

16. The Copyright Act contains two provisions that explicitly exclude certain kinds of subject matter from protection. According to section 10 paragraph 2, layout designs (topographies) of semiconductor products are not protected under the Copyright Act but are protected under the provisions of the Act on Protection of Topographies of Semiconductor Products.[6] By virtue of section 9 paragraph 1, acts, administrative orders, legal decisions and similar official documents are not subject to copyright, no matter whether the documents have been created at the State level or at the municipal level. Hence, for example, final patent documents are not subject to copyright protection. The provision is relatively narrow since it does not apply to works appearing as independent contributions in the documents mentioned in section 9 paragraph 1. Such works may, however, be reproduced in connection with the document. The right to further use shall be subjected to the provisions otherwise in force.[7] It is significant to the public interest that statutory rules, case law, etc., are widely disseminated, ensuring the rule of law and that is the rationale

5. Cf. s. 4 para. 1 of the Act.
6. *See* Ch. 8.
7. Cf. s. 9 para. 2 of the Act.

behind section 9. Informative publications published by governmental bodies (e.g., annual reports, speeches, contributions to debates) are not excluded subject matter unless they must be considered equivalent to acts, administrative orders or legal decisions.[8] Reports from committees established by public bodies are not subject to copyright even in cases where the report is not considered to form part of the preparatory work of a statute. Research reports and consultant reports created by private research institutions are only excluded subject matter if they are presented as originating in public authority. Section 9 only applies to works in written form, including maps and drawings and other works of a descriptive nature. Thus, for example, cinematographic works, photographies, and works of architecture are not covered by the exclusion; additionally, computer programs in written form are not excluded as subject matter under section 9.[9]

Notes issued by the National Bank of Denmark have been held to be protectable subject matter under the Copyright Act.[10] Works containing soft law rules, such as codes of conduct created by business associations, are not excluded from protectable subject matter. Subject matter excluded under section 9 is also excluded from protection by the sui generis right in section 71 of the Act.[11]

III. Special Categories of Works

A. *Computer Programs*

17. By the amendment of the Copyright Act in 1989, computer programs were listed explicitly as protectable subject matter. The amendment did not result in any changes in substantive law because, prior to 1989, the predominant opinion was that computer programs were protected under the Copyright Act. The implementation in 1992 of the Council Directive 91/250/EEC of 14 May 1991 on the legal protection of computer programs involved only minor amendments of the Copyright Act in relation to computer programs. Computer programs are not defined in the Copyright Act, but in the preparatory works related to the 1989 Act, a computer program is defined as a series of instructions fixated in any form or on any medium with the purpose of directly or indirectly enabling a computer to execute a particular function.[12] The definition is not authoritative; thus, it is stated in the preparatory works that the definition may be used as a guideline. Nevertheless, computer software is considered a computer program within the meaning of the Copyright Act, no matter whether it is manifested in object code or source code or stored on a disk, in a ROM,

8. Cf. FT 1988–1989, A, col. 3212 ff.
9. Cf. FT 1988–1989, col. 3212 ff. In general, *see* P. Schønning, 'Retsbeskyttelse af offentlige dokumenter – ophavsretslovens § 9', *Juristen* (1990): 270–282.
10. Cf. *Ugeskrift for Retsvæsen* 1997.691 H; and *Ugeskrift for Retsvæsen* 1993.183 Ø.
11. Cf. s. 71 para. 5 of the Act.
12. FT 1988–1989, A, col. 3210. The definition is in conformity with the Computer Program Directive.

or in written form on paper.[13] Contrary to databases, computer programs are not granted protection by the sui generis right in section 71 of the Act.[14]

B. Databases

18. The EC Directive 96/9 of the European Parliament and of the Council of 11 March 1996 on the legal protection of databases was implemented in Danish copyright law by Act No. 407 of 26 June 1998. Prior to the 1998 amendments to the Copyright Act, databases were eligible for copyright protection under section 1 of the Act, and, in addition, databases were qualified for protection under the sui generis right in section 71 of the Act. In the preparatory works leading to the 1995 Copyright Act, it is stated that a work in digital form, including a compilation of unprotectable data, shall be granted protection pursuant to section 1 paragraph 1 of the Act, provided the creation constitutes a work within the meaning of the Act, that is, if the creation is a result of the author's own intellectual creative contributions.[15] Protection under section 1 of the Act relates to compilations of unprotectable data. Compilations of existing works or parts of works are protected under section 5 of the Act. The conditions of protection under section 1 and section 5 respectively are identical. If the conditions of copyright protection are not satisfied, that is, if the compilation is non-original, protection may be granted under section 71 of the Act. Protectable subject matter under section 71 are catalogues, tables, databases and similar works; that includes, for example, exhibition catalogues, library catalogues, telephone directories, arithmetical tables, timetables, price lists, exchange lists, calendars, lists of books and prize lists.

Copyright protection and protection by the sui generis right in section 71 are cumulative. A database is eligible for protection under the Copyright Act irrespective of the form in which the database is manifested; hence, protection also applies to non-electronic databases.

The implementation of the Database Directive did not result in any changes as regards protectable subject matter under sections 1 and 5 Copyright Act.

C. Works of Applied Art

19. Danish copyright law is not rigorous in granting protection of works of applied art, including industrial designs, even if the creations have a dominant purpose of application. Among others, the following types of products have been held to be protectable subject matter under the Copyright Act: furniture, lamps, carpets, vases, candlesticks, cutlery, silverware, service, shoes and garments. Works of

13. Cf. H. Udsen, *IT-ret*, 5th edn (Copenhagen: Ex Tuto Publishing, 2021), 117 ff, M.B. Andersen, *IT-retten*, 2nd edn (Copenhagen: Gjellerup, 2005), Ch. 7; T. Riis, *Immaterialret og IT* (Copenhagen: Jurist-og Økonomforbundets Forlag, 2001), 19 ff; and M. Rosenmeier, *Værkslæren i ophavsretten* (Copenhagen: Jurist-og Økonomforbundets Forlag, 2001), 193 ff.
14. Cf. FT 1988–1989, A, col. 3233.
15. Cf. FT 1994–1995: A, 1332.

applied art are considered artistic works within the meaning of the Act. The specific form of a protectable work of applied art shall be motivated by artistic or aesthetic considerations; if the form of the work is dictated by a practical function, as a main rule, the work does not qualify for copyright protection.[16]

§3. Conditions of Protection

I. Formal Requirements

20. In Danish copyright law, protection is not contingent on registration of the work. Copyright notice (©) is not required in order to obtain protection under the Act; however, it may serve the interest of the author to apply © on copies of the work because it indicates that the right owner intends to enforce the right.

21. The scope of the Copyright Act is laid down in section 85 of the Act. The provision of the Act is applicable to: (i) works of persons who are nationals of or who have their habitual residence in a country within the European Economic Area (EEA); (ii) works first published in a country within the EEA or first published simultaneously in a country within the EEA and in another country; (iii) cinematographic works, the maker of which has his/her headquarters or his/her habitual residence in a country within the EEA; (iv) buildings situated in a country within the EEA; and (v) works of art incorporated in a building or other structure in a country within the EEA.[17] The Minister for Culture may define more detailed rules under which the application of the provisions of the Copyright Act may be extended to other countries conditional upon reciprocity.[18] The Minister for Culture may also define more detailed rules under which the Act may be made applicable to works first published by international organizations and to unpublished works that such organizations are entitled to publish.[19]

II. Substantive Requirements

22. The central condition of copyright protection is originality. Only works that are considered original are protectable by copyright. The originality requirement is not explicitly stated in the Act but is derived by interpretation of the terms 'literary and artistic works' in section 1 paragraph 1 of the Act. The originality requirement implies that a work shall originate in the author and be the result of the author's own intellectual creative contributions; in other words, an original work will be marked

---

16. *See* in general, P. Møgelvang-Hansen, T. Riis & J. Trzqaskowski, *Markedsføringsretten*, 4th edn (Copenhagen: Ex Tuto, 2022), 565–566, E. Borcher, *Produktefterligninger*, 2nd edn (Copenhagen: Forlaget Thomson. GadJura, 2003), 72–115.
17. Cf. s. 85 para. 1 of the Act. The provisions in s. 85 are based on Arts 3, 5(4), 14*bis* and 15(2) of the Berne Convention.
18. Cf. s. 88 para. 1. Under this provision, Ordinance No. 218 of 9 Mar. 2010 on the Application of the Copyright Act in Relation to other Countries has been issued.
19. Cf. s. 88 para. 2 of the Act.

by the personality of the author. Hence, things pre-existing in nature passed on without being arranged by the author are not original. Originality shall not be construed as novelty. That means it is possible two identical works created independently – that is, if the author of the latest work did not know of the existence of the first work – can both satisfy the originality requirement. It is required that a work shall be created by a human in order to be considered original; works created by minors, mentally deranged persons, drunk persons, etc., are subject to the same originality requirement as works created by other persons.

As regards traditional literary and artistic works such as works of fine art and fiction, the originality threshold has been considered to be relatively low,[20] and practical problems seem not to have resulted for that reason. However, in *Ugeskrift for Retsvæsen* 1998.946 SH, it was held that the World Wide Fund for Nature's famous panda mark did not satisfy the conditions of protection under the Copyright Act; similarly, in *Ugeskrift for Retsvæsen* 2007.1112 H the Supreme Court found that two T-shirt designs were not eligible for protection under the Copyright Act on the ground that the two designs were created by juxtaposing known figures and forms found in a book. The number of different possible forms of expression for these kinds of works, in principle, is indefinite, and consequently, a low originality threshold does not create practical impediments for other authors in creating their own works.

The same does not apply to works of a mainly functional character, for example, works of applied art and industrial designs because the number of different possible forms of expression for these kinds of works is limited. If copyright protection of works of a mainly functional character is granted too generously, the production and marketing of certain ordinary and useful products may be monopolized by a few right owners, stifling competition in the markets for these products in a harmful way. Therefore, the originality threshold for works of a mainly functional character may appear relatively rigorous. As a practical guideline, it may be said that if there exists a risk of two authors creating identical works independently of each other, the works will probably not satisfy the originality requirement, or at least in that situation, the range of creations that are considered original is narrow.[21]

In several cases, the Danish courts, including the Supreme Court, have stated that a more rigorous originality requirement applies to works of applied art compared to other categories of works.[22] Arguably, this position is not in conformity with case law of the Court of Justice of the European Union (CJEU) that, in a number of cases,[23] has implied that the originality requirement has been harmonized in a uniform manner applying to all categories of works by means of the Infosoc Directive.[24] Thus, it is possible that a differentiated originality requirement, as applied by the Danish courts, is in conflict with the Infosoc Directive.

20. For various aspects of the originality requirement, *see* Rosenmeier (2001), and in relation to musical works, M. Rosenmeier, *Ophavsretlig beskyttelse af musikværker* (Copenhagen: Jurist-og Økonomforbundets Forlag, 1996).
21. *See* J. Schovsbo, M. Rosenmeier & C.S. Petersen, *Immaterialret,* 7th edn (Copenhagen: Jurist- og Økonomforbundets Forlag, 2024), 71 ff.
22. For example, cf. *Ugeskrift for Retsvæsen* 2012.229 H.
23. For example, case C-5/08 (Infopaq I), at 36–37.
24. Directive (2001/29/EF).

In the Supreme Court case reported in *Ugeskrift for Retsvæsen* 1993.17 H, the court should decide whether a system for betting in the State football pools was original within the meaning of the Copyright Act and hence protected by copyright. The court held that the fundamental ideas and methods were so simple that two creators with knowledge of this kind of system independently of each other were likely to create identical systems; consequently, such a system would not qualify for copyright protection unless a specific system is based on particularly original combinations that deviate from the fundamental ideas and methods, and two creators independently of each other are less likely to create identical systems.

In practice, most literary creations are considered original. However, printed forms and formulas are assumed not to qualify for copyright protection. Contract forms and similar legal documents may be considered original if they are the results of the author's creativity.[25]

23. Photographic pictures are protected by copyright if the originality requirement is satisfied; otherwise, photographic pictures are protected by the neighbouring right in section 70. The precise distinction between original and non-original photographic pictures is difficult to establish. According to the preparatory works to the 1995 Act, the following elements may be taken into account in determining originality: composition, cutting, choice of motif, perspective, angle, depth of field and light setting; furthermore, it is stated that originality requires that the author has made artistic choices.[26] Originality of photographic pictures has to be assessed on the basis of Article 6 of the Council Directive 93/98/EEC of 29 October 1993, harmonizing the term of protection of copyright and certain related rights. According to Article 6 interpreted in the light of No. 17 of the directive's recitals, a photograph is original if it is the author's own intellectual creation reflecting his/her personality; no other criteria such as merit or purpose shall be applied to determine a photograph's eligibility for protection.

24. No authoritative case law exists on the originality requirement in relation to computer programs. After the implementation of the Computer Programs Directive, the originality requirement in Article 1(3) applies, according to which a computer program is original if it is the author's own intellectual creation. No other criteria – such as tests as to the qualitative or aesthetic merits of the program – shall be applied to determine its eligibility for protection.[27] Probably, the originality threshold in Danish copyright law for computer programs has been reduced by the implementation of the Computer Programs Directive.

25. The Database Directive establishes a similar originality criterion, which is applicable to databases.[28] Thus, a database, which by reason of the selection or arrangement of its contents constitutes the author's own intellectual creation, is

25. Cf. Schovsbo, Rosenmeier & Petersen (2024), 83–84; and P. Schønning, *Ophavsretsloven med kommentarer*, 8th edn (Copenhagen: Karnov Group, 2024), 158.
26. FT 1994–1995, A, 1333.
27. Cf. the Recitals No. 8.
28. Cf. Art. 3(1) and the Recitals No. 16.

original and no other criteria shall be applied to determine its eligibility for protection. Interpreting the originality requirement in relation to databases, one should consult the case law on non-electronic databases and compilations. In the case reported in *Ugeskrift for Retsvæsen* 1980.689 Ø, the court should decide whether a 'Nature Almanac' qualified for copyright protection. The 'Nature Almanac' was a combined almanac and notebook. At each date in the almanac, a couple of short sentences describing events of nature which took place at that date, were adduced, for example, 3 January: 'The minimum distance between the sun and the earth is due.' In consideration of the information contained in the short sentences in total was not available from one source prior to the almanac, the court held that the compilation of the information in the 'Nature Almanac' and the idea of adducing one or more events of nature at each date in the almanac constituted an original work eligible for copyright protection under section 1 of the Act.

26. Early case law was rather restrictive in granting copyright protection of works with a dominant purpose of application. Accordingly, in several cases, works of applied art within the functionalistic style were not granted copyright protection. This situation was changed by a Supreme Court decision in 1961.[29] A cutlery set with polished and grooved handles was held to be eligible for copyright protection. According to an expert opinion, the grooved handles were the most characteristic part of the cutlery, but it was not considered anything new or an original idea in itself. The Supreme Court held that the specific form of the cutlery and the combination of particulars created an aggregate artistic effect that should be considered original. However, the court provided the right owner with a narrow scope of protection; hence, other authors were not excluded from creating cutlery with grooved handles. Apparently, copyright protection of a work of applied art within the functionalistic style requires an expert opinion on the specific character of the work, which can convince the court that the work is an original artistic creation.[30]

27. Works shall not satisfy a requirement of quantity or size; however, the quantity or size of a work may be so modest that the originality requirement cannot be satisfied; that is, the work cannot be considered the author's own intellectual creation. It has been held that the advertising slogan '*At købe sengeudstyr er en tillidssag*' (Buying bedding is a matter of confidence) is not an original literary work.[31] However, the title of the Ernest Hemingway novel *For Whom the Bell Tolls* was translated into *Hvem ringer klokkerne for?* and the Danish translation was held to be an original literary work.[32] It must be assumed that only in extraordinary cases do sentences as short as the translated titled of the Hemingway novel qualify for copyright protection.

28. Danish copyright law does not contain a requirement for fixation of the work. Accordingly, improvisations are eligible for copyright protection, cf. section

29. *Ugeskrift for Retsvæsen* 1961.1027 H.
30. Cf. M. Koktvedgaard & J. Schovsbo, *Lærebog i immaterialret*, 7th edn (2005), 70.
31. Cf. *Ugeskrift for Retsvæsen* 1932.211 Ø.
32. Cf. *Ugeskrift for Retsvæsen* 1951.725 H.

1 paragraph 1 of the Act: 'a literary or artistic work … expressed … in speech … '. However, in most cases, copyright protection gains practical significance only when the work is fixated. For example, in a court case concerning infringement of a work, the right owner has to provide evidence as to the existence of the work and that is difficult without some kind of manifest of the work; obviously, this may not apply if the alleged infringing act is the actual fixation of the work.

§4. Ownership

I. The Author

29. The owner of copyright is the person creating the work. Copyright cannot originate in a legal person; however, a legal person can be assigned the copyright.

Section 7 paragraph 1 of the Act contains a legal presumption as to who is entitled to make decisions on the exploitation of a literary or artistic work. It is stipulated that, when not otherwise stated, the person whose name or generally known pseudonym or signature is indicated in the usual manner on copies of the work or when the work is made available to the public, that person shall be deemed to be the author. Section 7 paragraph 2 adds that if a work is published without the author being indicated in accordance with section 7 paragraph 1, the editor, if named, and otherwise the publisher, shall act on behalf of the author until the latter is named in a new edition of the work. The section contains a rule of evidence that is based on Article 15 of the Berne Convention.

II. Multi-author Works/Works Created by Several Persons

30. When a work has two or more authors, without the individual contributions being separable as independent works, the copyright in the work shall be held jointly. Each of the authors, however, may bring an action for infringement.[33] In the preparatory works to the 1961 Act, it is stated that the use of a multi-author work requires authorization from all authors involved unless something else is implied under the circumstances. Presumably, the statement in the preparatory work shall not be construed too rigorously, resulting in a situation where a single author of the multi-author work always has the opportunity to block the use of the work.

If a work can be separated into two or more independent works, such as lyrics combined with a musical composition and illustrations used in a literary work, it is not a multi-author work within the meaning of section 6, but each author can decide on the exploitation of his/her own independent work unless the authors have agreed that the works shall be exploited jointly. When a work is the result of contributions of several persons, a distinction of large practical importance concerns the question of who is considered an author and who is merely considered a technical assistant. The contribution of a technical assistant is not granted copyright protection. The

33. Cf. s. 6 of the Act.

contribution of each person has to be assessed with respect to the conditions of protectability, in particular, with respect to the originality requirement. A person who executes directions from others does not benefit from copyright protection; thus, the bronze founder who is following the directions of the sculptor is not granted copyright in the final sculpture. Co-ownership of copyright requires that the author has made independent artistic choices, perhaps within certain limits. A person other than the author who makes a fair copy of a literary work, does proofreading, edits notes, prepares index and table of contents, and researchers used by a journalist for an article are not co-owners of copyright in the work. Usually, the copyright to an interview is owned by the interviewer, but it may be shared by the person interviewed.[34]

III. Works Made for Hire

31. A person who has commissioned an author to create a literary or artistic work is not granted co-ownership of the copyright in the work. As a general rule, the commissioner of a work is not granted any rights in the work. The commissioner only acquires the right to the copy of the work, unless the author has assigned his/her right to the commissioner or some other arrangement has been agreed upon. However, even if no agreement between the author and the commissioner has been entered into to that effect, normally, certain limitations on the author's use of a commissioned work apply. As a practically occurring situation, it is often implied between the parties that the author is not entitled to produce more copies of the work than the one acquired by the commissioner. The rationale behind this principle is expressed in the Copyright Act in relation to copyrighted portraits. By virtue of section 60 of the Act, the author shall not have the right to exercise his/her right in a commissioned portrait without the consent of the commissioner. The limitation applies to photographic pictures, paintings, drawings and portraits in other forms. Consent shall be given by the commissioner, who is not necessarily the same person portrayed. The right of the commissioner is not subject to succession; when the commissioner is deceased, the author can exercise his/her copyright without limitations. Furthermore, the right of the commissioner is closely connected to the existence of copyright in the portrait; if the portrait is not copyrighted, for example, if the copyright has expired, the commissioner has no rights pursuant to section 60 of the Copyright Act.

Copyright in works created and submitted as contributions to a prize competition is owned by the creator unless otherwise clearly provided under the terms of the competition.

34. Cf. Schovsbo, Rosenmeier & Petersen (2024), 83, and M. Rosenmeier, 'Har intervieweren ophavsret til den interviewedes udtalelser? Nogle bemærkninger til Högsta domstolens dom af 26.11.1996, NJA 1996 s. 712 ff; NIR 1997 s. 277 ff', *Nordiskt Immateriellt Rättsskydd* (2003), 57 ff.

§5. TRANSFER

32. Sections 53–62 contain various provisions on the transfer of copyrights. These provisions are, to a large extent, non-mandatory rules; hence, the provisions of sections 54–59 on assignment of copyright may be deviated from by agreement between the parties except where otherwise provided in the individual provisions.[35]

I. Assignment of Copyright[36]

33. Subject to the limitations following from section 3 on moral rights and section 38 on *droit de suite*, the copyright owner may wholly or partially assign his/her rights under the Copyright Act.[37] Future rights (e.g., copyright on unspecified works that have not yet come into existence) are assignable provided the parties involved are informed of the consequences of the assignment and provided the assignment is not void according to the rules of the Contracts Act; the grounds of voidability primarily are fraud, duress, undue influence, unconscionability and forgery. In the case reported in *Ugeskrift for Retsvæsen* 2002.1224 H, a composer entered into an agreement in 1925 with a music publisher on the assignment of the copyright to a musical work and the division of royalties from that work. In the following decades, the musical work proved to be extremely successful, and in conformity with the contract during the years, the music publisher received very high sums of royalties from the work. On the basis of section 36 of the Contracts Act on unconscionability, the Supreme Court in 2002 declared the contract void on the grounds that the contract provided the music publisher significant benefits without imposing countervailing duties.

34. In the case reported in *Ugeskrift for Retsvæsen* 2022.2949 H, a rock band had, by means of a music publishing contract in 1993, assigned the exclusive rights to all compositions worldwide to a music publisher. Decades later, a dispute arose between the parties on whether the assignment included rights to use the compositions in music dramatical works (musicals, etc.). The Supreme Court held that the provisions on the assignment of rights were detailed and clear, and it appeared from the contract that the list of possible forms of exploitation of the compositions was not exhaustive. According to the wording, the publishing agreement thus implied a complete transfer of all rights to commercial exploitation of the compositions in question. As a consequence, the publishing contract could not be declared void pursuant to section 36 of the Contracts Act on unconscionability.

35. Cf. s. 53 para. 4 of the Act.
36. In general on the assignment of copyrights, *see* J. Blomqvist, *Overdragelse af ophavsrettigheder. Rettighedsoverdragelsen og dens fortolkning* (Copenhagen: Jurist-og Økonomforbundets Forlag, 1986); and J. Schovsbo, *Immaterialretsaftaler* (Copenhagen: Jurist-og Økonomforbundets Forlag, 2001), 255–308.
37. Cf. s. 53 para. 1 of the Act.

35. The obvious principle that the transfer of copies shall not include an assignment of the copyright is included in section 53 paragraph 2 of the Act. The principle also applies in cases where only one copy of the work exists. In a case before the Maritime and Commercial Court,[38] an engineer had created a twenty-one-foot-long boat. In agreement with the engineer, a boat builder produced a plastic mould on the basis of a copy of the boat made of wood and used the plastic mould to produce identical boats in fibreglass. The boat builder sold the wooden boat to a private person; the boat was resold twice and ended up in the possession of another boat builder. In the last sales agreement, the good was described as 'a wooden boat for *moulding*'. The boat builder who had acquired the boat used the boat to produce identical boats made of fibreglass. The moulds used were sold to a Norwegian boat builder, and according to the contract, all rights to production and sales of boats made by the moulds in Norway and Sweden were assigned to the Norwegian. When the first boat builder was informed of the production of the identical boats by the other boat builders, he claimed that it constituted infringement of his/her copyright in the boat. The court held that the wooden boat qualified for copyright protection, and this right should not be considered lost just because the wooden boat was sold. The fact that the first buyer had the technical skills to build boats, even though he was not a professional boat builder, did not imply that the right owner explicitly should have reserved his/her copyright in the boat. The infringing boats and moulds possessed by the defendant were ordered to be destroyed.

36. An important principle of interpretation is contained in section 53 paragraph 3. It stipulates that where a right to exploit the work in a specific manner or through specific means has been assigned, the assignment does not give the assignee the right to exploit the work in any other manner or through any other means. According to this principle, assignments of copyright have to be interpreted narrowly, and, consequently, only the rights clearly specified and expressly assigned are comprised by the assignment. In the Supreme Court case reported in *Ugeskrift for Retsvæsen* 1974.167 H, a writer had assigned the right to make a screen version of one of his plays in 1944 and additionally the right to perform the film in Scandinavia. In 1952, the writer made a written statement to the effect that all performance rights to the film were assigned to the producer. The assignment did not include any time limits or other reservations. In 1971, the film was broadcast on national television, and the writer claimed that he had not assigned the right to broadcast the film publicly. At the time the assignment was concluded, it did not appear to the writer that public broadcasting was a pertinent way of exploiting the film, and in 1952, television broadcasting in Denmark had just started. A majority of the Supreme Court held that since the assignment did not include any reservations on the performance right, and, additionally, since 1944 television broadcasting was effective in the United States and in 1952 also in Denmark, the producer had acquired the necessary performance rights to transmit the film on national television at a later time.

38. *Ugeskrift for Retsvæsen* 1978.944 SH.

37. According to section 54 of the Act,[39] the assignee is under an obligation to exploit the work. The author may terminate an agreement on assignment of exclusive rights with six months' notice if the exploitation has not been initiated within a reasonable time after the time when the agreement has been fulfilled by the author. However, this does not apply if the exploitation is initiated before the expiry of the notice period. The obligation of exploitation cannot be derogated unless this follows from a collectively negotiated agreement.[40]

38. When the author has assigned the copyright in whole or in part, the author is entitled to an appropriate and proportionate remuneration for the exploitation of the work, cf. section 55 of the Act.[41] The provision on appropriate and proportionate remuneration is supplemented by the 'bestseller clause' in section 55 b, according to which the author shall have the right to claim additional appropriate and fair remuneration from the assignee if the originally agreed remuneration proves to be disproportionately low compared to all subsequent relevant revenues derived from the exploitation of the work. The right to additional remuneration only applies in the absence of a collectively negotiated agreement providing for a contractual adjustment scheme comparable to that provided for under section 55 b.[42] Thus, sections 55 and 55 b not only ensure the author appropriate and proportionate remuneration at the time when the contract is entered into but also that the remuneration continuously remains fair and proportional when the scope of exploitation expands. The provision in sections 55 and 55 b cannot be derogated to the detriment of the author.

39. Pursuant to section 56 of the Act, assignment of copyright does not give the assignee any right to alter the work unless the alteration is usual or obviously presumed, and, in addition, assignment of the copyright does not give the assignee any right to reassign the copyright unless the reassignment is usual or obviously presumed. The assignor remains liable for the performance of the agreement with the author.

40. The usual provisions of the inheritance laws apply to the copyright upon the author's death. If the author has several heirs, the work shall be dealt with under the rules of multi-author works. With many heirs, the exercise of the copyright may be impeded. The Act does not solve this problem; however, the author may give directions in his/her will with binding effect also for the spouse and issue concerning the exercise of the copyright or may authorize somebody else to give such directions.[43]

41. The large investments required to produce, in particular, feature films substantiate the rule of assignment by way of legal presumption in section 58 of the Act. Section 58 paragraph 1 states that an agreement to take part in the recording of

---

39. The provision implements Art. 22 of DSMD.
40. This provision does not apply to the assignment of copyright in works in the form of computer programmes, cf. s. 54 para. 2.
41. The provision implements Art. 18 of DSMD.
42. The provision implements Art. 20 of DSMD.
43. Cf. s. 61 of the Act.

a film shall imply that the author shall have no right to oppose that: (i) copies of the film are made; (ii) copies of the film are distributed to the public; (iii) the film is performed in public; or (iv) the film is subtitled or dubbed in another language. According to section 58 paragraph 2, the provisions of paragraph 1 shall not apply to: (i) works already existing; (ii) script, dialogues and musical works created for the purpose of making the film; or (iii) the principal director of the film.[44] The scope of section 58 is relatively narrow. In the preparatory work to the 1995 Act, it is stated that section 58 paragraph 1 primarily applies to the rights of assistant directors, producers, set designers, film editors and cameramen.[45] Hence, section 58 does not preclude the need to enter into agreements on assignments of rights in film production. Solely as regards rental rights, assignment by way of legal presumption also applies to the neighbouring rights of performers.[46]

42. Section 55 a–55 c of the Act contain transparency provisions that shall enable the author/assignor to control that the author's remuneration is calculated according to the agreement.[47] These provision originating in DSMS is supplemented by the transparency provision in section 57 that was introduced in the 1995 Copyright Act.

II. Licences

43. The Copyright Act does not contain provisions on licences, and hence, a valid licence agreement is not contingent on any formalities. As a practical matter, copyright licence agreements are almost always in written form.[48] The general rules on assignment of copyright also apply to licenses.

III. Works Made in the Course of Employment

44. Besides section 59 of the Act, which exclusively applies to computer programs, works made in the course of employment are not subject to specific provisions of the Copyright Act. Many copyrightable works are created in the course of employment, and the issue has great practical importance. In the final report prior to the revision of the Copyright Act in 1995, the Copyright Committee (*Ophavsretsudvalget*) proposed a general rule to the effect that copyright to works made in the course of permanent employment should be presumed to have passed to the employer to the extent necessary for the normal business activities of the employer. The proposal was not adopted, and the reason for this was, according to the preparatory works, that such a rule would have fundamental consequences for existing

44. The provisions are based on Art. 14*bis* of The Berne Convention.
45. Cf. FT 1994–1995, A, 1386.
46. Cf. s. 65 para. 3. *See infra* para. 116.
47. Sections 55 a–55 c implement Arts 19–21 of DSMD.
48. In general on license agreements, *see* J. Hansen, *Licensaftalen* (Copenhagen: Udenrigstjenestens eksportinformation, 1981), and M.B. Andersen, *Enkelte transaktioner*. 4th edn (Copenhagen: Gjellerup, 2022), 443–472.

collective agreements on the labour market, and these collective agreements formed part of a tradition where agreements could be made freely independent of legal presumptions.[49]

The affected parties apparently considered the proposal controversial, even though the proposal probably did not deviate from valid case law to any significant extent. The copyright originates from the creator of the work, and the creator is often the employee. However, depending on the circumstances, the copyright may pass to the employer. In the case reported in *Ugeskrift for Retsvæsen* 1978.901 H, the Supreme Court decided on a journalist's copyright to his own articles. The journalist was permanently employed by a major national Danish newspaper. One of the journalist's articles was published in the newspaper, and the following day, a local newspaper reprinted the article with permission from neither the national newspaper nor the journalist. Before the Supreme Court, it was undisputed that the local newspaper had infringed the copyright; the remaining question was whether the copyright was owned by the national newspaper or the journalist. The Supreme Court held that the copyright had passed to the national newspaper but only to the extent necessary for the normal business activities of the national newspaper, and the exploitation of an article by reprint of the article in a local newspaper could not be considered a normal business activity of a national newspaper. Hence, the right to control this form of exploitation of the article remained with the journalist. More precisely, how normal business activities shall be construed must be decided in consideration of the normal exploitation of similar works made by other employers in the same line of business. The partial copyright acquired by the employer remains at the employer as long as necessary for normal business activities. Consequently, the employer does not lose the partial copyright when the employment ceases.

45. Section 59 of the Act stipulates that where a computer program is created by an employee in the execution of his/her duties or following the instructions given by his/her employer, the copyright in such a computer program shall pass to the employer. A rule to that effect was already included in the Copyright Act in 1989; minor amendments were made in 1992 in order to implement Article 2(3) of the Council Directive 91/250/EEC on the legal protection of computer programs. Section 59 applies to computer programs exclusively, and it cannot be used by analogy in relation to other categories of works, for example, databases. The copyright only passes to the employer if the employee has been employed with reference to create computer programs or if the employee has been instructed by the employer to create computer programs and that task falls within the limits of the employment. It is not decisive whether the employee has created the computer program at the working place or at home in his/her leisure time using his/her privately owned hardware

49. Cf. FT 1994–1995, A, 1331. In 2003, the Ministry for Culture appointed a committee with the task of analysing, among other things, copyright to works made in the course of employment and in that connection the need for new rules. The committee published a comprehensive report in 2006 (Report No. 1480 Copenhagen 2006 '*Revision af ophavsretslovens kapitel 3*') but was not able to draw any concurrent conclusions on the need to amend the Copyright Act and, consequently, the Minister decided to repeat the statement in the preparatory works to the 1995 Act that copyright issues in employment relationships should be left for the existing collective agreements on the labour market.

facilities. The only crucial factor is the duties of the employee as expressed in the employment agreement or by the instructions of the employer.

Pursuant to section 59, the rights are transferred fully and finally to the employer. In one respect, the Danish rule is broader than Article 2(3) of the European Economic Community (EEC) Directive since the moral rights of the author are also transferred to the employer.[50]

The application of the rule in section 59 is strictly limited to cases of permanent employment with normal rights of instructions on the employer. In cases where a software producer has commissioned the labour of, for example, a software expert of some sort or employed such a person on a freelance basis, section 59 is not applicable, and the prospective copyright remains at the software expert. Where section 59 is not applicable, the copyright will only be transferred to the software producer by way of assignment according to the general rules and principles and that will usually require an explicit assignment of the right.

§6. Scope of Exclusive Rights

46. Copyright protects the ideal as well as the economic interests of the author. Basically, the economic interests are protected by section 2 of the Act, which grants the author the exclusive right to control the work by making copies thereof and by making it available to the public. The ideal interests are protected by the moral rights under section 3 of the Act.

I. Moral Rights

47. The moral rights are divided into the right of paternity and the right of integrity. By virtue of section 3 paragraph 1, the right of paternity implies that the author of a work shall be identified by name as the author in accordance with the requirements of proper usage on copies of the work as well as if the work is made available to the public, for example, by public performance. The duty to state the name of the author is dependent on what is considered proper usage. If it is impossible, unreasonably burdensome or unreasonably disturbing, given the context in which the work is used, to state the name of the author, it is in compliance with proper usage not to do so. Consequently, the meaning of proper usage may differ from one category of work to the other and from one form of exploitation to the other. For example, it is in accordance with proper usage not to state the name of the author as regards musical works performed as a part of religious ceremonies such as weddings and funerals, and according to the preparatory works to the 1961 Act, it is in accordance with proper usage not to state the name of the author to works of applied art in the form of glassware. As a general rule, the right of paternity has a rather limited scope in relation to works of a primarily functional character. The large and often changing numbers of authors who have created a specific computer program implies, normally, that there is no duty under section 3 paragraph 1 to state the

50. Cf. FT 1992–1993, A, col. 1961.

names of these authors. Business practices may influence the way in which proper usage is to be construed, but every widespread business practice is not necessarily proper usage within the meaning of section 3 paragraph 1.[51]

48. The right of integrity is worded in section 3 paragraph 2 of the Act: The work must not be altered nor made available to the public in a manner or in a context which is prejudicial to the author's literary or artistic reputation or individuality. For example, the use of a musical work in a televised advertising spot was held to infringe the integrity right of the author pursuant to section 3 paragraph 2 of the Act.[52]

The rights of paternity and integrity of the author pursuant to section 3 cannot be waived except in respect of a use of the work that is limited in nature and extent.[53] One implication of section 3 paragraph 3 is that if the author assigns the copyrights in a large number or in all his/her works, he/she cannot, in the same general way, waive his/her moral rights in the same works. An agreement stating, in general terms, that the author has waived his/her moral rights in a number of works is not valid.

When the copyright has been assigned, the first part of section 3 paragraph 2 shall be seen in connection with the non-mandatory rule in section 56 paragraph 1, which states that assignment of copyright does not give the assignee any right to alter the work unless the alteration is usual or obviously presumed. In a case before the Eastern Court of Appeal, the scope of the right of integrity was determined in relation to the editing of a film by the process of panscanning.[54] Previously, it was a normal process in the film industry to panscan films made in a wide film format when they were televised. The feature film *Three Days of the Condor*, directed by Sidney Pollack, was transmitted on national television in a panscanned version. The court held that the comprehensive editing of the film, which resulted from panscanning, was not technically necessary for the purpose of televising the film because, alternatively, the film may have been transmitted in the so-called Letter Box Format. Hence, the process of panscanning the film originally produced in cinemascope format infringed the right of integrity by virtue of section 3 paragraph 2. However, Sidney Pollack had entered into a contract with the producer of the film that entitled the producer to arrange for a special television version of the film by way of cutting and editing the original film. At the time in 1975, when the contract was entered into, panscanning was a normal way of adjusting films produced in wide formats to the television medium. By accepting the contract, Sidney Pollack had waived his right in respect of a use of the film that was limited in nature and extent, cf. section 3 paragraph 3, and therefore, he did not obtain relief.

In the case, *Ugeskrift for Retsvæsen* 1979.685 Ø, the soundtrack of a television production was performed at a campaign meeting for a political party. The court

51. *See* Schovsbo, Rosenmeier & Petersen (2024), 161f f; and Schønning (2024), 234 ff.
52. *Ugeskrift for Retsvæsen* 2000.2359 Ø.
53. Cf. s. 3 para. 3 of the Act. *See also* s. 53 para. 1 of the Act.
54. *Ugeskrift for Retsvæsen* 1997.975 Ø.

held that by solely performing the soundtrack instead of the work in total, the defendant infringed the author's right of integrity. The fact that the performance took place at a political meeting, apparently, did not influence the decision.

49. Use of a copyrightable work based on specific provisions and exemptions to copyright protection does not limit the scope of moral rights. The exemptions on copyright are compiled in Chapter 2 of the Act, and according to section 11 paragraph 1, the provisions of this chapter do not limit the author's moral rights under section 3, except as provided in section 29. Pursuant to section 29, buildings may be altered by the owner without the consent of author if this is done for technical reasons or for the purpose of their practical use, and furthermore, articles for everyday use may be altered by the owner without the consent of the author.

Where a work is used in accordance with the provisions of Chapter 2 on exemptions, the work may not be altered more extensively than is required for the permitted use.[55] If the work is used publicly, the source shall be indicated in accordance with the requirements of proper usage, cf. section 11 paragraph 2 last sentence. The last sentence of section 11 paragraph 2 provides the author with stronger protection against alteration of his/her work than section 3 paragraph 2, since alterations of the work may be in violation of section 11 without being prejudicial to the author's literary or artistic reputation, or to his/her individuality.

50. Violation of the right of integrity without altering the work may occur in numerous situations – for example, by placing a picture on the dust jacket of a book that counteracts the idea and spirit of the book, displaying a work in compromising surroundings, using a work in a pornographic context or using a religious work in a blasphemous context.[56]

The use of copyrightable works or quotes from copyrightable works in advertising is a significant practical issue. *Ophavsretsudvalget* concluded in 1990 with reference to a Supreme Court decision from 1936[57] that to a limited extent quotes from copyright-protected works used in advertising could be allowable in respect of the right of integrity but added that normally such use of a work will not be in compliance with the right of integrity. In particular, *Ophavsretsudvalget* found that the use of quotes from newspaper articles in advertising should require consent from the author.[58] In the district court decision reported in *Ugeskrift for Retsvæsen* 1981.693 B, a candidate used two humorous drawings in her campaign for the general election. The candidate owned the original drawings and changed the original text with political slogans. The author of the drawings was deceased and had bequeathed the copyright of his/her works to a foundation. The foundation claimed that the use of the drawings constituted infringement of copyright. The court held that the use of the drawings qualified as infringement of the author's right of integrity.

55. Section 11 para. 2 first sentence.
56. Cf. Schønning (2024), 244 ff.
57. *Ugeskrift for Retsvæsen* 1936.707 H.
58. Report No. 1197 Copenhagen 1990 '*Slutbetænkning*', 166 ff.

In deciding whether the use of a work is infringing the moral rights of the author, the author's subjective assessment is not a crucial factor. The fact that an author feels a certain use of his/her work is prejudicial to his/her reputation or individuality does not imply that his/her moral rights have been infringed. The decision must have a more objective basis, taking into account the point of view of society at large.

Whether the author's right of integrity can be extended to cover private acts is debatable.[59]

51. When the copyright expires seventy years after the death of the author, moral rights continue to exist; however, this is only to a very limited extent. By virtue of section 75 of the Act, although the copyright has expired, a literary or artistic work may not be altered or made available to the public contrary to section 3 paragraphs 1 and 2 of the Act if cultural interests are thereby violated. The right to take proceedings according to section 75 lies with the appropriate public authority and not with the author's heirs. An unambiguous understanding of 'cultural interests' within the meaning of section 75 is very difficult to determine in the modern pluralistic world. In a set of guidelines produced by the Ministry for Culture in 1967, it is said that the purpose of the rule in section 75 is to protect the cultural heritage. This implies that the rule can only be applied to works that are considered part of cultural heritage. In addition, however, the Ministry found that section 75 was applicable to works of authors who otherwise had created works of existing value. Thus, section 75 also applies to works of authors who are considered part of the cultural heritage even if the specific work is not part of the cultural heritage.[60] The bottom line reads that the moral rights protection under section 75 is very narrow. In a Supreme Court case from 1965,[61] section 75 was found to be violated by an adaptation of a musical work. The modern way of adapting older musical works does not correspond with the 1965 decision, and the decision is probably no longer valid case law.[62] In the case reported in *Ugeskrift for Retsvæsen* 1990.856 Ø, it was assumed that a film manuscript entitled *The Many Faces of Jesus Christ* that elaborated on the Gospels and added some pornographic aspects did not constitute a violation of section 75.

52. Solely the rights of paternity and integrity are recognized among the moral rights under Danish copyright law.[63] Hence, the moral rights do not include a right of divulgation or a right to repent or to withdraw. However, similar protection may be obtained under the economic rights of the author. According to section 8 paragraph 1 of the Act, a work shall be considered to have been made public when it has lawfully been made available to the public, and making copies of the work available to the public is comprised by the exclusive right of the author pursuant to section 2 paragraph 1 of the Act. However, a work may have been made public within the meaning of section 8 paragraph 1 even if the first copy is made available

59. *See* Schovsbo, Rosenmeier & Petersen (2024), 165 and Schønning (2024), 244.
60. Cf. Schønning (2024), 804.
61. *Ugeskrift for Retsvæsen* 1965.137 H. *See also* the comments in *Ugeskrift for Retsvæsen* 1965 B.229.
62. Cf. Schovsbo, Rosenmeier & Petersen (2024), 166.
63. Cf. Schønning (2024), 234.

to the public without the consent of the author. For example, if the author has made the first sale of a copy of the work to a person within his/her private sphere, the right of distribution to the copy of the work will be exhausted by virtue of section 19 of the Act, and if the owner of the copy sells the copy, that act will imply that the work is made public according to section 8 paragraph 1.[64]

Presumably, in certain cases, the courts will accept that the author withdraws from an agreement on assignment of rights substantiated by the ideal interests of the author (*droit de repentir*) – for example, by denying a publisher the right to reprint a book on grounds of changed circumstances.[65]

53. In connection to the protection of the ideal interests of the author, one should note the provisions in section 74 of the Act on signing of works of art:

> Para. 1. The name or signature of the artist may not be placed on a work of art by others than himself without his consent. Para. 2. The name or signature of the artist may not in any case be put on a reproduction in such a manner that the reproduction may be confused with the original.

The purpose of paragraph 2 is to prevent copies of the work from being confused with the original work of art.

II. Exploitation Rights

54. Copyright implies the exclusive right to control the work by reproducing it and by making it available to the public, whether in the original form or in an amended form, in translation, adaptation into another literary or artistic form, or in another technique, cf. section 2 paragraph 1 of the Act. It follows from section 2 paragraph 1 that copyright protects against more than just literal copying. However, copyright protection is confined to the specific expression of a work and does not encompass rights in the underlying idea of the work or any facts, information or opinions. In connection to the right of adaptation specified in section 4 paragraph 1 of the Act, it is stated in section 4 paragraph 2 that copyright in a new and independent work created through the free use of another work shall not be subject to copyright in the original work.

The scope of copyright protection was the crucial issue in the Supreme Court case reported in *Ugeskrift for Retsvæsen* 1987.882 H. The defendant marketed an online news information service comprising summaries of the most important political and economic news from the national newspapers. The organization of Danish newspapers claimed on behalf of the national newspapers that the online news information service infringed the copyright of the newspapers. The online news information service consisted of short summaries of actual circumstances described in the newspapers and to a limited extent quotes from the newspapers; it included references to the respective newspapers. The Supreme Court held that according to the merits of

64. *Ibid.*, 271.
65. *Ibid.*, 619.

the case, the online news information service did not infringe the copyright of the newspapers. Accordingly, the summaries of the newspaper articles did not constitute copyright infringement, and the quotes were permissible under section 14 of the Act (now section 22) concerning the right to quote copyrightable works.[66]

55. By virtue of section 2 paragraph 1, the copyright comprises two specific rights: the right to reproduce the work and the right to make the work available to the public. The reproduction right is not contingent on whether the work subsequently is made available to the public. The right to make the work available to the public is subdivided into more specific rights. By virtue of section 2 paragraph 3 of the Act, the work is made available to the public if:

- copies of the work are offered for sale, rental or lending, or distribution to the public in some other manner (distribution right);
- copies are exhibited in public (display right); or
- the work is performed in public (performing right).

A. *Reproduction Right*

56. In conformity with Article 2 of the Infosoc Directive (2001/29/EF), any direct or indirect, temporary or permanent reproduction, in whole or in part, by any means and in any form shall be considered reproduction. The recording of the work on devices that can reproduce it shall also be considered a reproduction (section 2 paragraph 2 of the Act).

Section 2 paragraph 2 of the Act implements Article 2 of the Infosoc Directive, the purpose of which is to clarify the scope of the reproduction right in respect of temporary acts of reproduction. The Directive opted for a broad scope of the reproduction right; hence, the copying of a computer program into the RAM of a computer, which is a precondition for using the program, constitutes reproduction. Similarly, the reproduction right covers cache copying in connection with browsing the Internet.

57. According to section 2 paragraph 1, the exclusive right of the author includes, among other things, the right to make copies of the work by making adaptation of the work into another technique. This implies that a two-dimensional copy of a three-dimensional work – for example, a photograph of a sculpture – constitutes reproduction of the three-dimensional work. Similarly, the exclusive right includes the right to make a screen version of a novel. In spite of the wording of section 2 paragraph 1, a copyrightable technical drawing (e.g., a blueprint) is not granted protection against the production of a creation made on the basis of the drawing. Thus, copyright protection of a technical drawing does not extend to the technical product. No current case law supports this conclusion, but it is widely

66. Besides, the Supreme Court found that the online news information service did not constitute unfair competition under s. 3 of the Marketing Practice Act.

accepted.[67] This limitation on the scope of protection only applies to technical drawings; copyrightable architectural drawings and copyrightable drawings of works of applied art provide protection of creations made on the basis of the drawings.[68] The architectural drawing and the final building are two different modes of manifestation of the same work.

B. Performing Right

58. By the performing right, the author is granted the exclusive right to control the work made available to the public by public performance. Public performance has to be distinguished from performances within the private sphere that are not restricted by copyright, and that distinction has resulted in comprehensive case law. Every time a work is performed to an unspecified group of persons, a public performance takes place, such as the performance of a musical work at a public concert. Additionally, modern forms of programme delivery such as pay-per-view, video-on-demand and broadcasting that can only be received with the use of a decoder are public performance within the meaning of the Act.

According to section 2 paragraph 4 (i) and (ii), public performance shall include:

- communication to the public of works by wire or wireless means, including broadcasting by radio or television and
- the making available to the public works in such a way that members of the public may access them from a place and at a time individually chosen by them.

The Act was amended in 2002 in order to implement the Infosoc Directive, which, among other things, clarifies the performance right in the information society. Thus, section 2 paragraph 4(ii) covers acts of making works available on the Internet, for example, by uploading works on a website, providing access to works on a local storage medium by means of file-sharing software or otherwise or making works available in a chat room.

59. 'Public performance' must be understood in accordance with normal terminology. A crucial element is whether the performance is part of a private or a public arrangement; however, public performance may take place in settings to which only a definite number of persons have access if it is obvious that it is more than just a private arrangement. A local association of pensioners with 225 members invited the members by public announcement to a breaking-up celebration. Only members of the association had access to the celebration. The performance of musical works at the celebration was found to constitute public performance within the meaning of the Act. In reaching this decision, the court emphasized that membership of the association was open to all persons belonging to a certain age group and, hence,

---

67. Cf. Schovsbo, Rosenmeier & Petersen (2024), 85, 94f; Schønning (2024), 174 f; Report No. 1063 Copenhagen 1986 '*Billedret*', 18 ff; and Report No. 1064 Copenhagen 1986 '*Ophavsret og edb*', 77 ff.
68. Cf. *Ugeskrift for Retsvæsen* 1984.201 Ø.

could not be considered a private group of persons.[69] In deciding whether performance of works by an association at a special event constitutes public performance, the courts make a general evaluation of the arrangement emphasizing the purpose of the association, limitations on the possibilities for memberships, the form of membership, the number of persons who are members of the association, the number of persons who participate in the arrangement and, finally, whether the performance has a commercial purpose.[70]

Some modifications to the construction of the concept 'public performance' have been developed in case law. In *Ugeskrift for Retsvæsen* 1999.2011 H, the Supreme Court found the performance of music in youth clubs and recreation centres, some of them with more than one hundred members, did not constitute public performance within the meaning of the Act. In its decision, the Supreme Court refers to the public policy objectives of these entities. A majority of the Supreme Court reached the same result in *Ugeskrift for Retsvæsen* 2004.2134 H in respect of performance of music in gymnastics clubs. The court noted that the clubs in question are locally based, non-commercial, financed by member fees and public grants, and their activities are to a large extent based on voluntary and unpaid labour. However, the performance of music in dancing schools and aerobic centres is considered public and is restricted by copyright, cf. *Ugeskrift for Retsvæsen* 2002.649 Ø and *Ugeskrift for Retsvæsen* 2003.212 Ø. The same applies to the use of music at dance, exercise and gymnastics classes, film screenings, prom, harvest, Christmas parties and live events at a municipality's care centres, to which citizens other than residents also had access, cf. *Ugeskrift for Retsvæsen* 2023.1448 V. In the same case, the court held that performance of music at events where only the residents of the care centres had access should not be considered to be public.

'Communication to the public' is a form of public performance that has been harmonized by Article 3(1) of the Infosoc Directive, and, by now, a relatively high number of court cases have been decided by the CJEU on how to determine 'the public' in respect of communication to the public. The harmonized right of communication to the public only applies to communication to the public not present at the place where the communication originates[71] which means that, for example, live performances are not covered by the right of 'communication to the public' and thus shall be decided on the basis of national copyright law. It would have been expedient if 'the public' had been determined in the same way, no matter whether the concept relates to the harmonized right of communication to the public or to the non-harmonized right of direct performances. However, that is not the case. The Supreme Court has decided that there is no basis for applying the criteria developed by the CJEU on how to determine communication to the public when it comes to direct performances.[72]

---

69. *Ugeskrift for Retsvæsen* 1978.610 Ø.
70. Cf. T. Lund, *Ophavsretsloven og fotografiloven* (Copenhagen: G E C Gads Forlag, 1961), 81; and Schønning (2024), 217 ff.
71. Cf. the Preamble of the Infosoc Directive at 23.
72. *Ugeskrift for Retsvæsen* 2018.516 H.

60. The performing right is not exhausted, which implies that the first performance of the work does not confine the author's right to control subsequent performances of the work. For example, if a musical work is performed by way of a radio broadcast, the broadcast may not be performed anew to the public – for example, at a discotheque – without the consent of the right owners. In that case, a renewed public performance will take place. An owner of a restaurant who places loudspeakers connected to a radio in the restaurant in order to play broadcast music to the guests in the restaurant is making a renewed public performance of the works.[73] A renewed public performance also takes place when an owner of a hotel arranges for television sets and radio receivers in each hotel room, enabling the guests to receive radio and television broadcasts in their respective rooms. In the case reported in *Ugeskrift for Retsvæsen* 1962.922 Ø, a farmer ran a boarding house with eighteen rooms in connection to his farm. In a common room of the boarding house, a television set was placed for the use of the boarders. In advertisements for the boarding house, it was said that the boarders had access to television reception. The Eastern Court of Appeal found that the use of the television set in the boarding house constituted an independent public performance.

A sanitation company that had installed radios/CD players in its dust carts for the use of its employees did not commit an act of public performance of the music the employees decided to listen to, cf. *Ugeskrift for Retsvæsen* 2007.1581 H.

Retransmission of broadcasts via cable systems is a form of renewed public performance. Cable retransmission of broadcast works is subject to extended collective licence, cf. section 35 paragraph 1 of the Act (*see infra* paragraph 110-111). However, according to section 35 paragraph 2 of the Act, no liability applies where broadcasts are received by way of the receivers' own community antennae and retransmitted via cable systems consisting of no more than two connections.

61. It was previously a much-debated issue whether linking to copyrightable works constitutes public performance within the meaning of the Copyright Act. It may be argued that linking is a form of renewed public performance. In a Court of Appeal case from 2001, the court decided on deep links to unlawful MP3 files containing copyrightable musical works. The court stated that the defendants had independently made works available to the public in a way equivalent to public performance pursuant to section 2 of the Act by making deep links to musical works that third persons had uploaded unlawfully.[74] The question of whether links to copyrightable works constitute communication to the public is now settled by CJEU case law and, as the main rule, this is not the case because the making available of the works by means of a clickable link does not lead to the works in question being communicated to a new public. *See* specifically Case C-466/12 (Svensson), Case C-348/13 (Bestwater) and Case C-160/15 (GS Media).

---

73. Cf. *Ugeskrift for Retsvæsen* 1930.646 H.
74. Cf. *Ugeskrift for Retsvæsen* 2001.1572 V.

C. Adaptation Right

62. The right to make an adaptation of a work follows from section 2 paragraph 1 of the Act but is more precisely defined in section 4 paragraph 1 of the Act: 'The person translating, revising or otherwise adapting a work, including converting it into some other literary or artistic form, shall have copyright in the work in the new form, but his right to control it shall be subject to the copyright in the original work.' The subject of protection under section 4 paragraph 1 is the adaptation, and the exercise of the right is contingent on the copyright in the original work. Examples of adaptations are translations of a literary work into another language, making a screen version of a novel, editing and rewriting of a book, for example, with the purpose of making a version for children, revising a play and orchestration and harmonization of a musical composition.[75] Protection requires, first, that an original work is adapted and, second, that the adaptation in its own right constitutes a work within the meaning of the Copyright Act. Accordingly, the adaptation shall satisfy the requirement of originality. The requirement is assumed to be identical to the originality requirement under section 1 of the Act. Normally, the mere translation of information will not be considered an intellectual creative contribution. Neither will technical conversions – such as compiling a computer program's source code into object code or converting an existing work into digital form – satisfy the originality requirement. The persons making the adaptation are granted the same rights as other authors, including moral rights, and the adaptation is subject to the same limitations on the scope of protection as other works.

D. Translation Right

63. The translation right is recognized as a part of the adaptation right. The translator is granted copyright in the translation – for instance, subtitles for a foreign language film are protected in their own right.[76]

The translator – as well as other persons making a copyrightable adaptation – shall respect the copyright of the original author and therefore cannot make copies of the work or make the work available to the public without the consent of the original author. Third parties planning to exploit a translation shall obtain consent from the original author as well as the translator. The title of Ernest Hemingway's novel *For Whom the Bell Tolls*, translated into Danish (*Hvem ringer klokkerne for?*), was held to be an original literary work. The film producer who made a screen version of the novel infringed the copyright of the translator by marketing the film using the Danish title.[77]

75. Cf. Schønning (2024), 251. In general, on adaptation of musical compositions, *see* Rosenmeier (1996), 63 ff.
76. Cf. *Ugeskrift for Retsvæsen* 2005.60 V.
77. Cf. *Ugeskrift for Retsvæsen* 1951.725 H.

E. Distribution Right

64. The distribution right confers on the author the exclusive right to control distribution of copies of a work to the public by way of sale, rental, lending and the like. The distribution right is of great practical importance, particularly when applied to works that are produced in large numbers and, subsequently, put on the market, such as books, phonograms and standard computer software. Distribution of copies within the private sphere by the owner of a copy of the work is not restricted by the distribution right. Online transmission of works by use of digital networks is not considered distribution of copies of a work.[78]

65. Section 19 paragraph 1 of the Act lays down a rule of exhaustion of the distribution right. Where a copy of a work has been sold or otherwise transferred to others within the EEA with the consent of the author, the copy may be further distributed. Exhaustion does not apply to the right to distribute the work as such but only to the right to control the further distribution of the specific copy of a work. Exhaustion only occurs when the work has been put on the market with the consent of the author, and that implies that the right to distribute a copy of a work produced by infringement of the copyright is not exhausted. Important exceptions to the rule of exhaustion are stipulated in the following paragraphs of section 19. Notwithstanding the provision of section 19 paragraph 1, copies may not be distributed to the general public through rental without the consent of the author. However, this does not apply to works of architecture and applied art.[79] Thus, as a general rule, the right to rental of copies of a work is not exhausted. Notwithstanding the provision of section 19 paragraph 1, copies of cinematographic works, including videograms and computer programs in digitized form, may not be distributed to the public through lending without the consent of the author. However, this does not apply if a copy of a computer program in digitized form constitutes part of a literary work or is lent together with it.[80] Consequently, categories of works other than cinematographic works and computer programs in digitized form can freely be distributed to the public by way of lending.

The author's exclusive right to certain forms of rental and lending, according to section 19 paragraphs 2 and 3, does not apply to works that are integrated parts of an industrial product. Thus, the distribution right does not extend to, for example, a computer program that controls the functions of a car, a washing machine, a camera, a calculator and the like and which is integrated into such a product. Usually, the author will be considered to have consented to such distribution of the work by way of explicit or implied agreement.[81]

---

78. *See* Riis (2001), 149 ff; and Schønning (2024), 205.
79. Cf. s. 19 para. 2.
80. Cf. s. 19 para. 3.
81. Cf. FT 1988–1989, A, col. 3222 f. *See also* Report No. 1064 Copenhagen 1986 '*Ophavsret og edb*', 62.

If a copy of a work of art is resold on a commercial basis and the author has not been remunerated in accordance with his/her *droit de suite* under section 38 of the Act, the distribution right has not been exhausted, and, formally, the copyright has been infringed.[82]

66. A special issue concerns the geographical scope of the rule of exhaustion. It is a well-established principle in the case law from the CJEU that the first sale in the Community of a copy of a work by the rightholder or with his/her consent shall exhaust the distribution right within the Community of that copy, with the exception of the right to control further rental of the work or a copy thereof.[83] The principle of European Union (EU) exhaustion has been included in several of the directives on harmonization of copyright law. When the EEA Agreement took effect on 1 January 1994, the principle was extended to countries within the EEA, which is now reflected in section 19 paragraph 1 of the Copyright Act. Accordingly, the first sale in the EEA of a copy of a work with the consent of the rightholder exhausts the right to control the further distribution of the copy within the EEA. Previously, it was assumed that a principle of global exhaustion applied in Danish copyright law.[84] However, it is not in conformity with EU law to apply a principle of global exhaustion within areas of copyright law that are harmonized by directives. In respect of the small parts of the distribution right that have not been harmonized, the principle of global exhaustion is still applicable.[85]

67. In relation to the distribution right, one should note the rule in section 77 paragraph 1 of the Act on importation of copies of a work. Where copies of works or of performances or productions that are protected under sections 65–71 have been produced outside Denmark under such circumstances that a similar production in Denmark would have been in conflict with the law, anyone who, with intent or by gross negligence, imports such copies with a view to making them available to the public shall be liable to a fine. Importation of copies of works for private use does not constitute a violation of section 77. The application of section 77 paragraph 1 does not depend on whether production of the work complies with the copyright law in the country of production; the decisive factor is whether the production of the work would have violated Danish copyright law if it had taken place in Denmark. Typically, the rule will be applied in cases where the work is protected in Denmark but has been produced in a country where the work is not copyrightable subject matter or has been produced in a foreign country under a compulsory licence or some other exception to the scope of copyright protection.

---

82. Cf. FT 1988–1989, A, col. 3224. *See* Schønning (2024), 519.
83. *See*, for example, *Ugeskrift for Retsvæsen* 1982.69 H.
84. Cf. FT for example, 1992–1993, A, col. 1960, FT 1994–1995, A, 1390; and P. Blok, *Patentrettens konsumtionsprincip* (Copenhagen: Juristforbundets Forlag, 1974).
85. Cf. Schovsbo, Rosenmeier & Petersen (2024) 236 f.

1. Public Lending Right

68. As it follows from section 19 paragraph 3, the author's lending right in Danish copyright law is very narrow since it only applies to cinematographic works and computer programs in digitized form. Furthermore, a copy of a computer program in digitized form is exempted from the lending right when it constitutes part of a literary work or is lent together with it. The purpose of this exemption is to ensure that public libraries do not incur copyright liability by lending electronic books that include an operative computer program in order to use the book (e.g., books on CD-ROMs). The exemption also applies to books and printed periodicals that are published with an attached CD-ROM storing a computer program.

The distinction between public lending and rental has been clarified by the Supreme Court in the case reported in *Ugeskrift for Retsvæsen* 1993.572 H. A public library issued a special card that entitled the person who obtained it to borrow phonograms from the library for one year. In order to obtain the card, a fee of *Danske kroner* (DKK) 100 had to be paid to the library. The crux of the matter is whether this arrangement constituted lending, which is not restricted by copyright, or rental, which requires the consent of the authors. The Supreme Court held that rental within the meaning of the Copyright Act shall be construed in accordance with the normal understanding in Danish law of rental of tangibles, and that implies that rental takes place when an object is handed over against payment with the purpose of use, and it is immaterial whether such rental is commercial or not. Hence, according to the Supreme Court, the arrangement constituted rental.

69. Lending by public libraries has traditionally been an important part of Danish cultural policy, and a significant number of books are lent to the public by the public libraries each year. The authors are not compensated for this lending under copyright law. However, provided the work is published in Danish, an author may claim remuneration from the treasury under the Act on Public Lending Right Remuneration. Remuneration is calculated on the basis of the number and the use of the copies of the work. Translators of foreign language books are entitled to compensation under the Act on Public Lending Right Remuneration but not the original author.[86] It is stipulated in section 19 paragraph 4 of the Copyright Act that the rule of exhaustion in section 19 paragraph 1 shall not carry any limitation in the right to receive remuneration, etc. under the Act on Public Lending Right Remuneration.

F. Display Right

70. The display right confers on the author the exclusive right to control the work by making the work or copies of the work available to the public by display (display right is used in the same meaning as exhibition right). If the work is displayed in a place to which the public has access, a public display takes place. Normally, the display right has practical significance only in cases where the visual

86. *See* Consolidated Act No. 1175 of 17 Dec. 2002 with amendments by Act No 676 of 8 Jun. 2017; and Order No. 1448 of 30 November on Public Lending Right Remuneration.

appearance is the central characteristic of the work, which is the case, for example, for works of art and photographs.[87] Literary works may be exploited by public display as well; for example, when newspapers are made available at cafés, when newspapers are displayed in showcases and when books are placed in show windows.[88]

71. The display right is exhausted by virtue of section 20 of the Act: 'Where a work has been published or if a copy of a work of art has been transferred to other parties by the author, the published or transferred copies may be exhibited in public.' A work is considered published if, with the consent of the author, copies of the work have been put on the market or otherwise distributed to the public, cf. section 8 paragraph 2 of the Act. Accordingly, for example, the right to place a book in a show window is exhausted when the book is published. Since the display right is not harmonized under EU law, a principle of global exhaustion applies, which used to be the traditional exhaustion rule in Danish copyright law.

Only the display right to the specific copy is exhausted; for example, if a published newspaper article is photocopied, which can be done legally under the provision on private copying in section 12 paragraph 1 of the Act, the public display of the photocopy in a showcase infringes the copyright.

Often, works of art are not published in the way prescribed in section 8 paragraph 2; therefore, the display right to a specific copy of a work of art is exhausted when the author has transferred the copy to third parties. Thus, a person who has bought a painting can display the painting publicly without infringing the copyright.[89]

Copyrightable works – for example, works of fine art – included in a television programme or in a transmission on the Internet are not 'displayed' within the meaning of the Copyright Act; instead, they are covered by the performing right.

G. *Other Rights*

1. *Droit de Suite*

72. A *droit de suite* (resale right) was introduced into Danish copyright law in 1989.[90] In the event of resale of copies of works of art, including paintings, collages, drawings, engravings, prints, lithographs, sculptures, tapestries, ceramic art, glass art and photographic works, the author is entitled to remuneration.[91] The resale right relates to copies of works of art that have been produced in one copy or in a limited quantity by the author himself/herself or with his/her permission. The resale

87. Cf. FT 1994–1995, A, 1334.
88. Cf. Schønning (2024), 208 f.
89. *See* Report No. 1197 Copenhagen 1990 '*Slutbetænkning*', 161.
90. In general on *droit de suite*, *see* Report No. 1063 Copenhagen 1986 '*Billedret*', 91–129. The provision was amended in 2005 in order to implement the EU Resale Rights Directive (2001/84/EC).
91. The enumerated categories of works are not exhaustive.

right does not comprise architectural works.[92] The *droit de suite* only affects resale, and it does not affect the author's first sale of a copy of a work of art; however, the right applies to all acts of resale in which sellers, buyers or agents are involved on a professional basis in the art market, including auction houses, art galleries, salesrooms and art dealers.[93] Hence, the right is not applicable to resale between commercial entities who are not art market professionals or resale between non-commercial entities.

The obligation to pay the resale right remuneration rests with the seller or the intermediary. Remuneration shall only be paid if the sales price exceeds EUR 300 (excluding value added tax (VAT)). The total remuneration cannot exceed EUR 12,500 (excluding VAT) per copy.[94] The resale right remuneration is calculated as:

- 5% for the portion of the sale price up to EUR 50,000 (excluding VAT);
- 3% for the portion of the sale price from EUR 50,000.01 to EUR 200,000 (excluding VAT);
- 1% for the portion of the sale price from EUR 200,000.01 to EUR 350,000 (excluding VAT);
- 0.5% for the portion of the sale price from EUR 350,000.01 to EUR 500,000 (excluding VAT);
- 0.25% for the portion of the sale price exceeding EUR 500,000 (excluding VAT).[95]

The right to remuneration lasts until the expiration of the term of copyright, cf. section 63 of the Act. The right is personal and unassignable. After the death of the author, the right shall, however, succeed to the spouse and issue of the author. Where the author does not leave any spouse or issue, the right of remuneration passes to the organization that is approved by the Minister for Culture as the only entity to claim the right of remuneration.[96]

According to section 85 paragraph 4 of the Act, the resale right shall apply to works of persons who are nationals of or who have their habitual residence in a country within the EEA.

73. The right of remuneration may be exercised only by an organization approved by the Minister for Culture. The organization shall be in charge of the collection and shall make the distribution to the beneficiaries.[97] The Minister for Culture has approved the collective administration organization *Copydan* as the said organization. *Copydan* can claim the remuneration even if the author is unaware of the resale, and furthermore, the author cannot prevent *Copydan* from claiming the remuneration. The beneficiary's claim against *Copydan* lasts until three years have

92. Cf. s. 38 para. 1 of the Copyright Act.
93. Cf. s. 38 para. 2.
94. *Ibid.*
95. Cf. s. 38 para. 3.
96. Cf. s. 38 para. 4.
97. Cf. s. 38 para. 5 of the Act.

elapsed from the end of the year in which the resale took place. The period of limitation can be suspended by written demand from the beneficiary.[98] In the event of a resale covered by the resale right, the seller or agent, etc., is under an obligation to forward to *Copydan* an annual statement of the sale of works of art covered by the resale right scheme attested by an authorized public accountant or a registered auditor.[99]

2. *Editio Princeps*

74. When a work has not been published previously, the person who lawfully makes the work public or publishes it for the first time after the expiry of copyright protection has rights in the work equivalent to the economic rights attributed by the Act to the person creating a literary or artistic work. This protection lasts for twenty-five years after the end of the year in which the work was made public or published.[100] The protection applies to publications, etc., made by persons who are nationals or who have their habitual residence in a country within the EEA or companies with headquarters in a country within the EEA.[101]

3. Circumvention of Technological Protective Measures

75. The Copyright Act contains prohibitions on the circumvention of technological protective measures (copy control devices and the like) and the marketing of means for that purpose. Strictly speaking, the prohibitions are not copyrights, but they may, in specific circumstances, provide an important legal instrument for the protection of the copyright holders' interest. The Act distinguishes between technological protective measures that are used to protect computer programs and technological protective measures used to protect other categories of copyrightable works.

In respect of computer programs, it is not permitted to market or for commercial purposes possess means the only purpose of which is to facilitate unlawful removal or circumvention of technical devices that are used to protect a computer program, cf. section 75b of the Act. Section 75b does not prohibit the actual circumvention of a technological protective measure nor, for private purposes, the possession of means for circumvention.

A more comprehensive prohibition applies to circumvention of technological protective measures used to protect other categories of copyrightable works since, in respect of such works, it is not permitted to circumvent effective technological measures without the consent of the rightholder.[102] In addition, it is not permitted to produce, import, distribute, sell, rent, advertise for sale or rental, or to possess for commercial purposes devices, products or components that:

98. *Ibid.*
99. Cf. s. 38 para. 7 of the Act.
100. Cf. s. 64 of the Act.
101. Cf. s. 85 para. 5.
102. Cf. s. 75b para. 1 of the Act.

- are promoted, advertised or marketed for the purpose of circumvention of effective technological measures;
- have only a limited commercially significant purpose or use other than to circumvent effective technological measures; or
- are primarily designed, produced, adapted or performed for the purpose of enabling or facilitating the circumvention of effective technological measures.[103]

These provisions apply correspondingly to services.[104] Violations of the provisions on technological protective measures may involve criminal liability.[105]

By means of technological protective measures and supported by the prohibition in section 75c, the rightholders can preclude users from taking advantage of the exemptions to the exclusive copyrights. In respect of some (but not all) of the exemptions, the Copyright License Tribunal may, upon request, order a rightholder who has used effective technological measures to make such means available to a user that are necessary for the latter to benefit from the provisions, cf. section 75d paragraph 1 of the Act. The provision on private use in section 12 is not among the exemptions listed in section 75d paragraph 1.

In order to further facilitate the copyright holders' usage of digital rights management systems, it is not permitted without the consent of the rightholder to: (i) remove or alter any electronic rights management information or (ii) distribute, import for distribution or communicate to the public works and performances or productions, etc., from which electronic rights management information has been removed or altered without consent.[106]

4. Use of Protected Content by Online Content-Sharing Service Providers

76. Article 17 of the DSMD on liability for online content-sharing service providers is implemented in section 52 c of the Act. An 'Online content sharing service provider' is defined in section 52 c, paragraph 1 of the Act as a provider of an information society service whose main purpose or one of its main purposes is to store and provide the public with access to a large amount of works or creations protected under neighbouring rights uploaded by its users, which it organizes and promotes with the aim of making a direct or indirect profit.

A provider of an online content-sharing service carries out a communication to the public or makes available to the public of works and creations protected under neighbouring rights when these are uploaded by users of the online content-sharing service. A provider of an online content-sharing service must seek authorization from the rightsholders for the use of such rights in accordance with this, unless the rightsholders do not wish to grant such authorization.[107]

---

103. Cf. s. 75b para. 2 of the Act.
104. Cf. s. 75b para. 3 of the Act.
105. Cf. s. 78 of the Act.
106. Cf. s. 75e para. 1 of the Act.
107. Cf. s. 52c para. 1 of the Act.

When an online content-sharing service provider has obtained an authorization from the rightholders, such authorization shall also cover the actions of the users of the online content-sharing service. However, this does not apply when the users act for commercial purposes, or their activity generates substantial revenue. The user does not obtain a better legal position than that granted by the rightholders to the provider of the online content-sharing service.[108]

If the rightholders do not grant authorization to the online content-sharing service provider, the provider may still escape liability by means of the exemption in Article 52 c, paragraph 4. Accordingly, providers of online content-sharing services are liable for unauthorized communication to the public, including making available copyrighted works and other subject matter, unless the provider demonstrates that it has met the following conditions:

(1) The provider has made its best efforts to obtain an authorization from the rightholders.
(2) The provider has made, in accordance with high industry standards of professional diligence, best efforts to ensure the unavailability of specific works and other subject matter for which the rightholders have provided the service providers with the relevant and necessary information.
(3) The provider, upon receiving a sufficiently substantiated notice from the rightholders, to disable access to, or to remove from their websites, the notified works or other subject matter, and made best efforts to prevent their future uploads in accordance with point (2).

In the main, section 52 c is worded in strict compliance with Article 17 of DSMD. However, there are two notable exceptions. First, the provision of Article 17, paragraph 3, according to which Article 14, paragraph 1 of the e-Commerce Directive does not apply to direct infringements and that this provision shall not affect the possible application of Article 14, paragraph 1 of the e-Commerce Directive to those service providers for purposes falling outside the scope of the DSMD has not been transposed into the Danish statutory text. The content of Article 17, paragraph 3 is, however, mentioned in the preparatory works to the Danish Act. Second, the de facto users' rights in Article 17, paragraph 7, have by the Danish legislator been construed as merely an obligation to provide for ordinary exceptions for the mentioned purposes. Article 17, paragraph 7 *in fine* stipulates that Member States shall ensure that users are able to rely on any of the existing exceptions or limitations on quotation, criticism, review, and use for the purpose of caricature, parody or pastiche when uploading and making available content generated by users on online content-sharing services. In the preparatory works for the Danish Act, there is a reference to the exceptions concerning quotation, criticism, review, caricature, parody and pastiche, and there is no text in the Act that ensures that the users actually can rely on those exceptions.

108. Cf. s. 52c para. 3 of the Act.

5. Others

77. A special protection of titles of literary and artistic work is provided by section 73 of the Act. A literary or artistic work may not be made available to the public under a title, pseudonym or signature which is likely to be confused with a work previously made public or with its author (cf. paragraph 1). Where the publication of the work made public previously has taken place less than three months prior to the publishing of the other work, the provision of paragraph 1 does not apply unless it may be presumed that the confusion was intentional (cf. paragraph 2). This kind of protection is more akin to protection against unfair competition than to copyright protection, and the provisions must be interpreted in accordance hereto. Accordingly, protection of a title under section 73 requires a certain degree of distinctiveness.[109] Protection under section 73 applies to any work[110] and is not limited in time.

78. A blank media levy was introduced into Danish copyright law in 1992. The pertinent provisions are found in sections 39–46 a of the Act.[111] Anyone who for commercial purposes produces or imports storage media onto which sounds or images can be recorded shall pay remuneration to the authors for storage media that are suitable for production of copies for private use. Remuneration shall only be paid for works that have been broadcast on radio or television, or that have been published on phonogram, film, videogram, etc., or have been made available in such a way that the public has access to them at a place and time individually chosen by them.[112] The blank media levy is a right of remuneration that is independent of the scope of copyright protection. Thus, the rightholder is entitled to remuneration regardless of whether the actual copying is legitimized, for example, under the provisions on private copying of section 12 of the Act. Similarly, the blank tape media does not extend the scope of legitimate private copying, according to section 12. Besides, a person who produces or imports blank tapes for commercial purposes and who is not paying remuneration to the authors is not infringing the copyright of the authors.

Pursuant to section 40 of the Act, by 1 January 2022, the remuneration is as follows:

(1) Hard disc ≤ 128 GB: DKK 4.00.
(2) Hard disc > 128 GB: DKK 16.00
(3) Tablet: DKK 45.00
(4) Smartphone: 45.00 kr.
(5) Laptop: 45.00 kr.
(6) Desktop computer: DKK 45.00.

109. Cf. Schovsbo, Rosenmeier & Petersen (2024), 116 f and Schønning (2024), 796 ff.
110. Cf. s. 85 para. 6 of the Act.
111. *See also* Ordinance No. 2659 of 28 Dec. 2021 on a Levy System for Reproduction for private Purpose. In general on blank tape levies, *see* Report No. 944 Copenhagen 1982 *'Båndafgift, sanktioner, påtale'*, 13–63.
112. Section 39 paras 1 and 2 of the Act.

The remuneration is adjusted annually by the rate adjustment percentage, cf. Act on Rate Adjustment Percentage.[113]

The administration and control, including collection, is carried out by a joint organization representing a significant proportion of authors, performers and other rights holders, including record producers, etc., and photographers whose works, performances, etc., are used in Denmark. The organization must be approved by the Minister of Culture. The Minister for Culture has approved *Copydan* as the said organization. The Minister may demand to be supplied with all information about collection, administration and distribution of the remuneration.[114] *Copydan* lays down guidelines for payment of the remuneration to the beneficiaries so that, to the greatest possible extent, distribution will take place in accordance with the copying actually made. One-third of the annual amount for payment shall, however, be used to support purposes common to the authors and others within the groups represented by *Copydan*.[115] On remuneration to be used to support purposes common to the authors, it is said in the preparatory works to the Act that, among other things, it aims to support individual authors and artists who make a significant and innovative contribution to the Danish art of music and film in the form of creations that, due to the relatively small Danish market for these products, are not commercially viable. A rightholder who has his/her habitual residence within the EEA is entitled to remuneration under section 39. Furthermore, a rightholder from a foreign country is entitled to remuneration provided that a blank media remuneration scheme has been implemented in the country concerned, which provides a possibility for payment of remuneration to Danish rightholders;[116] thus, a principle of material reciprocity applies.

§7. Limitations or Exemptions to the Scope of Copyright Protection

79. The various exemptions to the scope of copyright protection comprise Chapter 2 of the Copyright Act. As a general rule, the legitimate use of protected works under the provisions in Chapter 2 requires that the works have been made public within the meaning of section 8 paragraph 1 of the Act. Some of the provisions require that the works have been published within the meaning of section 8 paragraph 2 of the Act. Accordingly, the provisions of Chapter 2 do not legitimize the use of works which have not been made public.[117]

As a further requirement, it is stipulated in section 11 paragraph 3 of the Act that where a work is used in accordance with the exemptions of Chapter 2, copies may not be made on the basis of a reproduction of the work that is contrary to section 2

113. Act No. 373 of 28 May 2003.
114. Cf. s. 39 para. 3 of the Act.
115. Cf. s. 39 para. 4 of the Act.
116. Cf. ss 18 and 19 of Ordinance No. 218 of 9 Mar. 2010. *See also* Schønning (2024), 533 ff.
117. Cf. Schovsbo, Rosenmeier & Petersen (2024), 201 f.

or on the basis of a circumvention of a technological measure that is contrary to section 75c paragraph 1.[118] Thus, the exemptions in Chapter 2 of the Act require that the original copy be lawful.

I. Temporary Reproduction

80. In conformity with the mandatory provision in Article 5(1) of the Infosoc Directive (2001/29/EF) and as a consequence of the broad scope of the reproduction right, according to section 11a paragraph 1 of the Acts, it is permitted to make temporary copies:

- that are transient or incidental;
- that are an integral and essential part of a technical process;
- the sole purpose of which is to enable a transmission of a work in a network between third parties by an intermediary or a lawful use of a work; and
- those that have no independent economic significance.

In the preparatory works to the 2002 amendment of the Copyright Act, it is explained that more incidental forms of copying, such as automatic copying of content in a computer's cache memory when browsing on the Internet, do not have a significant economic impact on the right owner. The preparatory works also state that temporary storing by Internet service providers with the purpose of making the transmission system more efficient (proxy caching) is covered by the exemption. Also, RAM copying is exempted from the reproduction right by means of section 11a paragraph 1. It should be noted that pursuant to section 11 paragraph 3, the exemption on temporary reproduction requires the original copy to be lawful.

In the Supreme Court decision reported in *Ugeskrift for Retsvæsen* 2013.1782 H, a media monitoring Company, Infopaq, used a data capture process that involved the scanning of news articles that were searched electronically for the purpose of extracting and printing short excerpts comprising eleven words, including the search word. The Supreme Court found that the scanning of articles was not covered by the exemption in section 11a paragraph 1 because the copying that took place by the process of scanning could not be considered transient. A number of questions on the interpretation of the pertinent provision of the Infosoc Directive were referred to the CJEU that has delivered one judgment in case C-5/08 of 16 July 2009 and one Order in Case C-302/10 of 17 January 2012. The judgment and the Order of the CJEU have clarified the conditions for making lawful temporary copies according to Article 5(1) of the Infosoc Directive which is implemented by section 11a paragraph 1 of the Copyright Act.

The provision in section 11a paragraph 1 on temporary reproduction does not apply to computer programs and databases. Exemptions to the exclusive rights in

118. The provision in the first sentence of s. 11 para. 3 does not apply to the production of copies pursuant to s. 16 para. 5 regarding copying in conformity with the Act on Legal Deposit of Published Material.

computer programs and databases are exclusively governed by sections 36 and 37 of the Copyright Act. On sections 36 and 37, *see infra* paragraph 82-83.

II. Reproduction for Private Use

81. The entitlement to reproduce copyrightable works for private use depends on whether the copy made is in digitized form or not. The main rule, which does not cover copies in digitized form, is stipulated in section 12 paragraph 1 of the Act, according to which anyone is entitled to make or have made, for private purposes, single copies of works that have been made public if this is not done for commercial purposes. Such copies may not be used for any other purposes. The terms 'single copies' and 'for private purposes' have to be interpreted narrowly. Only natural persons, not legal persons, are entitled to reproduction for private use under section 12; however, legal persons may reproduce copies of protected works according to the provisions on extended collective licences in section 14 of the Act (*see infra* paragraph 94). A natural person may reproduce copies for his/her own use and for the use of others within his/her family and his/her private sphere, no matter whether the copies are used for research, study, entertainment or hobby activities. Copying by members of closed associations or study groups of a private character can take place in compliance with section 12 paragraph 1, and also when the copies are used by other members of the association or the group. Copying made by one person for the use of another person is in compliance with section 12 paragraph 1 provided a personal tie exists between the two persons. A person is entitled to reproduce copies of periodical articles and other works at his/her place of employment for the use of conducting the tasks comprising his/her job function. However, he/she may not produce a number of copies for general distribution among the other employees at the place of employment. A teacher is entitled to make copies for his/her personal teaching preparations and for a few particularly interested pupils, but he/she is not entitled to make copies for the whole class. Doctors and lawyers and the like, as a part of their own business, can make copies for personal and professional use in compliance with section 12 paragraph 1, and, in addition, they may hand over such copies for the use of colleagues provided a personal tie exists between the persons in question.[119]

Reproduction for private use is not limited to one copy; how to construe 'single copies' must be decided in each specific case. A person may engage another person to make the reproduction for private use on his/her behalf, for example, by commissioning a public library employee to photocopy a periodical article. In that case, it is a prerequisite that the commissioner has initiated the copying, and whether the copying is in compliance with section 12 has to be decided on the basis of circumstances surrounding the commissioner.

According to section 12 paragraph 4, the provision of section 12, paragraph 1 does not confer a right to engage another person to make copies of: (i) musical works; (ii) cinematographic works; (iii) literary works if the other person assists for commercial purposes; (iv) works of applied art; or (iv) works of art if the copying

---

119. Cf. FT 1994–1995, A, 1337 ff.

is in the form of an artistic reproduction. Section 12 paragraph 4 subparagraph (iii) was adopted in 2003 in order to clarify the legal situation concerning the activities of copy shops.

Under section 12, it is permissible to use copying machines made available to the public for the purpose of private copying; however, section 12 paragraph 1 does not entitle the user to make copies of musical works and cinematographic works by using technical equipment made available to the public in libraries, on business premises or in other places accessible to the public. The same applies to literary works if the technical equipment has been provided for commercial purposes.[120]

The provision of section 12 paragraph 1 does not provide the right to: (i) construct a work of architecture; (ii) make a copy of a work of art by casting, by printing from an original negative or base or in any other manner implying that the copy can be considered an original; (iii) make copies of computer programs in digitized form; (iv) make copies in digitized form of databases if the copy is made on the basis of a reproduction of the database in digitized form; or (v) make single copies in digitized form of other works than computer programs and databases unless this is done exclusively for the personal use of the copying person himself/herself or his/her household.[121]

Section 12 paragraph 2 subparagraph (v) applies to copies in digitized forms of works other than computer programs and databases and narrows down the entitlement to reproduction for private use to 'exclusively personal use of the copying person himself or his household'. Contrary to the main rule in section 12 paragraph 1, under section 12 paragraph 1 subparagraph (v), a person is not entitled to make copies for the use of close friends and colleagues or family members who do not belong to the same household.

An additional restriction on digital reproduction for private use is stipulated in section 12 paragraph 3, which was adopted in 2003 with the purpose of preventing an allegedly widespread practice of borrowing namely film and musical works at public libraries and copying them for private use. Accordingly, it is not permitted without the consent of the author to produce copies in digital form on the basis of a copy that has been lent or hired.

A. *Computer Programs and Databases*

82. Traditionally, it has been widely accepted that anyone ought to have the possibility of making copies of protected works for private use. When computer programs were included as protectable subject matter under the Copyright Act, it was disputed whether the provisions on private reproduction should apply to these creations. The market value of a computer program is allegedly very susceptible to private reproduction.[122] In order to ensure the significant investments made in the creation of a computer program, in 1989, the Act was amended *inter alia* to the effect that private reproduction of computer programs constituted infringement of

120. Cf. s. 12 para. 5 of the Act.
121. Cf. s. 12 para. 2 of the Act.
122. *See* Report No. 1064 Copenhagen 1986 '*Ophavsret og edb*', 52 ff.

copyright. Now, the provision is found in section 12 paragraph 2 subparagraph (iii) of the Act, and it should be understood in connection to sections 36 and 37 of the Act, which to a certain extent allow copying of computer programs.[123] By virtue of section 36 paragraph 1, the person who has the right to use a computer program shall be entitled to: (i) produce such copies of the program and to make such alterations of the program that are necessary for the person to use the computer program in accordance with its intended purpose, including error correction; (ii) make a backup copy insofar as it is necessary for the use of the program; and (iii) observe, study or test the functioning of the program in order to determine the ideas and principles that underlie any element of the program if he/she does so while performing any of the acts of loading, displaying, running, transmitting or storing, etc. the program that he/she is entitled to.[124] The provision in subparagraph (i) allows the lawful user to make the copying that is a technical prerequisite for the normal use of the program; it does not allow a company to buy one computer program and install it on several of the company's computers. In spite of the wording of subparagraph (ii), the lawful user's right to make a backup copy of the program is not confined to one copy but covers the number of copies that are necessary for the use of the program. The right to make backup copies is inextricably bound to the lawful user and lapses if the lawful user distributes the program to other persons or if the right to use the program expires. Further distribution of lawfully made backup copies infringes the copyright. Subparagraph (iii) stipulates a rule on reverse engineering, but arguably, it does not confer on the lawful user any rights that he/she did not already have under subparagraph (i). Hence, the primary function of subparagraph 3 is to specify the rights of the lawful user. Contrary to subparagraph (i), subparagraphs (ii) and (iii) may not be deviated from by agreement.[125] In comparison with the general provision on reproduction for private use in section 12 paragraph 1, section 36 paragraph 1 is broader in one respect because legal persons are also entitled to copy under section 36 paragraph 1; in other respects, it is narrower, in particular, because section 36 paragraph 1 only allows copying that is necessary for the lawful use of the computer program.

83. As regards databases, a provision somewhat similar to section 36 paragraph 1 is found in the same section's paragraph 2: The person who has a right to use a database may perform such actions that are necessary for the person to obtain access to the contents of the database and make normal use of it.[126]

---

123. In general on ss 36 and 37, *see* Riis (2001), 50 ff.
124. The provisions implement Art. 5 of the Council Directive 91/250/EEC on the legal protection of computer programs.
125. Cf. s. 36 para. 3 of the Act. The question of which provisions can be deviated from by agreement is complicated and not always clear, *see* in Case C-13/20 (*Top System SA v. Belgian State*), ECLI: EU:C:2021:811; and Thomas Riis & Jens Schovsbo, 'How Much "Freedom of Contract" in EU Copyright Law?', in Florent Thouvenin, Alexander Peukert, Thomas Jaeger & Christophe Geiger (eds) 'Kreation Innovation Märkte – Creation Innovation. Festschrift Reto M. Hilty' (Springer 2024), pp. 335–345.
126. The provision implements Art. 6(1) of the Parliament and Council Directive 96/9/EC on the legal protection of databases.

B. Decompilation

84. Certain forms of reverse engineering of a computer program require copying of the program. One form of reverse engineering is decompilation, which is subjected to the provisions of section 37 of the Act. Reproduction of the code of a computer program and translation of its form is permitted where this is indispensable to obtain the information necessary to achieve the interoperability of an independently created computer program with other programs, provided the following conditions are met: (i) these acts are performed by the licensee or by another person having a right to use a copy of a program, or on their behalf by a person authorized to do so; (ii) the information necessary to achieve interoperability has not previously been readily available to the persons referred to in (i); and (iii) these acts are confined to the parts of the original program that are necessary to achieve interoperability.[127] The provision also permits decompilation in order to obtain interoperability between a computer program and computer hardware. When the producer of a computer program has revealed the principles underlying the interfaces of the computer program, for example, in a manual, and, thus, the information necessary to achieve interoperability, decompilation of the program is not permitted.[128] Decompilation is not permitted for purposes other than obtaining interoperability, for example, for the purpose of correcting errors. Section 37 paragraph 2 of the Act restricts the use of information obtained by the act of decompilation: The provisions of section 37 paragraph 1 shall not permit the information obtained through its application: (i) to be used for goals other than to achieve the interoperability of the independently created computer program; (ii) to be given to others, except when necessary for the interoperability of the independently created computer program; or (iii) to be used for the development, production or marketing of a computer program substantially similar in its expression, or for any other act that infringes copyright. Section 37 paragraph 2 subparagraph (iii) implies that the use of the expression of the interface of the decompiled program in a new such program infringes the copyright to the decompiled program.[129] By this, it is emphasized that interfaces as such are not exempted from copyright protection. The provisions on decompilation of section 37 paragraphs 1 and 2 may not be deviated from by agreement.

III. Quotations

85. A person may quote from a work that has been made public in accordance with proper usage and to the extent required for the purpose, cf. section 22 of the Act. The provision applies to categories of works that have been made public, including works of art and works of a descriptive nature. Applied to works of art, the right to quote is very limited because, normally, it is not possible to use extracts

127. Cf. s. 37 para. 1 of the Act. The provision implements Art. 6 of the Council Directive 91/250/EEC on the legal protection of computer programs.
128. Cf. FT 1992–1993, A, col. 1956.
129. Cf. FT 1992–1993, A, col. 1958.

from a work of art without infringing the moral rights of the author. However, one should note the special provision in section 23 paragraph 1 of the Act, which, from the user's point of view, pursues the same purpose as section 22:

> Works of art and works of a descriptive nature that have been made public, cf. section 1 paragraph 2, may be used in critical or scientific presentations in connection with the text if fair practice is observed and to the extent justified for the purpose. Reproduction for commercial purposes is not permitted.

It is not possible to state some objective limits within which extracts of a work constitute a lawful quote. In *Ugeskrift for Retsvæsen* 1991.744 Ø, a one-minute-and-fifty-two-second sequence from a fifty-minute television transmission was found to be a lawful quote under section 22. In another case,[130] a television station produced a programme on the South American writer Isabel Allende, which included a ten-minute-and-twenty-four-second interview with the writer. Another television station used a one-minute-and-second sequence of the interview in a programme on the film director Bille August. The court held that this use of the interview was not a legitimate quote, according to section 22.

Under section 22, still pictures from cinematographic works and other photographs cannot be lawfully quoted, for example, by reproduction in a newspaper.[131]

The right to quote has most practical importance in relation to literary works. In the case reported in *Ugeskrift for Retsvæsen* 1977.175 V, apart from a short introduction, a press release concerning a forthcoming city festival consisted of an extract from a newspaper article. The extract comprised 20% of the article. Nevertheless, the Western Court of Appeal found that it was precarious to hold that the use of the extract from the article fell outside the right to quote. Consequently, the use of the extract constituted a lawful quote. In *Ugeskrift for Retsvæsen* 1987.204 Ø, the state-owned television company *Danmarks Radio* produced a booklet on Roman agriculture for use in connection to educational radio programmes. The written part of one of the chapters of the booklet consisted primarily of extracts from one other book, and one-third of another chapter consisted of extracts from another book on the pertinent subject. The court held that these quotations were not lawful under the Copyright Act.

In the preparatory works to the 1961 Act, it is said that the right of newspapers and periodicals to quote from articles of other newspapers and periodicals is relatively broad as regards topical issues of political, economic, religious and cultural interests. Accordingly, a lawful quotation may comprise a relatively large part of such an article.[132] Normally, the use of quotations for the purpose of advertising is not considered proper usage of the quotations; in addition, such use typically infringes the author's moral rights.

130. *Ugeskrift for Retsvæsen* 1993.180 Ø.
131. Cf. FT 1994–1995, A, 1355; and *Ugeskrift for Retsvæsen* 2007.280 SH.
132. *See* Schønning (2024), 425 f.

In principle, small parts of musical compositions may be used for the purpose of 'sampling' in accordance with section 22, but it is presumed that the access to sample parts of a musical composition as a lawful quotation under section 22 is very narrow.[133]

IV. Exceptions Grounded on the Public Interest in Freedom of Information

86. The provisions of sections 26–28 of the Act serve the purposes of ensuring free debate related to public proceedings and ensuring the legal requirement of public access. Proceedings in Parliament, municipal councils and other elected public authorities, as well as judicial proceedings and public meetings held to discuss general matters, may be used without the author's consent. However, the author shall have the exclusive right to publish compilations of his/her own statements.[134] With specific reference to radio and television transmission, a provision pursuing the same aim of free debate is included in section 32 of the Act; thus, broadcasts of debate programmes in which general questions are discussed may be reproduced without the consent of the author. However, the author shall have the exclusive right to publish compilations of his/her own statements.

87. Where copies of works protected under the Copyright Act have come into an administrative authority or court in connection with its activities, the copyright does not prevent other parties from demanding access to copies of works, including demanding a transcript or a copy, in accordance with the provisions of the legislation on access to public documents. The same shall apply to works produced within the administrative authority or court.[135] The application of this provision is not confined to works that have been made public but is extended to all protected works; pursuant to the provision, public access to the work does not imply that the work has been made public. The copyright does not prevent that records and files delivered to a public record office or an institution that the Minister for Culture has decided shall be considered equivalent hereto are made available to the public in accordance with the provisions of the legislation on archives. However, it is prohibited to issue transcripts or to make copies of private documents.[136] To the extent justified by the purpose, works may be used in connection with: (i) judicial proceedings and proceedings before administrative tribunals, etc. and (ii) proceedings within public authorities and institutions under Parliament. The right to further exploitation is subject to the provisions otherwise in force.[137]

88. If performance or exhibition of a work is part of a current event and it is used in film, radio or television, the work may be included to the extent the work forms

133. Cf. Schovsbo, Rosenmeier & Petersen (2024), 99, 243; Schønning (2024), 425; and Rosenmeier (1996), 97 ff.
134. Cf. s. 26 of the Act.
135. Cf. s. 27 para. 1 of the Act.
136. Cf. s. 27 para. 2 of the Act.
137. Cf. s. 28 paras 1 and 2 of the Act.

a natural part of the reporting of the current event, cf. section 25 of the Act.[138] For example, the provision is applicable to a television recording of the performance of a musical work or the recitation of a poem at a celebration. Under section 25, it is not permitted to include old recordings of previous current events into a new recording of a current event; however, the provision does not prevent a television station from retransmitting unaltered old recordings of current events.[139]

Works of art made available to the public may be used in newspapers and periodicals in connection with the reporting of current events in accordance with proper usage and to the extent required for the purpose. The provision does not apply to works produced with a view to use in newspapers or periodicals, cf. section 23 paragraph 3 of the Act. For example, under this provision, it is permissible for a newspaper to print photographs of paintings in connection to the obituary of the painter who has created the paintings.[140] The exclusion of works of arts produced with a view to use in newspapers and periodicals aims at works such as press photographs, newspaper drawings and still pictures from a television programme, provided the programme is reporting current events. The Act contains various other exemptions to the protection of works of art that support the public interest in the free flow of information. Published works of art or copies of works of art that have been transferred to others by the author may be used in newspapers, periodicals, film and television if the use is of subordinate importance in the context in question.[141] Works of art included in a collection or exhibited publicly or offered for sale may be reproduced in catalogues of the collection. Such works of art may also be used in notices of exhibitions or sale, including in the form of communication to the public.[142] Furthermore, works of art may be reproduced in pictorial form and then made available to the public if they are permanently situated in a public place or road. This provision does not apply if the work of art is the chief motif and its reproduction is used for commercial purposes.[143] Buildings may be freely reproduced in pictorial form and then made available to the public.[144]

V. Educational Activities

89. In respect of the performing right, it is stipulated in section 21 paragraph 1 subparagraph 1 that a published work other than dramatic or cinematographic works may be performed in public on occasions where the audience or spectators are admitted free of charge if the performance is not the essential part of the event in question and if it is not organized for commercial purposes. The exemption applies

138. The provision is based on Art. 10*bis* of the Berne Convention.
139. Cf. FT 1994–1995, A, 1360.
140. Cf. Report No. 1197 Copenhagen 1990 '*Slutbetænkning*', 174.
141. Cf. s. 23 para. 4 of the Act.
142. Cf. s. 24 para. 1 of the Act. *See Ugeskrift for Retsvæsen 2001.1291 Ø*, where the publication was considered an art book rather than as a catalogue of the collection.
143. Cf. s. 24 para. 2 of the Act. *See* the Supreme Court decision reported in *Ugeskrift for Retsvæsen* 2001.1691 H.
144. Cf. s. 24 para. 3 of the Act.

to perfomances that take place at, e.g., public schools. It is assumed that the performance of copyright-protected works for educational purposes, at least in primary school classes, is not considered public performance. Obviously, section 21 paragraph 1 subparagraph 1 is applicable only to cases where the performance is public within the meaning of the Act (*see supra* paragraph 59). Section 21 paragraph 1 subparagraph 1 does not cover the right of communication to the public.[145] In practice, this means that the provision only allows for direct performances (live performances) and performances on radio, television and the Internet.

90. The exemption on reproduction for private use in section 12 paragraph 1 is applicable for natural persons only. Legal persons, such as institutions of education, need another legal basis for lawful reproduction of protected works. Reproduction and communication to the public of protected works for the purpose of education is controlled by the extended collective licence in section 13 paragraph 1 of the Act. The copies thus made may be used only in educational activities comprised by the agreement presumed in section 50. An extended collective licence may be invoked by users who have made an agreement on the particular exploitation of the work with an organization comprising a substantial number of Danish authors; the extended collective licence grants the users a right to exploit other works of the same nature although the authors of those works are not represented by the organization (In general, on section 50 and extended collective licences, *see infra* paragraph 110-111). The extended collective licence in section 13 paragraph 1 applies to photocopying and the like, digital copying and the recording of works broadcast on radio and television and is confined to published and broadcast works. The agreement underlying the extended collective licence provides the authors' organizations the opportunity to decide which institutions and which categories of works should be subject to the extended collective licence. If an authors' organization demands unfair terms included in such an agreement, the issue can be referred to the Copyright License Tribunal. The Tribunal has the power to determine the terms of the agreement, including the remuneration.[146]

91. According to section 13 paragraph 1, 'published works' only cover computer programs in digital form to the extent that the work has been communicated to the public.[147] Use of works under the extended collective licence through secure electronic environments that are only accessible to pupils, students and teaching staff of an educational institution shall be deemed to take place in Denmark if the educational institution is established in Denmark.[148]

92. If no suitable licences are available, copies may be made and made available to the general public for the sole purpose of illustration for educational purposes, provided that this is not done for commercial purposes, jf. Section 13 a paragraph 1. The author is entitled to reasonable compensation unless the damage

145. Cf. s. 22 para. 2.
146. Cf. s. 13 para. 5 of the Act.
147. Cf. s. 13 para. 3 of the Act.
148. Cf. s. 13 para. 4 of the Act. Se also s. 88 a of the Act.

is minimal. This provision cannot be deviated from the agreement. Use under Section 13 a paragraph 1 is conditional on it taking place under the responsibility of an educational institution on its premises or elsewhere or via a secure electronic environment that is only accessible to the educational institution's pupils, students and teaching staff. Use of works via secure electronic environments is deemed to take place in Denmark if the educational institution is established in Denmark.[149]

93. Finally, production of anthologies for educational use is subject to compulsory licensing according to section 18 of the Act. Minor portions of literary works and musical works or such works of small proportions may be used in composite works compiling contributions by a large number of authors for use in educational activities, provided that five years have elapsed since the year when the work was published. In connection with the text, works of art and works of a descriptive nature, cf. section 1(2), may also be used, provided that five years have elapsed since the year when the work was made public. The author shall be entitled to remuneration. If the parties cannot agree on the remuneration, the issue can be referred to the Copyright License Tribunal.[150] The compulsory licence does not apply to works prepared for use in educational activities or if the use is for commercial purposes.[151] In order to benefit from the compulsory licence in section 18 paragraph 1, the resulting compilation or anthology shall constitute a copyrightable work in its own right. Such a compilation shall not necessarily be in print but may as well consist of sound recordings or be a digitized multimedia work. How to construe the term 'short works' within the meaning of section 18 paragraph 1 is not elaborated in the preparatory works to the Act; however, lyrics and poems are mentioned as examples.[152]

VI. Reproduction by Business Enterprises, Etc.

94. Reproduction by business enterprises does not benefit from the exemption on reproduction for private use in section 12 paragraph 1 because these institutions are not natural persons. This kind of reproduction is subject to an extended collective licence. Public and private institutions, organizations and business enterprises may for internal use for the purpose of their activities by photocopying, etc., make or have copies made of descriptive articles in newspapers, magazines and collections, of brief excerpts of other published works of a descriptive nature, of musical works and of illustrations reproduced in association with the text, provided the requirements regarding extended collective licence according to section 50 have

149. Cf. s. 13 a of the Act. The provision implements parts of Art. 5 of the DSMD.
150. Cf. s. 18 para. 1 of the Act.
151. Cf. s. 18 para. 2 of the Act.
152. Cf. FT 1994–1995, A, 1350.

been met. Such copies may be used only for activities that are covered by the agreement presumed in section 50. The extended collective licence applies only to published works and does not cover recordings of broadcasts on radio or television. Individual rightholders may opt out of the extended collective licence and exercise their exclusive rights.[153]

The agreements concluded under the provision are administered by the collective administration organization *Copydan*. If an authors' organization demands unfair terms included in such an agreement, the issue can be referred to the Copyright License Tribunal. The Tribunal has the power to determine the terms of the agreement, including the remuneration.[154]

VII. Reproduction for Visually Handicapped and Hearing-Impaired Persons

95. To the benefit of certain handicapped persons, special provisions are included in sections 17–17 e of the Act. According to the general rules in section 17, paragraph 1, it is permitted to reproduce and distribute copies of published works when the reproduction and the distributed copies are specifically intended for use by deaf and speech-impaired persons, to the extent that sections 17 a-17 e do not apply. Section 17, paragraph 1 does not apply to reproduction or distribution of copies for commercial purposes, to sound recordings of literary works or to reproductions consisting exclusively of sound recordings of musical works.

Sections 17 a-17 e provide exceptions for the benefit of persons with visual or reading disabilities. Accordingly, a person with a visual or reading disability or a person acting on their behalf may produce an accessible format. An accessible format is works that are presented in an alternative way or in an alternative form that allows a person with a visual or reading disability to access the work as easily and comfortably as a person without those impairments or disabilities.[155] An accessible format may only be used by a person with a visual or reading disability. An authorized entity may produce, transfer, make available, disseminate or lend an accessible format to a person with a visual or reading disability or another authorized entity within the European Union. The acts referred to may only be carried out on a non-commercial basis for the use of persons with visual or reading disabilities.[156]

Sections 17 a–17 e are not confined to particular kinds of handicaps but cover physical as well as psychical handicaps. The provisions cover the making of copies in Braille, synthetic speak and the like, when such copying is in digitized form. If the said usage is done for commercial purposes, it is subject to protection under exclusive rights.

As the general rule, the author shall be entitled to remuneration unless the damage to the author is minimal. Furthermore, no compensation is payable when an authorized entity established in Denmark produces, transmits, makes available, disseminates or lends an accessible format in Braille or other formats normally used

153. Cf. s. 14 para. 1 of the Act.
154. Cf. s. 14 para. 4 of the Act.
155. Section 17 a para. 2.
156. Section 17 c paras 1–2.

only by persons with visual or reading disabilities.[157] The provision is thus a combination of a compulsory licence and a traditional exception. If the parties cannot agree on the remuneration, the issue can be referred to the Copyright License Tribunal.

VIII. Radio and Television: Cable Retransmission

96. Radio and television broadcasts of copyright-protected works by State-owned broadcasting stations are subject to extended collective licence pursuant to section 30 of the Act. The State-owned broadcasting stations, *Danmarks Radio*, TV 2/DANMARK A/S, the regional TV 2 companies, *Færøernes Fjernsyn* and *Grønlands Radio,* may on radio or television broadcast published works provided the requirements regarding extended collective licence according to section 50 have been met. However, the provision does not apply to dramatic or cinematographic works.[158] If an authors' organization demands unfair terms included in a collective agreement in relation to section 30, the issue can be referred to the Copyright License Tribunal. The Tribunal has the power to determine the terms of the agreement, including the remuneration.[159] Works of art are covered by the extended collective licence when the author has transferred one or more copies to others; thus, it is not a requirement that works of art have been published.[160] The author, who is not represented by the organization that is party to the agreement underlying the extended collective licence, may issue a prohibition to the radio or television organization against the broadcast of the work.[161] Local radio and television stations and programme production companies supplying the State-owned radio and television stations do not benefit from the extended collective licence. The application of the extended collective licence is limited in regard to satellite broadcast. Thus, the extended collective licence under section 30 paragraph 1 does not apply to broadcasts on radio and television via satellite unless the broadcaster makes a simultaneous broadcast via a terrestrial network.[162]

97. The Danish State-owned broadcasting stations are permitted to broadcast repeats of their own productions and to make their own productions available to the public (e.g., on the Internet) under the conditions of extended collective licence. Accordingly, works that have been made public and are a part of DR's, TV 2/DANMARK A/S' and the regional TV 2 companies' own productions can, by the mentioned broadcasters, be repeated and made available in such a way that members of the public may access them from a place and at a time individually chosen by them provided that the requirements regarding extended collective licence according to section 50 have been met. The provision applies correspondingly to the

157. Section 17 d paras 1–2.
158. Cf. s. 30 para. 1 of the Act. In general, on the extended collective licence on radio and television broadcasts, *see* Report No. 1197 Copenhagen 1990 '*Slutbetænkning*', 187 ff.
159. Cf. s. 30 para. 5 of the Act.
160. Cf. s. 30 para. 3 of the Act.
161. Cf. s. 30 para. 2 of the Act.
162. Cf. s. 30 para. 4 of the Act.

making of the necessary copies. However, the provision applies exclusively to works that are a part of productions broadcast before 1 January 2007, cf. section 30a paragraph 1 of the Act. The author may issue a prohibition to the broadcaster against the making available of the work pursuant to section 30 a paragraph 1.[163] The provision covers all categories of works made public, including dramatic works and cinematographic works, but it is confined to the broadcasting stations' own productions; thus, the general cinema repertoire of feature films is excluded. The concept of 'own productions' includes television productions made by independent production companies provided that the production has been ordered and financed by the State-owned broadcasting station. The decisive factor is whether the State-owned broadcasting station has financed the production.

98. Broadcasters may, for the purpose of their broadcasts, record works on tape, film or any other device that can reproduce them, provided they have the right to broadcast the works in question. The right to make such works available to the public is subject to rules otherwise in force, cf. section 31 paragraph 1 of the Act.[164] The provision that applies to all broadcasters and not exclusively the ones owned by the State grants the broadcasters a right to make ephemeral recordings, which enable the broadcasters to transmit non-live telecasts. The right to make ephemeral recordings is inextricably bound to the right to broadcast copyright-protected works. In the case reported in *Ugeskrift for Retsvæsen* 2003.284 H, the Supreme Court held that section 31 paragraph 1 allowed the broadcasting station *Danmarks Radio* to copy published musical recordings into a digital database for the purpose of facilitating radio broadcasts.

99. Section 25 a of the Copyright Act stipulates that works which are part of short reports are given access to under section 90, paragraph 3 of the Radio and Television Broadcasting Act and provisions issued according to section 90, paragraph 5 of the same Act may be reproduced in accordance with section 90, paragraph 4 of the Radio and Television Broadcasting Act and in accordance with provisions issued according to section 90, paragraph 5 of the same Act. Section 90, paragraph 3 of the Radio and Television Broadcasting Act gives access to short extracts of transmissions of significant interest to the public, and according to section 90, paragraph 4 of the Radio and Television Broadcasting Act, extracts to which access is given under paragraph 3 may only be used in general news programmes. Extracts in a general news programme may only be used in on-demand audiovisual media services when the same programme is offered with a time lag by the same media service provider. The Minister for Culture is empowered to lay down detailed rules on access to and use of extracts under these provisions.[165]

163. Cf. s. 30a para. 2 of the Act.
164. The provision is based on Art. 11*bis*(3) of the Berne Convention.
165. Cf. s. 90 para. 5 of the Radio and Television Broadcasting Act. The Minister has laid down such rules in Ordinance No. 106 of 28 Jan. 2010.

100. Broadcasters may on request deliver recordings of broadcasts to persons who have taken part in the broadcasts in question or who feel offended by comments in a specific broadcast or through public mention of the broadcast in question. Recordings delivered according to the first sentence may be used for internal use only.[166] The provision applies to recordings of all broadcasts of a particular radio or television station regardless of whether the broadcast has been produced by another radio or television station or by an independent production company. Section 34 does not put broadcasters under an obligation to deliver recordings of broadcasts to the persons mentioned in section 34 but provides them with the possibility of doing so without infringing the copyrights.

101. Cable retransmission of radio and television broadcasts is governed by section 35 of the Act, which in paragraph 1 contains an extended collective licence. Copyrightable works that are broadcast over the air on radio or television may simultaneously and without any alterations be retransmitted by cable systems and may in the same way be retransmitted to the general public by means of radio systems if the conditions concerning the extended collective licence under section 50 of the Act have been met. The provision also applies to the rights of performing artists, phonogram producers, film producers and photographers but not to the rights owned by broadcasting organizations. Irrespective of the provision under section 35 paragraph 1, works that are included in a broadcast over the air and that are received by way of the receivers' own antennae may be retransmitted via cable systems that consist of no more than two connections.[167] Accordingly, retransmission by cable systems of no more than two connections is not restricted by copyright. The extended collective licence covers all kinds of terrestrial and satellite broadcasts, including broadcasts of fixed service satellites. Coded broadcasts are covered by the extended collective licence, provided decoding facilities have been made available to the public by the broadcasting organization or with the consent of the broadcasting organization.[168] Broadcasts that originate as cable transmissions are not covered by the extended collective licence but are subject to the exclusive rights of the rightholders. The owner of a cable system is liable to ensure that an agreement has been concluded on the retransmission of broadcasts via cable systems. If the remuneration payable by the owner of a cable system according to an agreement between the parties pursuant to section 35 paragraph 1 or to a decision made by the Copyright License Tribunal (*Ophavsretslicensnævnet*) has been fixed as an amount per connection, the user of the individual connection is under an obligation to pay the owner a corresponding amount.[169]

By an amendment to the Copyright Act in 1996, the extended collective licence substituted a compulsory licence due to the obligations under the Council Directive 93/83/EEC on the coordination of certain rules concerning copyright and rights related to copyright applicable to satellite broadcasting and cable retransmission.

166. Cf. s. 34 of the Act.
167. Cf. s. 35 para. 2 of the Act.
168. Cf. FT 1996–1997, A, 1932.
169. Cf. s. 35 para. 3 of the Act.

IX. Text and Datamining

102. By the implementation of the last part of the DSMD in June 2023, two exceptions on text and data mining were introduced into the Act. The provisions are worded in strict compliance with the corresponding provisions of the directive. The general rule in section 11 b stipulates that anyone who has legal access to a work may extract and produce copies of the work for the purpose of text and data mining, provided that the rightholder has not expressly reserved the use of the work in an appropriate manner. Extracts made and copies produced in accordance with this provision may be stored for as long as necessary for the purpose of text and data mining.

The general rule in section 11 b thus enables the rightholders to opt out of the exception. That option is not available under the special rule that applies to research organizations and cultural heritage institutions. If such institutions have legal access to a work, they may extract and produce copies of the work in order to carry out text and data mining, cf. section 11 b(1), for the purpose of scientific research. The exception applies regardless of whether the scientific research is carried out within the framework of public-private partnerships, and the exception cannot be derogated from by agreement, cf. section 11 c. Copies of works produced in accordance with section 11 c(1) shall be stored with an appropriate level of security and may be stored for the purpose of scientific research. Under the provision, rightholders are authorized to take measures to ensure the security and integrity of the networks and databases in which the works are stored. Such measures shall not go beyond what is necessary to achieve this objective.

X. Other Exceptions to the Scope of Copyright Protection

103. The Copyright Act contains a number of more specific exemptions to the scope of copyright protection.

A few published songs may be freely reproduced in small song sheets produced solely for the use of participants in a particular meeting. However, no more than 300 copies of each song sheet may be produced.[170]

104. Hospitals, nursing homes, prisons, other twenty-four-hour institutions within the social and welfare sector, the prison service and similar institutions may for the brief use of the inmates and others of the institution make recordings of works broadcast on radio and television if this is not done for commercial purposes. Such recordings may be used only within the institution in question.[171]

105. Various provisions of the Act grant special exemptions to the benefit of archives and libraries. According to section 16 of the Act, public archives, public libraries and other libraries that are financed in whole or in part by the public authorities, as well as State-run museums and museums that have been approved in

170. Cf. s. 18 para. 3 of the Act.
171. Cf. s. 15 of the Act.

accordance with the Museums Act, may use and distribute copies of works in their activities in certain specified situations if this is not done for commercial purposes. However, this does not apply to computer programs in digital form, with the exception of computer games.[172] The following situations are listed in section 16:

- The institutions may make copies for the purpose of backup and preservation (paragraph 2).
- If a copy in an institution's collection is incomplete, the institution may make copies of the missing parts, unless the work can be acquired through general trade or from the publisher (paragraph 3).
- Libraries may make copies of published works that should be available in the library's collections but which cannot be acquired through general trade or from the publisher (paragraph 4).
- The copyright does not prevent the making of copies in accordance with the provisions of the Act on Legal Deposit of Published Material (paragraph 5).

As the main rule, copies that have been made in accordance with the said provisions of section 16 or delivered pursuant to the Act on Legal Deposit of Published Material may be loaned to users.[173] The right to further exploitation of copies made pursuant to section 16 is subject to the provisions otherwise in force.[174]

Published works may be made available to individuals at the institutions specified in section 16[175] for personal viewing or study on the spot by means of technical equipment. Notwithstanding this provision, copies that are made or deposited pursuant to the Act on Legal Deposit of Published Material may only be made available at the Royal Library, the State and University Library and the Danish Film Institute for separate individual persons. The said institutions may communicate and hand over legal deposited copies of works that have been broadcast on radio and television, films and works published on electronic communication networks for research purposes, if the work cannot be acquired through general trade. Such copies may not be used in any other way.[176]

Libraries are entitled to lend certain works by means of digital transmission subject to extended collective licence. Thus, pursuant to section 16 b of the Act, public libraries and other libraries financed in whole or in part by the public authorities may upon request in digital form reproduce articles from newspapers, magazines and composite works, brief excerpts of books and other published literary works, as well as illustrations and music reproduced in connection with the text, provided the requirements regarding the extended collective licence according to section 50 have been met. This provision does not comprise broadcast by radio or television or the making available to the public of works in such a way that members of the public may access them from a place and at a time individually chosen by them.

172. Cf. s. 16 para. 1 of the Act.
173. Cf. s. 16 para. 6 of the Act.
174. Cf. s. 16 para. 7 of the Act.
175. Public archives, public libraries and other libraries that are financed in whole or in part by the public authorities, as well as State-run museums and museums that have been approved in accordance with the Museums Act.
176. Cf. s. 16 a paras 1–3 of the Act.

106. Regarding the performance right, section 21 paragraph 1 subparagraph 2 of the Act stipulates that a published work, which is not a dramatic work or a cinematographic work, may be performed in public on occasions when the audience is admitted free of charge, where the performance is not the main feature of the event, where the event does not occur for commercial purposes and where the performance occurs in the case of divine services. This exemption does not apply to performances on radio or television.

107. Sections 16 c–16 f contain exceptions related to out-of-commerce work and implement Articles 8–11 of the DSMD. Traditionally, acts concerning copyright-protected out-of-commerce works have been governed by extended collective licensing. The provision on extended collective licensing of out-of-commerce works is maintained in Section 16 c of the Copyright Act, and it is the reason why the alternative way of clearing rights to out-of-commerce works by means of diligent search (Sections 16 d – 16 f) is not expected to be of any significant practical importance.

108. Previously, the Copyright Act did not include an explicit exception for parodies, etc. It was generally assumed that a non-statutory parody exception existed, but it was disputed, which created uncertainty as to the actual legal position concerning parodies.[177] In June 2024, a parody exception was adopted and included in the Copyright Act. The provision in Section 24 b now stipulates that it is permitted to use works for the purpose of parody, caricature or pastiche. The provision does not apply to computer programs and databases. Contrary to the other exceptions in Chapter 2 of the Act, the parody exception is not only an exception from economic rights but also from moral rights. Furthermore, the parody exception also exempts from the provision in Section 11 paragraph 2 of the Act, according to which the exceptions in Chapter 2 may not be used in a way that allows the original work to be modified to a greater extent than the authorized use requires.

XI. Compulsory Licences: The Copyright License Tribunal

109. The compulsory licences are found in section 17 d paragraph 2 (exceptions concerning persons with visual or reading disabilities) and section 18 paragraph 1 (anthologies for educational use, etc.), regarding copyrights, and in section 68 (use of sound recordings in broadcasts on radio and television) regarding neighbouring rights. If no agreement can be reached on the amount of remuneration under the compulsory licences, each party may submit the question to a tribunal: the Copyright License Tribunal (*Ophavsretslicensnævnet*) set up by the Minister for Culture. The decision of the Tribunal may not be brought before any other administrative authority.[178] In the Order No. 25 of 14 January 2004, the Minister has laid down the rules governing the activities of the Tribunal.

177. *See* the case reported in *Ugeskrift for Retsvæsen* 2023.3772 H.
178. Cf. s. 47 para. 2 of the Act.

If an organization of right owners approved in accordance with section 50 paragraph 4 of the Act or a broadcaster unreasonably refuses to consent to retransmission via cable systems or wireless of works and broadcasts that are broadcast wireless simultaneously and without alteration or if such retransmission is offered on unreasonable terms, the Copyright License Tribunal may at request grant the necessary permission and lay down the conditions in this respect. However, in such a case, the Copyright License Tribunal's decision is not binding on radio and television companies.[179]

XII. Extended Collective Licences

110. The notion of extended collective licences originates in Nordic copyright law. For the system to work efficiently, it is a prerequisite that collective organizations representing the rightholders exist. On behalf of their members, the collective organizations enter into agreements with users of copyright-protected works specifying the permitted use of the works and the conditions in this respect. Due to the statutory provisions on the extended collective licences, the effects of the collective agreements are extended to the rightholders who are not represented by the collective organizations. Thus, in respect of rightholders who are not represented by the collective organizations, extended collective licences have the same effect as compulsory licences. In areas where the only practical way of clearing copyrights for the use of protected works is by way of collective licencing, the users cannot be sure that all works and all rightholders are covered by the licence agreement and, thus that all relevant rights have been cleared. Consequently, the users run the risk of copyright infringement. This so-called outsider problem is solved by the extended collective licences.[180]

The Act includes various extended collective licences, and common provisions on these are contained in sections 50–52 of the Act. Extended collective licences according to sections 13, 14 and 16 b, 16 c, 17 paragraph 3, 24 a, 29 a, 30, 30 a and 35 of the Act may be invoked by users who have made an agreement on the exploitation of works in question with an organization comprising a substantial number of

179. Cf. s. 48 para. 1 of the Act.

180. In general on extended collective licences, *see* Thomas Riis & Jens Schovsbo, 'Extended Collective Licenses in Action', *International Review of Intellectual Property and Competition Law* (2012): 930–950; Thomas Riis & Jens Schovsbo, 'Extended Collective Licenses and the Nordic Experience: It's a Hybrid but Is It a Volvo or a Lemon', *The Columbia Journal of Law and the Arts* (2010): 471–498; Martin Kyst, 'Aftalelicens – Quo Vadis?', *Nordiskt Immmateriellt Rättsskydd* (2009): 44–55; Ole-Andreas Rognstad, 'Avtalelisenser', *Nordiskt Immmateriellt Rättsskydd* (2004): 151–159; G.W.G. Karnell, 'Outsiders' Rights: A Dilemma for Collective Administration of Authors' Rights in a Present and Enlarged European Community', *European Intellectual Property Review* (1991): 430–435; H. Lund Christiansen, 'The Nordic Licensing Systems – Extended Collective Agreement Licensing', *European Intellectual Property Review* (1991): 346–349; G.W.G. Karnell, 'Avtalslicenskonstruktionen principiella och praktiska frågor', *Nordiskt Immateriellt Rättsskydd* (1981): 255–267; and Report No. 912 Copenhagen 1981 '*Licenskonstruktioner og fotokopiering*'.

authors[181] of a certain type of works that are used in Denmark.[182] The extended collective licence grants the users a right to exploit other works of the same nature, although the authors of those works are not represented by the organization. The extended collective licence gives the user the right to exploit the unrepresented works only in the manner and on the terms that follow from the agreement made with the organization.[183]

A provision on a general extended collective licence that is not restricted to specific forms of usage was adopted in 2008, cf. section 50 paragraph 2 of the Act. The provision was adopted in order to accommodate the need for effective clearing of rights that originate from rapid technological development, for example, in respect of orphan works.[184] Under section 50 paragraph 2, the unrepresented author may issue a prohibition to one of the parties from the collective agreement.

Authors' organizations that make collective agreements in relation to extended collective licences must be sufficiently representative of the authors of a certain type of works used in Denmark and shall be approved by the Minister for Culture. The Minister may decide that an approved organization shall, in certain areas, be a joint organization comprising several organizations, each of which shall be deemed to meet the requirements of representativeness.[185] While it is not explicitly mentioned in the Act (anymore), however, only one organization can be approved for each type of works. Approved organizations shall take appropriate notice measures prior to the use of works under the agreement to inform rightholders of the collective management organization's ability to conclude agreements on the use of works and of the rightholders' right to seek injunctions.[186]

For exploitation of works under the extended collective licences, the rules laid down by the organization with regard to the distribution of remuneration between the authors represented by the organization apply correspondingly to unrepresented authors.[187] Unrepresented authors may claim individual remuneration, although such a right appears neither in the agreement with the user nor in the organization's rules on remuneration. The amount of the individual remuneration may be fixed according to the provision of section 47 of the Copyright License Tribunal. The claim for remuneration shall be advanced against the organization only.[188]

111. In the absence of any result of negotiations on the making of agreements directed at an extended collective licence under sections 13, 14, 16b, 17 paragraph 3, 24 a, 29 a and 30a, each party may demand mediation.[189] The request may be made if one of the parties has broken off the negotiations or rejected a request for

181. In this connection the term 'authors' includes persons who have been assigned the copyright from the authors.
182. Cf. s. 50 para. 1 of the Act.
183. Cf. s. 50 para. 3 of the Act.
184. Rights to orphan works can also be cleared by means of diligent search, cf. Ch. 6 b of the Copyright Act.
185. Cf. s. 50 para. 4 of the Act.
186. Cf. s. 50 para. 5 of the Act.
187. Cf. s. 51 para. 1 of the Act.
188. Cf. s. 51 para. 2 of the Act.
189. Cf. s. 52 para. 1 of the Act.

negotiations or if the negotiations do not appear to lead to any result.[190] The mediator may make proposals for the solution of the dispute and may demand that such a proposal be submitted to the competent bodies of the parties for adoption or rejection within a time limit fixed by the mediator.[191] The mediator may decide that agreements shall remain in force although the terms of the agreement have expired or will expire in the course of the negotiations. However, the agreement cannot be prolonged for more than two weeks after the parties have decided on a final mediation proposal or proposal for arbitration or after the mediator has notified that there is no basis to make such proposals.[192]

XIII. Orphan Works

112. Chapter 6b (section 75f–75m) of the copyright Act implements the provisions of the Orphan Works Directive.[193] Chapter 6b provides a limited number of organizations with the opportunity to clear rights to orphan works by means of a diligent search. In order to achieve aims related to their public interest missions, the following organizations established in Denmark may use orphan works after having carried out a diligent search:

(i) Publicly accessible libraries, educational establishments and museums.
(ii) Archives, film and audio heritage institutions.
(iii) Public service broadcasting organizations.[194]

An orphan work is defined as a work or a sound recording where none of the rightholders in such work or sound recording is identified or, even if one or more of the rightholders is identified, none is located despite a diligent search for the rightholders having been carried out and recorded, cf. section 75 j.[195] Section 75j stipulates that for the purposes of establishing whether a work or a sound recording is an orphan work, the organizations that benefit form the provisions in Chapter 6b (cf. section 75 h) shall ensure that a diligent search is carried out for each work or sound recording prior to use.[196] As the main rule, the diligent search shall be carried out in the country in the EEA of first publication of the work or sound recording or, in the absence of publication, of first broadcast. If the producer of a cinematographic work has his headquarters or habitual residence in a country within the EEA, the diligent search shall be carried out in the country of the producer's headquarters or habitual residence.[197] Further provisions specifying where the diligent search shall be carried out are contained in section 75j paragraphs 2–5 of the Act.

190. Cf. s. 52 para. 2 of the Act.
191. Cf. s. 52 para. 4 of the Act.
192. Cf. s. 52 para. 5 of the Act.
193. Directive 2012/28/EU of 25 Oct. 2012 on certain permitted uses of orphan works.
194. Cf. s. 75 h of the Act.
195. Cf. s. 75 f of the Act.
196. Cf. s. 75 j, para. 1 of the Act.
197. Cf. s. 75 j, para. 2 of the Act.

The organization that carries out the diligent search shall provide the following information to the Danish Ministry of Culture: (i) The results of the diligent search, (ii) The use of the orphan works, (iii) Any change of the orphan work status and (iv) Relevant contact information.[198]

In Ordinance No. 1146 of 25 October 2014 on the diligent search for and registration of orphan works, the Ministry of Culture has laid down rules governing the content of the diligent search, including the sources to consult in connection with the diligent search and the database for orphan works maintained by European Union Intellectual Property Office (EUIPO).

A work or sound recording which, pursuant to the legislation in another country within the EEA, is considered an orphan work shall be considered an orphan work in Denmark as well.[199]

In order to achieve aims related to their public-interest missions, the organizations that benefit from the provisions in Chapter 6b are permitted to: (i) make the orphan work available in such a way that the public acquires access to it at an individually chosen place and time and (ii) reproduce the orphan work for the purposes of digitization, making available to the public, indexing, cataloguing, preservation or restoration.[200]

If a rightholder approaches the organization using the orphan work, the orphan work or sound recording in question shall cease to be orphan. If a work ceases to be an orphan work, the rightholder has a right to receive a reasonable compensation from the organization which has used the orphan work in accordance with the provisions of Chapter 6 b.[201]

113. Rights to orphan works can also be cleared by means of extended collective licence, cf. section 50, paragraph 2 of the Copyright Act. The possibility of clearing rights to orphan works by extended collective licence is not limited to the public interest organizations mentioned in section 75h of the Act but is available to all types of users.

§8. DURATION OF COPYRIGHT PROTECTION

114. The copyright in a work comes into existence when the work is created. The copyright lasts for seventy years after the year of the author's death. With regard to multi-author works, according to section 6 of the Act, the copyright lasts for seventy years after the death of the last surviving author. With regard to cinematographic works, the copyright, however, lasts for seventy years after the year of death of the last of the following persons to survive: (i) the principal director; (ii) the author of the script; (iii) the author of the dialogue; and (iv) the composer of music specifically created for use in the cinematographic work.[202] Where a work is

198. Cf. s. 75 j, para. 7 of the Act.
199. Cf. s. 75 k of the Act.
200. Cf. s. 75 l, para. 1 of the Act.
201. Cf. s. 75 m, paras 1–2 of the Act.
202. Cf. s. 63 para. 1 of the Act.

made public without indication of the author's name, generally known as a pseudonym or signature, the copyright lasts for seventy years after the year in which the work was made public. Where a work consists of parts, volumes, instalments, issues or episodes, a separate term of protection runs for each item.[203] If, within the period mentioned, the author is indicated in the usual manner on copies of the work by his/her name, generally known as pseudonym or signature, or if it is established that he/she had died before the work was made public, the duration of copyright is calculated in accordance with section 63 paragraph 1.[204] Copyright in a work of unknown authorship that has not been made public shall last seventy years after the end of the year in which the work was created.[205] This provision prevents that copyright in unpublished works never expires.

The provisions of section 63 on the term of protection apply to Danish works and works from a country within the EEA. The term of protection of other foreign works is calculated on the basis of a principle of material reciprocity. Accordingly, a foreign work is protected for a period equal to the term of protection in the country where the work originates. However, the term of protection of a foreign work cannot exceed seventy years after the death of the author.[206]

§9. Neighbouring Rights

115. As a general observation, the protection under the neighbouring rights is in various respects weaker compared to copyright protection.

I. Performing Artists

116. The performance of a literary or artistic work by a performing artist is protected by virtue of section 65 of the Act. Section 65 only applies to performances of a literary or artistic work; other kinds of performances are not protected.[207] Thus, normally, the performances of clowns, circus performers, acrobats, athletes and the like are not protected. It has been argued that this requirement results in inadequate protection of performers since, as a consequence, not all artistic performances are protected.[208] In a Supreme Court case from 1977,[209] it was held that the protection of a stage director should be compared to the protection of performing artists, and consequently, the stage director was protected under the provision of the 1961 Act, similar to section 65. The works of stage directors are eligible for copyright protection under sections 1 and 4 of the Act as well.

203. Cf. s. 63 para. 2 of the Act.
204. Cf. s. 63 para. 3 of the Act.
205. Cf. s. 63 para. 4 of the Act. The provisions of s. 63 are based on the Council Directive 93/98/EEC of 29 Oct. 1993 harmonizing the term of protection of copyright and certain related rights.
206. Cf. s. 3 of Ordinance No. 218 of 9 Mar. 2010.
207. The provision is in conformity with Art. 3 of the Rome Convention.
208. *See* Report No. 962 Copenhagen 1982 '*Beskyttelse af kunstneriske præstationer*'; and Schovsbo, Rosenmeier & Petersen (2024), 107 f.
209. *Ugeskrift for Retsvæsen* 1978.42 H.

117. The performance right of a performing artist does not presuppose originality in the performance. In practice, most performances of literary and artistic works are protected irrespective of the degree of artistic content. However, the mechanical recitation of a text with the sole purpose of providing information is probably not protectable.[210] Notwithstanding, it is stated in the preparatory works that the performance that leads to the creation of an audio book used by blinds and persons with low reading skills is protected if it implies an artistic interpretation of the text.[211]

118. The performance of a literary or artistic work by a performing artist may not without his/her consent: (i) be recorded on tape, film or any other device by means of which it can be reproduced or (ii) be made available to the public.[212] Where a performance has been recorded, it must not without the consent of the performing artist be copied or made available to the public until fifty years after the end of the year in which the performance took place. However, if a recording of the performance is lawfully published or lawfully communicated to the public during this period, the rights shall expire fifty years from the date of the first such publication or the first such communication, whichever is the earlier.[213] However, if the recording is a sound recording and the sound recording is published or communicated to the public within the period mentioned in section 65(2) (i.e., a period of fifty years), the copyright protection shall last until seventy years passed from the end of the year of first publication or communication to the public, whichever is the earlier.[214]

119. The object of protection is exclusively the original performance. The performing artist is not granted any rights against another performing artist copying the performance (e.g., sound alikes) or against adaptations of the performance.

Pursuant to section 65 paragraph 6, a number of provisions on copyright protection apply to the protection of performing artists as well, including most of the exemptions from the scope of protection and the moral rights under section 3 of the Act.

120. A provision corresponding to section 58 on the transfer of rights in relation to film production contracts is contained in section 65 paragraph 5: 'An agreement between a performing artist and a film producer to take part in the recording of a film implies that in the absence of any opposite agreement the performing artist is assumed to have assigned his right to the rental of the film to the producer.'[215]

---

210. Cf. Schønning (2024), 620 f; and Schovsbo, Rosenmeier & Petersen (2024), 108.
211. Cf. FT 1994–1995, A, 1392.
212. Cf. s. 65 para. 1 of the Act.
213. Cf. s. 65 para. 2 of the Act.
214. Cf. s. 65 para. 4 of the Act. The provision is implementing Directive of the European Parliament and of the Council 2011/77/EU of 27 Sep. 2011 amending Directive 2006/116/EC on the term of protection of copyright and certain related rights.
215. The provision is based on Art. 2(5) of the Council Directive 92/100/EEC of 19 Nov. 1992 on rental right and lending right and on certain rights related to copyright in the field of intellectual property.

121. The rights of performing artists are subject to compulsory licence as regards published sound recordings used in broadcasts on radio and television and for other public performances, cf. section 68 paragraphs 1 and 2 of the Act. The rights of producers of sound recordings are covered by the compulsory licence under section 68 as well. Performing artists and producers of sound recordings are entitled to remuneration, and the claim for remuneration may be made only through a joint organization approved by the Minister for Culture, which comprises performers as well as producers of sound recordings.[216] The said organization approved by the minister is the collective administration organization *Gramex*. The compulsory licence does not apply to public performance in the form of the making available to the public of published sound recordings in such a way that members of the public may access them from a place and at a time individually chosen by them;[217] additionally, it does not apply to broadcasts on television and other public performances of cinematographic works if sound and images are broadcast or performed simultaneously.[218] Consequently, the soundtrack to a moving picture is covered by the compulsory licence only in situations where the soundtrack and not the associated moving picture is performed publicly. The common provisions of sections 47 and 49 on compulsory licences apply to the compulsory licence under section 68.

II. Producers of Sound Recordings

122. By virtue of section 66 of the Act, sound recordings may not without the consent of the producer be copied or made available to the public until fifty years have elapsed after the end of the year in which the recording was made. If a sound recording is published during this period, the protection shall, however, last until seventy years have elapsed after the end of the year of the first publication. If a sound recording is not published but is made public in any other manner within the period mentioned in the first sentence, the protection shall, however, last until seventy years have elapsed after the end of the year in which it was made public.[219]

123. Protection under section 66 is granted regardless of the character of the sounds recorded, which is an anomaly in Danish copyright law. In other words, all kinds of sound recordings are protected, including recordings of sounds that are not protectable subject matter. The protectable subject matter under section 66 can be described as the technical contribution of the phonogram producer in making the recording.

124. Similar to the protection of performing artists, producers of sound recordings are not protected against adaptations of the recordings. Most of the exemptions from the scope of copyright protection apply to the protection of producers of sound

216. Cf. s. 68 para. 2 of the Act.
217. Cf. s. 68 para. 1 of the Act.
218. Cf. s. 68 para. 3 of the Act.
219. Cf. s. 66 para. 1 of the Act. The provision is implementing Directive of the European Parliament and of the Council 2011/77/EU of 27 Sep. 2011 amending Directive 2006/116/EC on the term of protection of copyright and certain related rights.

recordings as well.[220] Due to the technical character of the protected subject matter, producers of sound recordings are not protected by moral rights.

The rights of producers of sound recordings are subject to compulsory licence as regards published sound recordings used in broadcasts on radio and television and for other public performances, cf. section 68 paragraphs 1 and 2 of the Act (*see supra* paragraphs 109 and 121).

The provisions of section 65 (performing artists) and section 66 (producers of sound recordings) concerning recording and copying apply to all performances and recordings that take place within the EEA. Hereby, the rightholders are granted an extended protection against bootleg recordings.[221]

III. Producers of Recordings of Moving Pictures

125. Producers of recordings of moving pictures are protected equally as producers of sound recordings. According to section 67 of the Act, recordings of moving pictures may not without the consent of the producer be copied or made available to the public until fifty years have elapsed after the end of the year in which the recording was made. If a recording of a moving picture is published or made public during this period, the protection shall, however, last until fifty years have elapsed after the end of the year in which it was first published or made public, whichever is earlier.[222] Most of the exemptions from the scope of copyright protection apply to the protection of producers of recordings of moving pictures as well.[223]

The provision was introduced into Danish copyright law by the 1995 Act, and it implements the pertinent provisions of the Council Directive 92/100/EEC of 19 November 1992 on rental rights and lending and certain rights related to copyright in the field of intellectual property. Protection under section 67 is granted irrespective of the quality and character of the moving picture. However, it is required that the pictures are moving; still pictures and the like are not protectable subject matter under section 67 but may be eligible for copyright protection under section 1 of the Act or protection by the neighbouring right in section 70 of the Act. The protection extends to the soundtrack of a moving picture.

IV. Broadcasters

126. Broadcasters are granted independent protection of their broadcasts. By virtue of section 69 of the Act, a radio or television broadcast may not without the consent of the broadcaster be rebroadcast by others or in any other manner performed in public. Neither may the broadcast without consent be photographed or recorded

220. Cf. s. 66 para. 2 of the Act.
221. Cf. s. 86 paras 1 and 2 of the Act.
222. Cf. s. 67 para. 1 of the Act.
223. Cf. s. 67 para. 2 of the Act.

on tape, film or any other device by means of which it can be reproduced.[224] Protected subject matter under section 69 is in fact the broadcast signals that are not dependent on the contents of the broadcast. Protection is granted for terrestrial broadcasts as well as for broadcasts by means of satellites and cable systems. Where a broadcast is photographed or recorded, it must not without the consent of the broadcaster be copied or made available to the public until fifty years have elapsed after the end of the year in which the broadcast took place.[225] Most of the exemptions from the scope of copyright protection apply to the protection of broadcasters as well.[226]

V. Producers of Photographic Pictures

127. By virtue of section 70 paragraph 1 of the Act, the person who produces a photographic picture (the photographer) shall enjoy the exclusive right to make copies of it and make it available to the public. Protection under section 70 is not contingent on the quality or any other characteristics of the photographic picture; consequently, all photographic pictures are protected under this provision. Photographic works are protected under section 1 if the more rigorous condition of copyright protection (i.e., originality) is satisfied. Where a photographic picture is subject to copyright according to section 1, such right may also be enforced. Section 2 paragraphs 2–4 of the Act specifying the content of the reproduction right and the right to make the work available to the public apply to the protection of photographers under section 70 in addition to the moral rights of section 3 and most of the exemptions from the scope of copyright protection.[227] In spite of the wording of section 70, the photographer is protected against others' reproduction of the photographic picture in amended form.[228] However, on two points, the protection of photographic pictures under section 70 is distinguished from copyright protection. First, the right in a photographic picture according to section 70 shall last only until fifty years have elapsed from the end of the year in which the picture was taken.[229] Second, the owner of the right according to section 70 is not necessarily the same as the author of a photographic work. Author of a photographic work is the person who makes the decisions that qualify the photographic picture as a work within the meaning of section 1 of the Act, such as composition, cutting, choice of motif, perspective, angle, depth of field and light setting. Often but not always the photographer makes those decisions. Whereas a photographic work may be held jointly by two or more authors, there is only one owner of the right, according to section 70, the photographer.

224. Cf. s. 69 para. 1 of the Act.
225. Cf. s. 69 para. 2 of the Act.
226. Cf. s. 69 para. 3 of the Act.
227. Cf. s. 70 para. 3 of the Act.
228. Cf. FT 1994–1995, A, 1405.
229. Cf. s. 70 para. 2 of the Act.

VI. Producers of Compilations, Databases, Etc.

128. According to section 71 of the Act, the person who produces a catalogue, a table, a database or the like, in which a great number of items of information have been compiled or that is a result of a substantial investment, shall enjoy the exclusive right to control the creation by making copies of the whole or of a substantial part of the creation and by making the whole or a substantial part of the creation available to the public.[230] Section 71 implements the provisions on a sui generis right of the European Parliament and Council Directive 96/9/EC of 11 March 1996 on legal protection of databases. Eligible for protection under section 71 are works such as telephone directories, arithmetical tables, dictionaries and timetables. The provision stipulates two conditions of protection of which only one has to be satisfied. Either the creation shall constitute a compilation of a great number of items of information or it shall be the result of a substantial investment. It has been questioned whether the two alternative conditions of protection in the Danish Act are in conformity with the directive on legal protection of databases, more precisely, whether the Directive is a total harmonization directive or a minimum harmonization directive.[231] In 2006, the Maritime and Commercial Court decided a case on the interpretation of section 71.[232] A web portal had made deep links to real estate advertisements in a database from a real estate franchise chain. The real estate chain claimed that its database was protected under section 71 and that the web portal infringed the database right by means of systematic deep linking. Congenial to the decisions of the European Court of Justice in the British Horseracing Board case[233] and the Fixtures cases,[234] the Court found that the collection of information in the database did not require a substantial investment because the creation of the database was mainly derived from the real estate chain's primary activity, which is to advertise and sell real estate. The decision reflects the so-called spin-off theory, according to which spin-offs and incidental by-products should not be eligible for protection under the sui generis right of the Directive. The real estate chain was denied protection under section 71, though it could not reasonably be disputed that the database comprised 'a great number of items of information'. The decision can hardly be construed in ways other than that, according to Maritime and Commercial Court, the Directive is a total harmonization directive and, thus, in respect of compilations that qualify as databases under the Directive, the only condition of protection is 'a substantial investment'.

129. In describing the rights conferred on the rightholder, the legislator chose not to use the terms 'extraction' and 'reutilization', which are used in the directive on the legal protection of databases. Instead, the rights are described by way of the

230. Cf. s. 71 para. 1 of the Act.
231. For example, Schovsbo, Rosenmeier & Petersen (2024), 112 f.
232. *Ugeskrift for Retsvæsen* 2006.1564 S. *See also* the case comment by M. Rosenmeier in *Nordiskt Immateriellt Rättsskydd* (2007), 405 ff.
233. C-203/02.
234. C-46/02, C-338/02 and C-444/02.

traditional copyright concepts of 'making copies' and 'making available to the public'. Whether the choice of terms in the Danish Copyright Act is in conformity with the directive must await a prospective decision on the issue from the European Court of Justice.

130. Where a database or another creation protected by section 71 is subject to copyright or some other form of protection, such rights may also be exercised.[235] The possibility of cumulative protection may be of significant importance, for example, to a producer of a database because the object of copyright protection is not identical to the object of protection under section 71. Copyright protects the selection or arrangement of a database, whereas section 71 provides protection against others' use of the content of the database in certain ways.[236]

Protection according to section 71 paragraph 1 applies correspondingly to the acts of making copies of insubstantial parts of the contents of a catalogue, a table, a database or the like and making insubstantial parts of the contents of a catalogue, a table, a database or the like available to the public if this is done repeatedly and systematically provided the said acts may be equalled to acts that conflict with normal exploitation of the products in question or that unreasonably prejudice the legitimate interests of the producer.[237]

The right under section 71 shall last until fifteen years have elapsed after the end of the year in which the creation was made. Where a creation of the said nature is made available to the public within this period of time, the protection shall, however, last until fifteen years have elapsed after the end of the year in which the creation was made available to the public for the first time. Section 2 paragraphs 2–4 of the Act specifying the content of the reproduction right and the right to make the work available to the public apply to the protection of catalogues, tables, databases or the like under section 71 in addition to most of the exemptions from the scope of copyright protection.[238] Terms of agreement that extend the protection of a catalogue, a table, a database or the like to the benefit of the producer are void.[239]

VII. Publishers of Press Publications

131. Article 15 of the DSMD granting publishers a neighbouring right in their press publication is implemented in section 69 a of the Act. According to this provision, press publications may not be made available online or made available in such a way that the general public can access them at an individually chosen place and time by providers of information society services without the publisher's consent until two years have elapsed after the end of the year in which the publication or publication took place.[240]

235. Cf. s. 71 para. 3 of the Act.
236. Cf. Riis (2001), 113 ff.
237. Cf. s. 71 para. 2 of the Act.
238. Cf. s. 71 para. 5 of the Act.
239. Cf. s. 71 para. 6 of the Act.
240. Cf. s. 69 a para. 1 of the Act.

The rights in press publications do not apply to the following:

(1) Individual users' use that is private or not made for commercial purposes.
(2) Hyperlinks.
(3) Single words or very short extracts from a press publication.[241]

The rights in press publications do not affect rights granted to authors and other rightholders in respect of the works and other subject matter contained in a press publication. The right may not be invoked against authors and other rightholders and may not deprive them of their right to exploit their works and other subject matter independently of a press publication in which they appear.[242]

Rights in press publications are subject to extended collective licensing, cf. section 29 a, and the collective management organization Danish Press Publications' Collective Management Organisation (DPCMO) has been established for the purpose of managing the rights collectively.

VIII. Press Releases

132. Pursuant to section 72 of the Act, a very limited form of protection is granted press releases supplied under contract from foreign news agencies or from correspondents abroad. Such press releases may not without the consent of the recipient be made available to the public through the press, radio or in any other similar manner until after twelve hours after they have been made public in Denmark. Apart from this provision, it must be noted that news as such is not protectable subject matter. The specific expression of a press release, however, is eligible for copyright protection as a literary work under section 1 of the Act.

§10. Infringement and Remedies

I. Infringement

133. The crucial issue in many cases of alleged copyright infringement is deciding the scope of protection. Copyright protects against more than just literal copying, but how much more? As the general abstract rule, the copyright is infringed if a new creation brings on the same aesthetical experience as an existing work.[243] This has to be construed in consideration of the central notion of copyright law that ideas, motifs, information and the like are not protected by copyright.[244] The

241. Cf. s. 69 a para. 2 of the Act.
242. Cf. s. 69 a para. 2 of the Act.
243. Cf. Schovsbo, Rosenmeier & Petersen (2018), 160.
244. In the case reported in *Ugeskrift for Retsvæsen* 1999.1762 Ø, a TV format for a quiz show was not found to infringe the copyright in an actual telecast of a similar quiz show. This case can be compared with *Ugeskrift for Retsvæsen* 2014.888 H where an advertising film was found to infringe an older advertising film because of a number of similarities between the two films, though the two films also had differences.

approach to deciding cases of alleged copyright infringement is based on a comparison of the general impressions of the two works and not particulars of the works.[245]

Whether a new creation is infringing an existing copyrightable work has to be decided in the concrete case, and the decision has a somewhat discretionary nature. In *Ugeskrift for Retsvæsen* 1962.254 SH, copying of 5%–6% of a descriptive literary work used in a competing work was found to constitute copyright infringement.

II. Remedies

A. *Injunctions*[246]

134. To the rightholder who finds his/her work infringed, it is of paramount importance to stop the infringing activities as soon as possible. Thus, from a practical point of view, an injunction is the primary remedy available to the rightholder. However, neither the Copyright Act nor any other intellectual property statutes contain provisions on injunctions. The pertinent legal basis in this respect is found in Chapter 40 of the Act on Civil Proceedings (sections 411–430). An interim injunction can be rescinded if the party applying for the injunction proves on a balance of probabilities or by clear and convincing evidence: (1) that the party holds the right for which protection by way of a injunction is sought; (2) that the conduct of the opposing party necessitates the granting of the injunction; and (3) that the ability of the party to enforce his right will be lost if the party has to await a full trial.[247] In addition, it is stated in section 414 of the Act on Civil Proceedings that no injunction may be granted if the general provisions on penalty and compensation and any security offered by the opposing party are deemed to provide adequate protection to the party and, furthermore, that the grant of an injunction can be refused if such injunction would cause the opposing party to suffer a detriment or disadvantage which is clearly disproportionate to the party's interest in obtaining the injunction.

135. Normally, adequate security is required in order to rescind an interim injunction.[248] The required security may prove a significant impediment for the rightholder in enforcing his/her rights since the demanded security occasionally is very large. Besides, the rightholder is liable for the loss of the alleged infringer if it turns out that the interim injunction was illegal and the rightholder ought not to have

245. Cf., for example, Ugeskrift for Retsvæsen 1991.847 H.
246. In general on injunctions in respect of intellectual property law, *see* C.S. Petersen, P. Møgelvang-Hansen & Thomas Riis, *Judicielle forbud/påbud og immaterialretsproces* (Copenhagen: Karnov Group 2015); C.S. Petersen, *Immaterialrettigheder og foreløbige forbud* (Copenhagen: Jurist-og Økonomforbundets Forlag, 2008); N.M. Andersen, A. Carlquist & A. Rubinstein, *Retshåndhævelse af immaterialrettigheder* (Copenhagen: Jurist- og Økonomforbundets Forlag, 2006), 265–340; and T. Riis, *Enerettigheder og vederlagsrettigheder. Håndhævelse af immaterialrettigheder i økonomisk perspektiv* (Copenhagen: Jurist- og Økonomforbundets Forlag, 2005), 119–157.
247. Cf. s. 413 of the Act on Civil Proceedings.
248. Cf. s. 415 of the Act on Civil Proceedings.

claimed the injunction.[249] To a limited extent, the alleged infringer may prevent an interim injunction by providing adequate security;[250] it appears that this opportunity has never been used in copyright infringement cases.[251] The crux of the problem in deciding whether an injunction shall be rescinded or not is related to the standard of proof. The burden of proof lies with the rightholder, and as the main rule, the rightholder shall produce a reasonable corroborated presumption.[252] An injunction does not require negligent or intentional acts on part of the alleged infringer.

The rightholder shall within two weeks take action to confirm the interim injunction.[253] In *Ugeskrift for Retsvæsen* 1974.944 Ø, an interim injunction was rescinded, and the rightholder pledged the required DKK 50,000 (approx. EUR 6,650) as security. Subsequently, the Eastern Court of Appeal found that the injunction was illegal because the defendant did not infringe the right of the plaintiff, and the defendant was awarded damages of DKK 75,000 (approx. EUR 10,000) as compensation for incurred costs and lost profits.

B. Liability[254]

136. Anyone who with intent or by negligence infringes copyrights or neighbouring rights granted by the Act shall pay: (i) reasonable remuneration to the infringed party for the exploitation and (ii) damages to the infringed party for any additional damage caused by the violation.[255] Liability under the Copyright Act conforms to the general principles of liability in tort law; it requires negligence, causality and adequacy.

Typically, in copyright infringement cases, damages are computed at the discretion of the court[256] and awarded damages are in general considered to be small, primarily because it is very difficult for the rightholder to provide sufficient evidence for all losses caused by copyright infringement.[257] However, in a case of video piracy from 1983,[258] the plaintiff was awarded DKK 1.2 million (approx. EUR 160,000) in damages, which is a large amount compared to other cases of infringement of intellectual property rights. The Eastern Court of Appeal found that the lost market sales of the rightholder were equivalent to the actual sales and rentals of

249. Cf. S. 428 of the Act on Civil Proceedings.
250. Cf. s. 414 para. 1 of the Act on Civil Proceedings.
251. In *Ugeskrift for retsvæsen* 1985.1014 H, the infringer tried to prevent an interim injunction by providing security, however, this was refused by the Supreme Court.
252. *See* A. Jacobi, 'Fogedforbud, særlig i patenttvister', *Ugeskrift for Retsvæsen* (1968 B): 51 ff.
253. Cf. s 425 para. 1 of the Act on Civil Proceedings.
254. In general on liability in respect of intellectual property law, *see* E.A. Skovbo, *Erstatning for ophavsretlige krænkelser* (Copenhagen: Forlaget Thomson. GadJura, 2005); Andersen, Carlquist & Rubinstein (2006), 419–495; and T. Riis, *Enerettigheder og vederlagsrettigheder. Håndhævelse af immaterialrettigheder i økonomisk perspektiv* (Copenhagen: Jurist- og Økonomforbundets Frorlag, 2005), 225–367.
255. Cf. s. 83 para. 1 of the Act.
256. *See*, for example, *Ugeskrift for Retsvæsen* 1994.132 Ø.
257. In general, *see* O. Eskildsen, 'Erstatningsberegning i immaterialretlige tvister', in *Vennebog til Mogens Koktvedgaard*, ed. M. Levin (Sweden: Nerenius & Santérus Förlag, 1993), 363–382.
258. *Ugeskrift for Retsvæsen* 1983.976 Ø.

infringing videograms by the infringer. On this basis, the rightholder was awarded damages of DKK 1 million. In addition, the rightholder was awarded DKK 200,000 in damages at the discretion of the court for lost sales in the future and market distortions.

Traditionally, damages for the infringement of copyright have been computed in conformity to the basic rule of tort law, according to which the claimant is entitled to damages for the full loss that the tortious act has caused. The most important element in the computation of damages is often the lost market sales of the rightholder. Lost sales are computed as the number of products that have not been sold due to the infringement multiplied by the loss connected to each product. In spite of the decision reported in *Ugeskrift for Retsvæsen* 1983.976 Ø on video piracy (mentioned *supra*), in general, it cannot be assumed that the computation of lost market sale equates the infringer's profits.

Another element in the computation of damages may be compensation for the distortion of the market for the rightholder's product. The market for the rightholder's product may be distorted if the infringer's product that is put on the market is similar to the rightholder's product but of poor quality. The result may be that the goodwill connected to the rightholder's product is significantly reduced, and, consequently, it requires large investments in marketing measures to re-establish that goodwill. However, it can be rather difficult for the rightholder to provide sufficient evidence to be awarded compensation for distortion of the market.

As a consequence of the implementation of the Directive 2004/48/EC on the enforcement of intellectual property rights (The Enforcement Directive), it is now stated in the Act that when setting the damages, consideration shall be given to such matters as the infringed party's loss of profits and the offender's unfair profits.[259] Computation of damages in consideration of the offender's unfair profits is an innovation in Danish law. This new provision provides the courts with the legal basis for the award of damages at a higher level than previously; however, it is doubtful whether this will happen to any significant extent.

According to section 24 paragraph 1 of the Damages Liability Act,[260] liability may be mitigated or lapsed, where liability would involve an unreasonable burden on the party liable or where very special circumstances otherwise make it reasonable. Copyright infringement that leads to claims from the rightholder usually takes place in a commercial context, and therefore, reduction of the award of damages pursuant to section 24 of the Damages Liability Act is not likely to occur.[261]

137. As indicated, it is difficult for the rightholder to provide evidence of the actual economic loss caused by the infringement, and often the result is small damages. In order to ensure the rightholder a kind of minimum compensation, according to section 83 paragraph 1 of the Copyright Act, he/she is entitled to a 'reasonable compensation' for the exploitation of his/her invention. The provision implies that the rightholder in all cases at a minimum is entitled to 'a reasonable royalty', notwithstanding that he/she cannot prove an actual loss caused by the infringement.

259. Cf. s. 83 para. 2 of the Act.
260. Consolidated Act No. 266 of 21 Mar. 2014.
261. Cf. Schovsbo, Rosenmeier & Petersen (2024), 794.

The provision was introduced in the 1995 Act. According to the preparatory works, 'reasonable remuneration' should be construed as a 'reasonable royalty'. However, case law indicates that it is difficult for the courts to establish a 'reasonable royalty', and the provision is primarily used to award discretionary damages without proof or other forms of documentation of an actual economic loss.

In cases of intentional or negligent copyright infringement, compensation can also be set to the infringed party for non-financial damage.[262] Compensation for non-financial damages prove most relevant in cases where the author's moral rights have been infringed but are not confined to the infringement of moral rights.

C. *Destruction, Seizure and Recall*

138. The risk of further infringements can justify destruction, seizure, etc., of existing infringing products. The court can by sentence decide that copies infringing the right to works or productions protected according to sections 65–71 shall:

- be recalled from the channels of commerce;
- be definitively removed from the channels of commerce;
- be destroyed; or
- be handed over to the infringed party.[263]

These provisions apply correspondingly to materials, tools, etc., that have primarily been used for illegal production or application of copies of the work or the production.[264] Destruction, etc., according to these provisions, shall be undertaken without any form of compensation to the offender and does not have any effect on any possible compensation to the infringed party. Furthermore, such measures shall be undertaken at the offender's expense, unless special reasons dictate otherwise.[265]

A principle of proportionality applies to these remedial measures. Thus, in considering a request for corrective measures, the need for proportionality between the seriousness of the infringement and the remedies ordered as well as the interests of third parties shall be taken into account by the court.[266] In the preparatory works of the 2005 amendment of the Copyright Act, it is stated as an example that the principle of proportionality as a main rule implies that the seizure or destruction of buildings may not be demanded in pursuance of these provisions even though the buildings infringe copyrights in architectural drawings.[267] Furthermore, the interests of third parties will normally preclude destruction, etc., of copies acquired in good faith for private use.[268]

---

262. Cf. s. 83 para. 3 of the Act.
263. Cf. s. 84 para. 1 of the Act.
264. Cf. s. 84 para. 2 of the Act.
265. Cf. s. 84 para. 3 of the Act.
266. Cf. s. 84 para. 4 of the Act.
267. Previously, the Act included an explicit provision to this effect.
268. Previously, the Act included an explicit provision to this effect.

D. *Search*[269]

139. Measures for preserving evidence in cases of infringement of intellectual property rights were included in Danish legislation in 2001 in order to satisfy the national obligations under the TRIPs Agreement. Subsequently, in 2006, the provisions were amended in conformity with Article 7 of the Enforcement Directive (2004/48/EC). The provisions are placed in Chapter 57a of the Act on Civil Proceedings (section 653–653d); nevertheless, they only apply in cases of infringement of intellectual property rights. In conformity with Article 7 of the Enforcement Directive, the purpose of such interim measures is to preserve relevant evidence in respect of an alleged infringement. On the request of the copyright holder, the bailiff's court can decide to search the premises of an alleged infringer in order to preserve evidence of the infringement or the extent of the infringement. The claimant shall produce a reasonable corroborated presumption that an infringement has taken place or will take place and that it is likely that the evidence for the infringement or the extent of the infringement can be found on the pertinent premises.[270] The search may involve, for example, a detailed description, with or without the taking of samples, or the physical seizure of the infringing goods, the materials and implements used in the production and/or distribution of these goods and the documents (including digitally stored information) relating thereto. The claimant's request may be denied in consideration of the privacy or trade secrets of the alleged infringer or if the interest of the claimant in the search is disproportionate to the harm the search is likely to cause on the alleged infringer.[271] The bailiff's court can decide to search the premises of the alleged infringer without the alleged infringer having been heard where there is a demonstrable risk of evidence being destroyed, removed or amended.[272] The search is an interim measure, and the claimant shall within four weeks after the bailiff's court decision on a search initiate a civil proceeding in respect of the alleged infringement of the search concern.[273]

E. *Right of Information*[274]

140. The provisions in Chapter 29a (sections 306–307) of the Act on Civil Proceedings were adopted in 2006 and implement Article 8 of the Enforcement Directive. This 'right of information' is an innovation in Danish law, and similar to the provisions in Chapter 57a of the Act on Civil Proceedings on search, the provisions in Chapter 29a only apply in cases of infringement of intellectual property rights. On the request of the claimant, the court can order that the infringer and/or any other

---

269. In general on measures for preserving evidence, *see* Petersen, C.S., P.M. Hansen & T. Riis. Judicielle forbud/påbud og immaterialretsproces. Copenhagen: 2015, Chs 7 and 8.
270. Cf. s. 653 para. 1 of the Act on Civil Proceedings.
271. Cf. s. 653 para. 4 of the Act on Civil Proceedings.
272. Cf. s. 653 a para. 2 of the Act on Civil Proceedings.
273. Cf. s. 653 c para. 1 of the Act on Civil Proceedings.
274. In general on the right of information, *see* Petersen, C.S., P.M. Hansen & T. Riis. Judicielle forbud/påbud og immaterialretsproces. Copenhagen: 2015, Ch. 9.

person provides information on goods or services that infringe an intellectual property right, provided the person in question:

(a) was found in possession of the infringing goods on a commercial scale;
(b) was found to be using the infringing services on a commercial scale;
(c) was found to be providing on a commercial scale services used in infringing activities; or
(d) was indicated by the person referred to in point (a), (b) or (c) as being involved in the production, manufacture or distribution of the goods or the provision of the services.[275]

The information that shall be provided includes:

(a) the names and addresses of the producers, manufacturers, distributors, suppliers and other previous holders of the goods or services, as well as the intended wholesalers and retailers the goods or services in question were aimed at, and
(b) information on the quantities produced, manufactured, delivered, received or ordered, as well as the price obtained for the goods or services in question.[276]

The provisions on the right of information enable that in a court case between A and B, C can be ordered to provide information on D even though the information is of no relevance in the conflict between A and B. In this way, the right of information departs from the tradition of the Danish law on civil procedure because according to the general principle of the law on civil procedure the courts shall deny all requests and evidence that bear no relevance to the litigated conflict. The right of information creates a risk of abuse of the procedural system; however, as the main safeguard against abuse, the court may deny a request if it must be assumed that the interest of the claimant in the information is disproportionate to the harm the provision of the information may cause on the person providing the information or on other persons.[277]

F. Penalties

141. Copyright infringement may involve criminal liability. According to section 76 paragraph 1 of the Act, anyone who with intent or by gross negligence infringes copyrights or neighbouring rights is liable to a fine. Copyright piracy is a more severe offence; thus, section 76 paragraph 2 stipulates that where an intentional infringement has been committed by using works, performances or productions protected by neighbouring rights or by distributing copies hereof among the general public, the punishment may under particularly aggravating circumstances be

275. Cf. s. 306 para. 1 of the Act on Civil Proceedings.
276. Cf. s. 306 para. 2 of the Act on Civil Proceedings.
277. Cf. s. 306 para. 3 of the Act on Civil Proceedings.

increased to imprisonment in one year and six months, unless a more severe punishment is provided by section 299b in the penal code. Particularly aggravating circumstances are deemed to exist, especially where the offence is commercial, concerns production or distribution of a considerable number of copies, or where works, performances or productions are made available to the public in such a way that members of the public may access them from a place and at a time individually chosen by them.

Violation of the provisions on technological protective measures in sections 75b, 75c and 75e of the Act is also penalized.

A company, etc. (legal persons) may be subject to criminal liability according to the rules of Chapter 5 of the Civil Penal Code.[278] Criminal liability under the Civil Penal Code requires, among other things, that the infringement can be imputed to a natural person who is associated with the legal person. The penalty provisions are not used very often in copyright infringement cases.

If customs and/or tax authorities presume a violation that is liable for penalties in accordance with section 76 or 77 of the Act, information relating to the presumption can be disclosed to the rightholder.[279]

G. Publication of Judgments

142. When the Enforcement Directive (2004/48/EC) was implemented, a new provision on publication of judgments was included in section 84a of the Act. In a judgment in which someone is sentenced according to section 83 (liability) or 84 (destruction, etc.), the court may upon request decide that the judgment shall be published in full or in part. The obligation to publish rests with the offender. Publication shall be arranged at the offender's expense and in as prominent a way as can reasonably be expected.

§11. Overlapping and Relation to Other Intellectual Property Laws

143. Copyrightable subject matter includes works of applied art and industrial designs that are the object of protection under design rights. Copyright protection and design right protection are cumulative; accordingly, protection under the Designs Act does not preclude copyright.[280]

144. Section 3 of the Marketing Practice Act, which in general terms provides protection against unfair competition, has proved to be an important supplement for the protection of works of applied art, most significantly in relation to creations that are distinctive but do not qualify as works within the meaning of the Copyright Act. Additionally, the rightholder may obtain relief under section 3 of the Marketing Practice Act in cases where such creations are considered works of applied art

278. Cf. s. 80 of the Copyright Act.
279. Cf. s. 84 b of the Copyright Act.
280. Cf. s. 10 para. 1 of the Copyright Act.

within the meaning of the Copyright Act but a similar creation is perceived as not being identical to the copyright-protected work and thus does not constitute infringement. Relief under section 3 of the Marketing Practice Act requires that the two creations are related in the marketplace, which, for example, is the case for actual competing products and, furthermore, that the competitor has acted unfairly by his/her production, marketing or distribution activities. In the majority of cases where a product has been copied from another product, the plaintiffs claim copyright infringement as well as violation of section 3 of the Marketing Practice Act, and when the courts conclude that unlawful copying has taken place, the conclusion is often based on both the provisions of the Copyright Act and section 3 of the Marketing Practice Act.

In addition, section 3 of the Marketing Practice Act provides supplementary protection of creations protected by neighbouring rights. Performing artists are not protected against soundalikes under the neighbouring rights of the Copyright Act; according to the circumstances, such protection may be granted under section 3 of the Marketing Practice Act.[281]

The case reported in *Ugeskrift for Retsvæsen* 1994.604 SH concerned bootleg recordings lawfully produced in countries that were not parties to the Rome Convention. The Maritime and Commercial Court concluded that the scope of protection of performing artists against recordings produced in foreign countries was exhaustively determined by the provisions of the Copyright Act and the Ordinance on the Application of the Copyright Act in Relation to other Countries (now Ordinance No. 218 of 9 March 2010); therefore, additional protection of the rightholders could not be obtained under section 3 of the Marketing Practice Act as claimed by the plaintiffs.

145. A trademark can be granted copyright protection as a work of fine art, provided the conditions of protection have been satisfied.[282] In almost all cases, trademarks consisting of words do not satisfy the conditions of copyright protection. In *Ugeskrift for Retsvæsen* 1998.1385 SH, a travel agency marketed particular travels under the slogan '*I Von Scholtens fodspor*' (In the footsteps of Von Scholten). The slogan was registered as a trademark but did not qualify for copyright protection.

146. Certain press releases are protected for twelve hours under section 72 of the Copyright Act. A supplementary protection of press releases is provided by basic principles of law developed in case law.[283]

281. Cf. Schønning (2016), 619.
282. *See*, for example, *Nordiskt Immaterieltlt Rättsskydd* 1985.332 V.
283. *See Ugeskrift for Retsvæsen* 1943.1063 H and 1982.179 H, cf. Schovsbo, Rosenmeier & Petersen (2024), 116.

Chapter 2. Patents

§1. Sources – Legislation

147. Danish patent law is statutory. The latest major revision of the Patents Act took place in 1967, but numerous amendments to the Act have been adopted since then. For example, the Act has been altered in order to comply with obligations, etc., stemming from international legal instruments in the field of patent law, that is, the Patent Cooperation Treaty (PCT); the European Patent Convention (EPC); the TRIPs Agreement; the Community Patent Convention (CPC) with subsequent amendments included in the Community Patent Agreement reached in Luxembourg 1989;[284] the Patent Law Treaty (PLT); the London Agreement on the translation of European patents; and the Package on Unitary Patent Protection in Europe (2012).[285] The PCT was ratified by Denmark in 1978, and the relevant provisions in this respect are included into Chapter 3 (sections 28–38) of the Patents Act. The EPC was ratified in 1989, and the relevant provisions are included into Chapter 10A (sections 75–90) of the Patents Act. After the ratification of the EPC, the decisions of the European Patent Organization (EPO) and the appeal boards on patentable subject matter and the conditions of patentability are decisive in obtaining a patent through the EPO. In order to avoid discrepancies as regards the formal part of patent law, the Danish Patent and Trademark Office (*Patent-og Varemærkestyrelsen*)[286] has expressed an intention to follow these decisions based on the EPC. Denmark ratified the Community Patent Agreement in 1993 and the relevant provisions are included in Chapter 10C (sections 92–97) of the Act. However, the Agreement and consequently the national provisions relating to the Agreement have not yet come into force.

Denmark is, since 1894, party to the Paris Convention for the Protection of Industrial Property, which is reflected in the provisions of the Patents Act. Furthermore, Denmark has ratified the Budapest Treaty on the International Recognition of Deposit of Micro-organisms for the Purposes of Patent Procedure of 1977, the Convention on International Classification of Patents on Inventions of 1971 and the European Council's Convention on Coordination of Certain Parts of the Material Patent Law of 1963.

148. As in other areas of Danish intellectual property law, Danish patent law has developed under the influence of the relatively close Nordic cooperation in this field. The consolidated Patents Act is at present Act No. 90 of 29 January 2019.[287]

284. O.J. 1989 L 401/1.
285. Cf. Act No. 551 of 2 Jun. 2014 on a Unified Patent Court etc.
286. The Patent Authority of Denmark is the Patent and Trademark Office (*Patent-og Varemærkestyrelsen*) and the Patent and Trademark Board of Appeal (*Ankenævnet for patenter og varemærker*), cf. s. 7 para. 1 of the Act.
287. Under the provisions of the Act important orders have been issued, especially Order No. 2111 of 24 Nov. 2021 on Patents and Supplementary Protection Certificates regarding applications for patents and supplementary protection certificates. Other orders under the provisions of the Act or related to the Act include Order. No. 450 of 16 Sep. 1983 on Patents on Pharmaceuticals as

In addition to the Patents Act, an act on secret patents concerning the protection of war materiel has been adopted.[288]

§2. PATENTABLE SUBJECT MATTER

149. A person who has made an invention which is susceptible of industrial application may on the basis of an application obtain a patent on that invention and thereby obtain an exclusive right to exploit the invention commercially. Patents shall be available for inventions in all fields of technology.[289] A patent claim can take three different forms: (1) a product or substance claim; (2) a process or a method claim; or (3) a use claim. Thus, an invention within the meaning of patent law may subsist in either a product, a method or the use of something known in the prior art, though there is not always a clear-cut distinction between these forms of inventions.

No definition of the concept of an 'invention' is stated in the Act; however, the concept should be understood in accordance with the generally accepted principles of European patent law. In general, it may be said that an invention is a solution to a technical problem. It follows that an invention covered by the Act has to comprise some sort of technical features. According to section 1 paragraph 2 of the Act, certain forms of subject matter are excluded from patent protection: thus, in particular: (1) discoveries, scientific theories and mathematical methods; (2) aesthetic creations; (3) schemes, rules and methods for performing mental acts, playing games or doing business, and programs for computers; and (4) presentations of information are not to be considered an invention if the claimed invention is directed to such subject matter as such.[290] Section 1 paragraph 2 is worded in a way that exemplifies excluded subject matter, and the content of the provision is not an exhaustive list in this regard.

150. It is a fundamental principle of patent law that discoveries are not patentable subject matter. Discovering an unknown law of nature implies that something new has been recognized, and it does not imply that something new has been created. Patentable subject matter has to be a creation that adds something that does

---

amended by Order No. 728 of 16 Sep. 1999, Order No. 511 of 23 Aug. 1988 on Patents on Inventions Related to Foodstuffs, Order No. 602 of 26 Aug. 1988 on the Coming into Force of Ch. II of the PCT with Respect to Denmark, Order No. 238 of 30 Mar. 1994 on Amendments of the Rules on Exhaustion of the Patents Acts, the Trademarks Act and the Act on Protection of Topographies of Semiconductor Products, Order No. 12 of 12 Jan. 2012 on the remuneration of the Patent and Trademark Office for the performance of tasks, specific transactions and transcripts, etc. Order No. 892 of 21 Sep. 2009 on the Patent and Trademark Board of Appeal (*Ankenævnet for patenter og varemærker*), Order No. 1578 of 14 Dec. 2016 on a special unit in the Patent and Trademark Office on enforcement and piracy and Order No. 459 of 22 Apr. 2023 on coming into force of the Act on a Unified Patent Court etc. Related to Patent Act is also Circular letter of 30 Apr. 2019 regarding Delegation of Powers to the Patent and Trademark Office (*Patent-og Varemærkestyrelsen*).

288. *See* now the consolidated Act No. 107 of 24 Jan. 2012. Various orders have been issued under the provisions of the Act.

289. Cf. s. 1 para. 1 of the Act.

290. The provision is similar to Art. 52(2) and (3) of the EPC.

not already exist in nature. A more practical reason for not granting patent protection of discoveries, scientific theories and mathematical methods is that such protection may have far-reaching adverse consequences for the technological progress and the conditions of the markets for products benefiting from the discovery, theory or method. Only discoveries, scientific theories and mathematical methods as such are excluded from subject matter. A specific invention created by applying, for example, a scientific theory may be patentable.

151. Normally, aesthetic creations have no technical function and no technical effect, and if that is the case, such creations are excluded from patentability. Aesthetic creations denote not only physical products such as paintings and sculptures but also creations such as works of music. This does not imply that devices and instruments used for aesthetic creations, for example, musical instruments, are excluded from subject matter.

152. It is often stated that the dominant reason for excluding schemes, rules and methods for performing mental acts, playing games or doing business, as well as programs for computers from patentability, is that such subject matter is assumed to be instructions to the human mind. The reason is not convincing, especially not in relation to computer programs that are in fact instructions to a machine (a computer). The reason for excluding this kind of subject matter is rather the apparent absence of any technical content or any technical features. Patentability of computer programs is a topical issue of great importance to the software industry. Computer programs as such are excluded from patent protection but are instead eligible for copyright protection. However, it is generally accepted that software-related inventions are patentable subject matter. Normally, a patentable software-related invention requires that the invention consist of something more than a computer program and that the invention taken as a whole demonstrate a technical effect.[291]

153. The exclusion of presentations of information is related to the exclusion of schemes, rules and methods for performing mental acts, etc. Presentations of information may take the form of a specific schedule of various information that enables the user to comprehend the information in a short time. Such a creation has no technical effect and, consequently, is not patentable.

154. According to section 1 paragraph 3 of the Act, methods for treatment of the human or animal body by surgery or therapy and diagnostic methods practiced on the human or animal body shall not be considered inventions within the meaning of section 1 paragraph 1. The provision does not apply to products, including substances and compositions, for use in any of these methods.[292] It is possible to find two reasons for the provision in section 1 paragraph 3. First, it may seem unethical to confer rights that may impede treatment of sick persons and animals, and second,

291. There exists no reported Danish case law on this issue and the relatively few decisions from the Patent and Trademark Board of Appeal do not provide substantial clarification. Instead one should consult the Guidelines for Examination in the EPO, G.II.3.6.
292. The provision is similar to Art. 52(4) of the EPC.

such methods are normally not susceptible of industrial application.[293] As mentioned, the provision does not exclude products from patentability only methods. Certain products for treatment of the human or animal body require specific methods to be used in that treatment; that fact, however, does not exclude patentability. Furthermore, methods with purely cosmetic purposes, for example, a method for permanent waving of hair, is not covered by the exclusion.[294]

155. Prior to the Patents Act of 1967, chemical compounds were not patentable subject matter. Patentability of chemical compounds was introduced in 1967, but only in a limited form. Not until the amendment of the Patents Act in 1978 was the limitation on the patentability of chemical compounds abolished. Chemical compounds, including pharmaceuticals, are patentable subject matter in spite of many kinds of chemical compounds that exist in nature, however, without being known or described. This implies that the traditional distinction in patent law between discoveries and inventions is somewhat blurred in this respect. Patentability requires that the applicant in a well-defined way makes the chemical compound at the disposal for the first time. The chemical compound may be defined, for example, by way of stating the chemical formula or other technical features of the compound. The same arguments may be put forward in favour of patentability of biotechnological creations that are in fact chemical compounds. Following the implementation of the Biotech Directive (98/44/EC), it is now stated in the Act that biological material that is isolated from its natural environment or produced by means of a technical process may be the subject of an invention even if it previously occurred in nature. Within the meaning of the Act, 'biological material' means any material containing genetic information that is capable of reproducing itself or being reproduced in a biological system.

156. Patent claims for pharmaceutical products were not admissible until 1983.[295] Prior to 1983, patents were only granted for processes for the production of a pharmaceutical, not for a pharmaceutical itself. The relevant provisions of the Act were interpreted in a way that de facto created a kind of indirect protection of the pharmaceutical itself since process claims to the production of a pharmaceutical were allowed to be constructed to cover elements of the claimed invention comprising the therapeutic effect. According to the applicable law, in the main, pharmaceuticals shall not be treated differently from other chemical compounds.

157. Deeply grounded in the Danish patent law tradition, foodstuffs and processes for the production of foodstuffs were for a long time excluded from patentability. This situation was changed by Order No. 511 of 23 August 1988, issued under the provisions of the Patents Act. The Order came into force on 1 January

293. Cf. M. Koktvedgaard & L. Østerborg, *Patentloven*, 2nd edn (Copenhagen: Juristforbundets Forlag, 1979), 81.
294. *Ibid.*
295. The situation was changed by Order No. 450 of 16 Sep. 1983, issued under the provisions of the Patents Act of 1978.

1989, providing patentability for foodstuffs and processes for the production of foodstuffs, and no special rules apply to this subject matter.

158. Plant and animal varieties are not patentable subject matter. However, inventions that concern plants or animals shall be patentable if the technical feasibility of the invention is not confined to a particular plant or animal variety.[296] Essentially, biological processes for the production of plants or animals are not patentable. A process for the production of plants or animals is essentially biological if it consists entirely of natural phenomena such as crossing or selection. However, the exclusion from patentability does not apply to inventions that concern a microbiological or other technical process or a product obtained by means of such a process. For the purpose of the Act, 'microbiological process' means any process involving or performed upon or resulting in microbiological material.[297] These rules implement various provisions of the Biotech Directive (98/44/EC).[298] The rapid development of biotechnology has created many complexities and uncertainties in patent law. The implementation of the Biotech Directive maintains that inventions can be patentable even if they concern a product consisting of or containing biological material or a process by means of which biological material is produced, processed or used.[299] However, in addition to plant and animal varieties, the human body, at the various stages of its formation and development, and the simple discovery of one of its elements, including the sequence or partial sequence of a gene, cannot constitute patentable inventions. However, an element isolated from the human body or otherwise produced by means of a technical process, including the sequence or partial sequence of a gene, may constitute a patentable invention, even if the structure of that element is identical to that of a natural element.[300]

159. Patents shall not be granted on inventions if the commercial exploitation of the inventions is contrary to public order or morality.[301] However, exploitation shall not be deemed to be contrary to public order or morality merely because it is prohibited by law or regulation.[302] On the basis of these rules, the following, in particular, shall be considered unpatentable:

(a) processes for cloning human beings;
(b) processes for modifying the germ-line genetic identity of human beings;
(c) uses of human embryos for industrial or commercial purposes;

296. The concept of 'plant variety' shall be construed in conformity with the definition in Art. 5 of Regulation (EC) No. 2100/94 on Community plant variety rights, cf. s. 1 para. 4 of the Act.
297. Cf. s. 1 para. 5 of the Act.
298. In general on the implementation of the Biotech Directive in Denmark, *see* T. Sommer, 'Den danske lovgivning vedrørende implementeringen af direktiv 98/44/EF af 6. juli 1998 om retlig beskyttelse af bioteknologiske opfindelser', in *Ugeskrift for Retsvæsen* 2004 B, 457–465.
299. Cf. s. 1 para. 6 of the Act.
300. Cf. s. 1a, paras 1 and 2 of the Act.
301. Cf. s. 1b, para. 1 of the Act.
302. Cf. s. 1b, para. 2 of the Act.

(d) processes for modifying the genetic identity of animals that are likely to cause them suffering without any substantial medical benefit to man or animal, and also animals resulting from such processes.[303]

160. Apart from biotechnological inventions, the exclusion of inventions, the exploitation of which would be contrary to morality or public order, seems to have no practical importance, and it has been called a patent law fossil.[304] A similar provision is included in the Act on Utility Models, and that provision was no hindrance to register a utility model for a penis extension device. Probably, the provision could be applied to an application for anti-personnel mines and letter bombs.

§3. Conditions of Patentability

161. A person who has made an invention that is susceptible of industrial application may obtain a patent on that invention. In addition to the condition of industrial application, section 2 paragraph 1 of the Act states that patents shall only be granted for inventions that are new and inventions that are considerably distinguished from the state of the art. Thus, section 2 paragraph 1 comprises two further conditions of patentability: one condition of novelty and one of inventive step.

I. Industrial Application

162. It is a fundamental condition of patent law that a patentable invention has to be susceptible to industrial application, and the notion emphasizes that patent protection closely relates to creations of a technical character. 'Industrial application' shall be understood in the light of Article 1(2) of the Paris Convention, which states that:

> Industrial property shall be understood in the broadest sense and shall apply not only to industry and commerce proper, but likewise to agricultural and extractive industries and to all manufactured or natural products, for example, wines, grain, tobacco leaf, fruit, cattle, minerals, mineral waters, beer, flowers, and flour.[305]

The broad interpretation of the word 'industrial' in conformity with Article 1(2) of the Paris Convention has been established in various decisions of the Patent and Trademark Board of Appeal.[306] A patentable invention must have practical application in one way or another. Further guidelines for interpretation can be found in Article 57 of the EPC, stating that an invention shall be considered susceptible of

303. Cf. s. 1b, para. 2 of the Act.
304. G. Karnell, *Nordiskt Immateriellt Rättsskyd* (1990), 179.
305. In that respect one should also note the provision in s. 1 para. 1 of the Act: 'Patents shall be available for any inventions in all fields of technology' (cf. Art. 27 para. 1 of the TRIPs Agreement).
306. For example, J No. 1-74/69 of 22 Feb. 1971.

industrial application if it can be made or used in any kind of industry, including agriculture. In principle, the law does not require that a patentable invention implies technological progress, though this will often be the case.

In the patent application, the invention shall be described in a way that expressly indicates how the invention can be applied industrially unless the industrial application clearly appears from the nature of the invention. If the invention relates to a gene, the industrial application of a sequence or a partial sequence of the gene must be disclosed in the patent application.[307]

163. Closely connected to the condition of industrial application, it is further required that the invention can be described in a patent document and can be reproduced on the basis of this description.[308] If an invention is not adequately disclosed by the description in the patent document and if the invention cannot be reproduced by a person skilled in the art on the basis of that description, the disclosed invention has no practical significance and, consequently, cannot be said to be susceptible of industrial application. Reproducibility within the meaning of the Act implies that a person arbitrarily can produce or recreate phenomena identical to the claimed invention when the necessary conditions are present. These necessary conditions have to be well-defined and be within reach of what is humanly possible at the state of the art.[309]

II. Novelty

164. A patentable invention must be new and is considered to be so if it does not form part of the state of the art. The state of the art shall be held to comprise everything made available to the public by means of a written or oral description, by use or in any other way.[310] The pertinent moment of assessing novelty of a claimed invention is the filing data; everything known prior to the filing date should be included in this assessment. The condition of novelty is an objective condition, which means that an invention is not considered new just because it is new to the inventor; it has to be new to everyone. Novelty within the meaning of the Act is not subject to territorial limitations. Hence, when the Act requires that the invention shall be new to everyone, it means that the invention shall be new to everyone worldwide, not just new to all Danes. Consequently, if an invention has been described in a local paper in Mongolia, it is not a new invention, irrespective of whether a person subsequently applying for patent on the same invention knows or ought to know of that description.

In order to be considered comprised in the state of the art, an invention must have been made available to a considerable or indefinite number of persons, enabling those persons, if they are skilled in the art, to carry out the invention. This does not

307. Cf. s. 18 para. 1 subpara. 5 of Order No. 93 of 29 Jan. 2009. Part of the provision implements Art. 5 para. 3 of the Biotech Directive.
308. *See* s. 8 para. 2 of the Act.
309. Cf. M. Koktvedgaard, *Nordiskt Immateriellt Rättsskyd* (1978), 76.
310. Cf. s. 2 para. 2 of the Act. The provision is similar to Art. 54(2) of the EPC.

apply if there exists a specific and close relationship between the said persons and the applicant. Such a relationship may exist, for example, between an employer and his/her employees and between an inventor and prospective customers or other business partners.

The contents of prior patent applications are considered comprised in the state of the art, provided the prior patent applications have been made available to the public according to section 22 of the Act.[311] Normally, patent applications are made available to the public eighteen months from the date of filing. Section 22 paragraph 1 states that the files of the application shall be available to the public from the date on which the patent is granted. However, according to section 22 paragraph 2, the application shall be available to the public when eighteen months have elapsed from the date of filing or from the date on which priority is claimed under the provisions of the Paris Convention, even if a patent has not yet been granted.[312] If a decision has been made to shelve or to refuse the application before eighteen months from the date of filing or the priority date has elapsed, the files of the application shall not be made available to the public. Similarly, the content of a utility model application as filed, with a prior date of filing, shall be considered comprised in the state of the art, provided the prior utility model application has been made available to the public according to the provisions in the Act on Utility Models.

165. The applicant's conduct in disclosing the invention prior to the date of filing is comprised in the state of the art irrespective of the form of disclosure. For instance, if the inventor has published a description of his/her invention or has lectured on his/her invention in a way that disclosed the invention to the public, the invention is comprised in the state of the art. Danish patent law does not grant a 'period of grace'. It is explicitly stated in section 2 paragraph 2 of the Act that an invention may be disclosed to the public by use. If the invention is only used within the four walls of the applicant's company, the invention is normally not considered to be comprised in the state of the art. Similarly, if the applicant demonstrates the invention to prospective customers, normally, the invention is not considered disclosed to the public within the meaning of section 2. However, if the number of prospective customers is sufficiently large, the invention is considered disclosed to the public. Experimental use of the invention does not disclose the invention to the public even if the experimental use due to the circumstances must take place where a large number of persons have access, for example, experimental use of a new type of aircraft.

166. By virtue of section 2 paragraph 6 of the Act, a disclosure of the invention shall not be taken into consideration if it occurred no earlier than six months preceding the filing of the patent application and if it was due to, or in consequence of: (i) an evident abuse in relation to the applicant or his/her legal predecessor (subparagraph 1) or (ii) the fact that the applicant or his/her legal predecessor has displayed the invention at an official, or officially recognized, international exhibition

311. Cf. s. 2 para. 2 of the Act.
312. On the request of the applicant the application can be made available to public at an earlier date, cf. s. 22 para. 3 of the Act.

falling within the terms of the Convention on international exhibitions signed at Paris on 22 November 1928 (subparagraph 2).[313]

The provision in subparagraph 1 aims at situations where the invention is disclosed to the public due to circumstances out of the applicant's control. The provision only applies in cases of an evident abuse, meaning that if the applicant or his/her legal predecessor has taken part in disclosing the invention, subparagraph 1 does not apply. Additionally, it is a condition for not taking the disclosure into consideration that someone other than the applicant or his/her legal predecessor has disclosed the invention by undue conduct, for example, by acquiring information on the invention by unlawful means or by passing information on the invention in breach of confidence. Thus, disclosure of the invention due to a mistake on part of the Patent Authority will exclude patentability.

As regards subparagraph 2, the provision seems to have no actual significance due to the rigorous conditions laid down in the said convention.

167. Section 2 paragraph 4 stipulates that the condition of novelty under section 2 paragraph 1 shall not exclude the patentability of any substance or composition, comprised in the state of the art, for use in a method referred to in section 1 paragraph 3 (i.e., methods for treatment of the human or animal body by surgery or therapy and diagnostic methods practised on the human or animal body), provided that the use of the substance or composition for any method referred to in that section is not comprised in the state of the art.[314] This means that a patent may be granted for the use of a substance or a composition even though the substance or composition in itself is comprised in the state of the art; but when a patent is granted for one specific form of use of the substance or composition within the said area (surgery, therapy and diagnostic methods), patentability is excluded for other forms of use within the same area no matter how different these other forms of use may be. The provision does not exclude patentability of the use of a substance or composition within another technical area. The scope of the exclusion and its interpretation is a much-debated issue, but it was adopted as part of the effort to harmonize Danish patent law with the EPC; hence, it should be understood in the light of EPC Article 54(5) and the relevant parts of the EPO Guidelines.[315]

In addition to section 2 paragraph 4, section 2 paragraph 5 of the Act stipulates that the condition of novelty under section 2 paragraph 1 shall not exclude the patentability of any substance or composition referred to in section 2 paragraph 4 for any specific use in a method referred to in section 1 paragraph 3 (i.e., methods for treatment of the human or animal body, etc.), provided that the invention relates to a specific use and such use is not comprised in the state of the art.

168. When the same person applies for patent in several countries, it proves a large practical difficulty to ensure the same date of filing in each country and that poses the question of whether the content of the application first time is considered

313. The provision is similar to Art. 55(1) of the EPC.
314. The provision is similar to Art. 54(5) of the EPC.
315. Cf. M. Koktvedgaard & L. Østerborg, 'Patent på lægemidler', in *Ugeskrift for Retsvæsen* (1984), 1–6.

comprised in the state of the art in relation to the subsequent applications in other countries. According to section 6 of the Act, an application for a patent on an invention that is contained in a prior application filed no earlier than twelve months for a patent or utility model in Denmark or in a prior application filed no earlier than twelve months for a patent, an inventor's certificate or a utility model in a country that has acceded the Paris Convention of 20 March 1883 or the World Trade Organization (WTO) Agreement, shall in relation to section 2 paragraphs 1, 2 and 4 and section 4 on request be considered filed on the same day as the prior application.[316]

The provision relates to the priority date, which is the date on which the application is tested against the state of the art, and it implies that the applicant is given a period of twelve months from the filing of the first application to decide whether he/she will apply for patent in other countries.

This principle of priority contained in section 6 also applies to applications originating in countries that have not acceded to the Paris Convention or the WTO Agreement provided that such a country due to a bilateral or multilateral agreement respects in the main on similar conditions a priority date in favour of applications for patent and utility model originating in Denmark.

The applicant has to claim priority in order to get it, and as an evidence of the right to priority, the applicant, among other things, has to submit a certified copy of the earlier application.[317]

III. Inventive Step

169. A patentable invention must be considerably distinguished from the state of the art. This condition of inventive step supplements the condition of novelty by making the conditions of protection more rigorous. The practical need of requiring an inventive step as a condition of protection manifests itself by the fact that it is possible to describe most inventions as new in relation to the state of the art, including inventions that are distinguished from the state of the art only by insignificant technical details.

Inventive step cannot be evaluated independently of novelty. Analogously with novelty, inventive step is an objective condition. However, contrary to novelty, it is more difficult to establish objective criteria on which the assessment can be based. Presumably, the principle in Article 56 of the EPC is applicable. Article 56 states that an invention shall be considered to involve an inventive step if, having regard to the state of the art, it is not obvious to a person skilled in the art. The EPO Guidelines elaborate on this point by stating that:

> the person skilled in the art should be presumed to be an ordinary practitioner aware of what was common general knowledge in the art at the relevant date. He should also be presumed to have had access to everything in the 'state of

---

316. The provision is based on Art. 4 of the Paris Convention.
317. Cf. s. 10 of Order No. 2111 of 24 Nov. 2021.

the art', in particular the documents cited in the search report, and to have had at his disposal the normal means and capacity of routine work and experimentation.

In assessing inventive step, the person skilled in the art shall not only confine his/her assessment to his/her immediate cognition of the invention and relate it to the state of the art but also he/she shall apply his/her ability to combine separate technical elements comprised in the state of the art in order to assess whether the combination of these separate technical elements makes the invention obvious to him/her.

170. It follows from the preparatory works of the Patents Act 1967 that one of the intentions of the Act was to make the condition of inventive step more rigorous. The subsequent case law and the decisions from the Patent and Trademark Board of Appeal provide to a minor extent support to such a development. Furthermore, it appears that the condition of inventive step is more rigorous in areas with rapid technological progress, ensuring that patent law does not curtail further technological progress.[318]

In a Supreme Court decision,[319] it was held that a remedy for dental care consisting of a combination of fluorine and abrasive, which separately was a well-known element of dental care, satisfied the conditions of protection. In reaching this decision, the Supreme Court argued that the fact that the use of the combination in dental care had a significant restrictive influence on caries was considered a surprising result for a person skilled in the art, and consequently, the combination involved an inventive step. Case law indicates that there does not exist a clear-cut distinction between the assessment of novelty and inventive step.[320]

§4. Formalities

171. National patents are based on registration. An application for a national patent shall be filed at the Patent and Trademark Office; after examining the application regarding patentable subject matter, novelty and inventive step on the basis of the Danish Patents Act, the Patent and Trademark Office may issue a patent.

I. The Patent Application

172. National patent applications are filed with the Patent and Trademark Office. International patent applications[321] covering Denmark are filed with a patent authority or an international organization that is competent under the PCT to receive such

318. Cf. Schovsbo, Rosenmeier & Petersen (2024), 353.
319. *Ugeskrift for Retsvæsen* 1980.557 H.
320. *See*, for example, the Supreme Court decision reported in *Ugeskrift for Retsvæsen* 1989.548 H.
321. An 'International patent application' means an application under the PCT, cf. s. 28 para. 1 of the Act.

applications (receiving authority). The Patent and Trademark Office receives authority of international patent applications from applicants who are Danish nationals and applicants who are domiciled in Denmark or who have a real and effective establishment in Denmark or who are recognized as legal persons according to Danish law. European patent applications covering Denmark are filed with an authority or a European organization that is the proper receiving authority, according to the EPC. If the Patent and Trademark Office receives a European patent application, the Patent and Trademark Office forwards the application to the EPO.[322]

173. A standard application form, which can be requested from the Patent and Trademark Office free of charge, may be used. The standard application form includes detailed guidelines. To file a patent application, the applicant shall pay the prescribed application fee of DKK 3,000 (basic fee). If the application contains more than ten patent claims, the applicant shall pay an extra fee of DKK 300 for each additional claim. In addition, the applicant shall pay a renewal fee in respect of each year. The renewal fee is raised progressively over the time of the patent life, amounting to DKK 535 for the first year and DKK 5,525 for the twentieth year; the fee shall the first time be reckoned from the filing date and thereafter from the corresponding day of the calendar year.[323]

The patent application shall contain an application document, a description of the invention including drawings where necessary, a precise statement of the matter for which protection by the patent is sought (one or more patent claims) and an abstract of the description and the claims. The application shall indicate the name of the inventor whenever the applicant and the inventor are the same person. If the applicant is not the inventor, it shall appear from the application that the applicant has acquired the right to the invention and that the inventor has been informed that a patent will be applied for.[324]

The description of the invention shall in the first part state a short and factual term for the invention. Additionally, the description shall state the technical field of the invention and explain the technical problem and how the claimed invention solves that problem, clarifying the contribution of the invention to the state of the art. Finally, the description shall expressly state how the invention may be applied industrially unless this is obvious from the rest of the description or from the character of the invention.[325] For most types of inventions drawings are necessary in order to describe the invention; however, as regards, for example, an invention in the form of a chemical substance, a description by the chemical formula may suffice. The description shall be sufficiently clear to enable a person skilled in the art to carry out the invention.[326]

Section 8 paragraph 2 and section 8a of the Patents Act stipulate certain additional requirements for the disclosure of inventions that relate to microbiological processes or the products thereof. If an invention of this kind in order to be carried

322. Cf. s. 28 para. 2 of the Act, and ss 2 and 87–89 of Order No. 2111 of 24 Nov. 2021.
323. Cf. s. 8 para. 5 of the Act.
324. Cf. s. 8 paras 2, 3 and 4 of the Act.
325. Cf. s. 16 para. 1 of Order No. 2111 of 24 Nov. 2021.
326. Cf. s. 8 para. 2 of the Act.

out involves the use of a microorganism that is neither available to the public nor describable in the documents of application so as to enable a person skilled in the art to carry out the invention, a sample of the microorganism shall be deposited the same day the application is submitted. These rules on deposit of microorganisms are related to the Budapest Treaty of 1977.[327]

174. The patent claims determine the scope of the patent protection and therefore must be worded very carefully. Consequently, it is stated in section 13 paragraph 3 of Order No. 2111 of 24 November 2021 that a patent claim shall not contain anything that is irrelevant to the claimed invention or that is inessential to the exclusive right applied for. Patent claims shall contain a precise statement of the matter for which protection is sought expressed by the technical features that are prerequisites in reaching the intended effect. Furthermore, the patent claims shall contain a term for the invention, an indication of the contribution of the invention to the state of the art and an indication of what is new and what are the characteristics of the invention. As far as possible, the patent claims shall relate the invention to one of the following categories: product, apparatus, process and use.[328]

A patent application may contain several patent claims. Section 14 paragraph 2 of Order No. 2111 of 24 November 2021 distinguishes between independent and dependent patent claims. A patent claim is independent if it exhaustively defines the invention concerned. A patent claim is dependent if it relates to a form of implementation of an invention contained in another patent claim and, consequently, has the same characteristics as the other patent claim. One or more dependent patent claims may be connected to an independent patent claim. A dependent patent claim shall refer to an independent patent claim and shall indicate the additional characteristics of the invention. By virtue of section 10 of the Act, in the same application, a patent may not be applied for in respect of two or more mutually independent inventions. This provision is not contravened by an application comprising several inventions provided that there exists a technical interrelationship between the inventions. Technical interrelationship denotes two or more inventions that in the whole or in parts share the same or similar specific technical features. Specific technical features shall be understood as the technical features each invention contributes to the state of the art.[329]

The fact that the invention relates to a chemical compound does not imply that specific use must be indicated in the claim.[330] The provision was introduced in 1978 when the limitations on the patentability of chemical compounds were abolished. Contrary to the former Act, this provision clarified that it is possible to obtain a patent on a chemical compound where the protection is not confined to certain expressly stated forms of use.

175. According to section 8 paragraph 3 of the Act, the abstract of the description and claims shall merely serve for use as technical information and may not be

327. *See* 20–22 of Order No. 2111 of 24 Nov. 2021.
328. Cf. s. 13 paras 1 and 2 of Order No. 2111 of 24 Nov. 2021.
329. Cf. s. 15 of Order No. 2111 of 24 Nov. 2021.
330. Cf. s. 8 para. 2 of the Act.

taken into account for any other purpose.[331] Among other things, this means that the abstract has no significance in determining the scope of protection.

The description, including drawings, photographs and a list of sequence, in addition to the claims, shall be worded in Danish or English. If a document contained in the application is worded in another language, the Patent and Trademark Office may demand that a translation be submitted to the Patent and Trademark Office. If an application has been examined for novelty and patentability on the basis of documents not worded in Danish, the patent claims shall be submitted in Danish when the Patent and Trademark Office finds that the patent can be granted.[332]

II. Examination

176. The Patent and Trademark Office conducts an examination of the patent application, and whether a patent is granted is contingent on the result of the examination. Primarily, a substantial material examination of the conditions of patentability is conducted (including patent search); the examination covers all conditions for obtaining patent protection.

If the applicant so requests, at the latest three months after the date of filing, and pays the prescribed fee, the Patent and Trademark Office shall with respect to the condition of novelty cause the application to be examined by an international examination authority under the provisions of Article 15(5) of the PCT.[333] Otherwise, the application is examined by the Patent and Trademark Office.

When examining the conditions of patentability under section 2 of the Act, the Patent and Trademark Office takes into consideration everything it knows of. Other available information is included in the examination where it is found necessary.[334]

In order to examine the patent application regarding patentable subject matter, novelty and inventive step, it is a prerequisite that the claimed invention is defined or described in a way that leaves no doubt as to what actually constitutes the invention. Therefore, the Patent and Trademark Office examines whether the description of the invention and the patent claims are sufficiently clear and precise.

177. In practice, the examination of the patent application often involves a comprehensive correspondence between the Patent and Trademark Office and the applicant. It is stated in section 15 paragraphs 1–4 of the Act that if the applicant has not complied with the requirements of the application or if the Patent and Trademark Office has other objections to the acceptance of the application, the applicant shall be notified accordingly and be invited to file his/her observations or to correct the application within a time limit to be specified. The Patent and Trademark Office may, however, make such amendments in the abstract as it finds necessary without consulting the applicant. If the applicant fails to file the required observation or to take steps to correct the application within expiry of the time limit, the application

331. *See also* s. 19 of Order No. 2111 of 24 Nov. 2021.
332. Cf. s. 6 paras 1–3 of Order No. 2111 of 24 Nov. 2021.
333. Cf. s. 9 of the Act, and ss 4 and 37 of Order No. 2111 of 24 Nov. 2021.
334. Cf. s. 35 of Order No. 2111 of 24 Nov. 2021.

shall be shelved. The notification of the applicant referred to *supra* shall contain information to that effect. The examination of the application shall, however, be resumed if the applicant submits his/her observations or takes steps to correct the application within four months after expiry of the specified time limit and pay the prescribed resumption fee. If any renewal fee is not paid according to sections 8, 41 and 42 of the Act, the application shall be shelved without previous notification. In the case of an application shelved for that reason, the proceeding for grant may not be resumed.

178. Typically, prospective objections to the application from the Patent and Trademark Office are based on a preliminary search and relate to limitations and specifications of the patent claims in order to consider the invention not being comprised in the state of the art. Accordingly, it is allowed to make amendments to the application; certain limitations, however, have to be respected. These limitations are primarily connected to the patent claims. By virtue of section 13 of the Act, an application for a patent may not be amended in such a way that protection is claimed for subject matter that was not disclosed in the application at the time when it was filed. This fundamental principle is further specified in Order No. 2111 of 24 November 2021: A patent claim cannot be amended in order to comprise elements that are not contained in the basic documents of the application.[335] The basic documents are the description of the invention, including necessary drawings, photographs, a list of sequence and the patent claims at the filing date.[336]

The description of the invention, drawings and photographs can only be subject to amendments and additions if such amendments and additions do not affect the understanding of the patent claims.[337] In general, it can be said that the patent application can be amended as long as it does not extend the claimed invention or introduce anything new to the application.

179. If, after having received the applicant's reply, the Patent and Trademark Office still has objections to the acceptance of the application, and the applicant has had an opportunity to comment on the objections, the application shall be refused, unless the Patent and Trademark Office considers it necessary once more to invite the applicant under section 15 of the Act,[338] as described *supra*.

180. The substantial examination ensures that a large proportion of the granted patents are valid and imply real protection. However, the examination is not final in the sense that the patent subsequently cannot be contested before the courts. For example, according to section 52 paragraph 1 subparagraph 1 of the Act, a patent may be revoked by a court decision if the conditions of protection under sections 1 and 2 of the Act are not complied with. Consequently, the owner of the patent has

335. Cf. s. 28 para. 1 of Order No. 2111 of 24 Nov. 2021.
336. Cf. s. 30 para. 1 of Order No. 2111 of 24 Nov. 2021.
337. Cf. s. 29 para. 1 of Order No. 2111 of 24 Nov. 2021.
338. Cf. s. 16 of the Act.

no absolute guarantee that the patent will not be revoked; for example, if after the grant of the patent, it becomes clear that the invention actually was comprised in the state of the art.

III. The Grant of a Patent

181. If the application complies with the requirements, and no objections have been found to the grant of a patent, and it has been established that the applicant approves the text on the basis of which a patent may be granted, the Patent and Trademark Office shall notify the applicant to the effect that patent may be granted against payment of the prescribed fee for publication of the patent specifications. This publication fee is separate from the application fee and the renewal fee. If the publication fee is not paid within two months after the Patent and Trademark Office has notified the applicant, the application will be shelved. However, the proceedings will be resumed if the applicant pays the publication fee and the prescribed resumption fee within four months after expiry of the time limit. After the Patent and Trademark Office has submitted notification to the applicant, the patent claims shall not be amended in such a manner that the scope of the patent protection is extended.[339]

When the requirements in section 19 of the Act as described *supra* have been complied with, the Patent and Trademark Office shall grant the patent and issue the letters patent. The grant of patent shall be advertised at the same time.[340] Granted patents shall be entered in a Register that shall be kept by the Patent and Trademark Office.[341]

IV. Oppositions

182. Prior to 1 January 1993, oppositions to the grant of a patent should be put forward before the patent actually was granted. However, according to the valid law, any person is entitled to file an opposition with the Patent and Trademark Office against a patent which has been granted. By 'any person' means a natural as well as a legal person irrespective of nationality and residence. The opposition shall be made in writing stating the grounds on which the opposition is filed and shall be submitted to the Patent and Trademark Office within nine months from advertisement of the grant of patent. The opposition shall be accompanied by the prescribed fee. An opposition shall only be filed on the grounds that the patent has been granted irrespective of the fact that the requirements in sections 1 and 2 of the Act (regarding patentable subject matter, industrial application, novelty and inventive step) are

339. Cf. s. 19 paras 1–3 of the Act, *see also* s. 39 of Order No. 2111 of 24 Nov. 2021.
340. Cf. s. 20 of the Act.
341. Cf. s. 27 of the Act. The rules governing the Register are laid down in ss 44–47 of Order No. 2111 of 24 Nov. 2021.

not complied with; it relates to an invention that has not been described in a sufficiently clear manner as to enable a person skilled in the art to carry out the invention on the basis of the description or the subject matter extends beyond the contents of the application field. The Patent and Trademark Office shall advertise the filing of an opposition.[342]

If an opposition has been filed, the owner of the patent shall be notified accordingly. After the expiry of the opposition period, and unless the opposition is refused, the patent owner is requested to file his/her observations on the opposition and possibly submit descriptions, claims, drawings or photographs in a changed form within six months. The Patent and Trademark Office may revoke a patent or maintain it unamended or amended. If the Patent and Trademark Office finds that the patent may be maintained as amended, the parties are informed, and the patent owner is requested to file his/her observations within two months. If it has been established that the owner of the patent consents to the patent as amended by the Patent and Trademark Office, the patent specifications shall be amended accordingly after the owner of the patent has paid the prescribed publication fee. In the case that the owner of the patent does not approve of the maintenance of the patent as amended, the opposition procedure may continue if the Patent and Trademark Office finds reason to do so. If the Patent and Trademark Office finds no such reason, the patent shall be revoked. Similarly, if the owner of the patent does not pay the fee for publication of new patent specifications in time, the patent shall be revoked.[343]

After the expiry of the opposition period, any person may file a written request with the Patent and Trademark Office to the effect that a patent granted by the Patent and Trademark Office or granted with effect for Denmark by the EPO be re-examined, cf. section 53b of the Act, *see infra* paragraph 231-232. on revocation.[344]

183. The opposition period of nine months from the grant of the patent requires that the application on which the patent is granted is available to the public. Thus, according to section 22 of the Act, the files of the application shall be available to the public as from the date on which the patent is granted. Furthermore, when eighteen months have elapsed from the date of filing or, if priority has been claimed under section 6 of the Act, from the date on which priority is claimed, the files shall be available to the public, even if patent has not been granted. From that date, everyone can request the files of the application from the Patent and Trademark Office.

V. Appeals

184. By virtue of section 24 paragraph 1 of the Act, an appeal from the final decision of the Patent and Trademark Office concerning a patent application may be filed by the applicant with the Patent and Trademark Board of Appeal. The owner

342. Cf. s. 21 of the Act.
343. Cf. s. 23 paras 1, 3 and 4 of the Act and ss 51–53 of Order No. 2111 of 24 Nov. 2021.
344. *See also* ss 55–57 of Order No. 2111 of 24 Nov. 2021.

of the patent may file an appeal with the Patent and Trademark Board of Appeal if a patent has been revoked or if the Patent and Trademark Office finds that the patent may be maintained as amended following an opposition. The opponent may file an appeal with the Patent and Trademark Board of Appeal if a patent is maintained unamended or if the Patent and Trademark Office finds that the patent may be maintained as amended despite a duly filed opposition. If the opponent withdraws his/her appeal, such appeal may nevertheless be examined when circumstances make it desirable. Appeals cannot be filed from other decisions than the ones stated in section 24 of the Act.

Appeals under section 24 of the Act shall be filed with the Patent and Trademark Board of Appeal not later than two months after the date on which the party concerned was notified of the decision by the Patent and Trademark Office. The prescribed fee shall be paid within the same time limit. Failure to do so shall cause the appeal to be refused. The decisions of the Patent and Trademark Board of Appeal may not be brought before any higher administrative authority. Proceedings to test decisions of the Patent and Trademark Office, which may be appealed to the Patent and Trademark Board of Appeal, may not be brought before the courts until the decision of the Patent and Trademark Board of Appeal has been given; however, this does not apply to the cases where a patent may be revoked by a court decision according to section 52 of the Act and cases where the court may transfer the patent where the patent has been granted to another person than the one entitled according to section 53 of the Act. Proceedings to test the decision by which the Patent and Trademark Board of Appeal refuses an application for a patent or revokes a patent shall be brought within two months after the date on which the party concerned was notified of the decision.[345]

The Patent and Trademark Board of Appeal is established by the Ministry of Business Affairs for the examination of appeals from decisions of the Patent and Trademark Office, cf. sections 25 and 67 of the Act.[346] The rules governing the Patent and Trademark Board are laid down in the Order No. 892 of 21 September 2009. In practice, a relatively large number of appeals are filed with the Patent and Trademark Board of Appeal; in comparison, only a few decisions are brought before the courts.

§5. Ownership and Transfer

185. Pursuant to section 1 of the Act, the right on application to be granted a patent is conferred on the inventor or his/her successor in title. The Act is based on the notion that the right of the invention originates from the inventor, and in that respect, the inventor will always be a natural person, not a legal person. However, the right of the invention may be transferred to another person, including a legal person, and in that case, the said person, whether natural or legal, acquires the right on application to be granted a patent. Accordingly, the applicant need not be the same

345. Cf. s. 25 paras 1–3 of the Act.

346. Cf. s. 7 para. 2 of the Act. The Patent and Trademark Board of Appeal is also examining appeals from decisions pursuant to the Danish Designs Act, the Danish Trademarks Act, etc.

person as the inventor. If the applicant is not the inventor, it shall appear from the application that the applicant has acquired the right to the invention and that the inventor has been informed that a patent will be applied for.[347]

186. If any person claims before the Patent and Trademark Office that he/she, and not the applicant, is entitled to the invention, the Patent and Trademark Office may, if it finds the question doubtful, invite him/her to bring it before the courts within a time limit to be specified. If the invitation is not complied with, the Patent and Trademark Office may disregard the claim when deciding on the patent application.[348] The provision is aimed at, for example, cases where the applicant has obtained detailed information on the invention from the actual inventor by breach of confidence. If any person proves to the Patent and Trademark Office that he/she, and not the applicant, is entitled to the invention, the Patent and Trademark Office shall transfer the application to the said person.[349]

187. When more than one person has cooperated in making the invention, they acquire the right of the invention jointly. In a Supreme Court decision from 1989, it was disputed who of two persons was the inventor of a specific technical device for sewing machines. On the grounds that the plaintiff conceived the idea of the invention and then asked the defendant to elaborate the idea into an applicable device, the right of the invention, though the elaboration of the idea took place in close cooperation with the plaintiff, was conferred on the plaintiff and the defendant jointly.[350]

The Act contains no provision governing joint ownership of the right of the invention. In practice, the involved parties solve the prospective problems by entering into agreements stipulating the rights to the invention. In the absence of such agreements, as the main rule, arrangements concerning the invention require unanimity among the entitled inventors.

188. When two or more persons have made the same invention independently of each other, they all have the right of the invention, and consequently, they all are entitled to apply for a patent for the invention. The right to the patent shall belong to the person whose application has the earliest filing date; that is, a first-to-file principle applies.

Often, the right of the inventor is transferred from the inventor to a company that, normally, will be better suited to apply for patent for the invention and exploit the patent commercially. When a patent has been obtained, the patent right is transferable, in the main, on the same lines as other kinds of property rights.

---

347. Cf. s. 8 para. 4 of the Act.
348. Cf. s. 17 para. 1 of the Act.
349. Cf. s. 18 para. 1 of the Act.
350. *Ugeskrift for Retsvæsen* 1988.991 H.

I. Licences

189. The Patents Act contains various provisions regarding specific aspects of patent licencing but no general rules on patent licences. In conformity with the general principles of contract law, there are no formal requirements for patent licence contracts; however, the practical needs result in probably all patent licence contracts being in writing.

The Supreme Court has held that a licence contract has not terminated on the sole fact that patent protection of the licenced invention had expired.[351] By stating that the period during which the licence contract was in force was not contingent on the term of patent protection, the Supreme Court pointed out that whether the licence contract was in force after the expiry of patent protection had to be decided on the basis of the content of the contract, the preparatory work leading to the contract and subsequent manifestations of the parties. Thus, the court applied general principles of interpretation of contracts. When the Supreme Court in the specific case concluded that the contract was in force after the expiry of patent protection, it was based on the facts that, first, the contract included terms on exclusive distribution of the patented product and, second, the contract had no direct reference to the subsistence of patent protection.

190. It is stipulated in section 43 of the Act that if the owner of a patent has granted another person a right to exploit the invention commercially (a licence), the licensee may not transfer that right to others in the absence of an agreement to the contrary. This provision applies to all different kinds of patent licences, including sublicences.

191. By virtue of section 44 paragraphs 1–2 of the Act, the transfer of a patent, the grant of a licence, pledging or execution proceedings shall on request be recorded in the Register of Patents. If it is proved that a registered licence has been terminated, the licence shall be deleted from the Register. Additionally, if a licensee transfers his/her right under the licence, with respect to section 43 of the Act, on request, the transfer may be recorded in the Register.[352] This kind of registration is not a condition of validity of the transfer, but it serves a formal purpose and provides information on various limited rights in patents. Accordingly, registration does not influence prospective conflicts between several licensees with conflicting rights. However, any person who institutes proceedings for the revocation of a patent, for the transfer of a patent or for the grant of a compulsory licence shall notify the Patent and Trademark Office as well as any licensees who are entered in the Register of Patents, and whose addresses are recorded in that Register, of the proceedings. Similarly, any person requesting administrative re-examination of a patent shall notify the said licensees to that effect.[353]

---

351. *Ugeskrift for Retsvæsen* 1991.652 H.
352. *See also* s. 47 of Order No. 2111 of 24 Nov. 2021.
353. Cf. s. 63 para. 1 of the Act.

192. The primary duty of the licensor is to place the patented invention at the disposal of the licensee in accordance with the terms of the licence agreement. The primary duty of the licensee is to pay the prescribed licence fee. Furthermore, if the licence fee is based on the volume of the licensee's production or sales, the licensee shall make arrangements that enable the licensor to monitor the extent of the production or sales if this is necessary for the licensor in assessing whether the licensee has paid the prescribed fee. In the absence of an agreement to the contrary, normally, the licensee has no duty to exploit the invention.[354] The licensee has unlimited capacity to institute proceedings for patent infringement.[355]

II. Inventions of Employees

193. The rights to inventions of employees have since 1955 been subject to a specific Act, the Act on Inventions of Employees.[356] The Act is in conformity with a central principle of Danish intellectual property law, according to which the rights originate in the physical creator of a good protected by intellectual property rights. Hence, an employee owns the rights to the inventions he/she has created unless other provisions of this Act or other Acts state otherwise.[357] Where an invention has been created by an employee in the execution of his/her duties, pursuant to section 5 of the Act, the employer is entitled to demand the right to the invention transferred to him/her for one or more countries, provided the exploitation of the invention lies within the field of activity of the employer. Even if the exploitation of the invention lies outside the field of activity of the employer, the employer is granted the same right if the invention of the employee is related to a specific task that has been assigned to the employee by the employer. If the right in the invention of the employee is transferred to the employer due to the provision of section 5 or on some other basis, the employee is entitled to reasonable remuneration unless the value of the invention does not exceed the value of the results that the employee reasonably could assume to have been created given the actual employment. The employee's right of remuneration cannot be waived by agreement.[358] The right to the invention has to be distinguished from the patent right. The right to the invention solely entitles the rightholder to apply for a patent.

The right to the invention is only transferred to the employer if the employer demands so. The decision on whether the right shall be transferred or not is facilitated by the provision of section 6 of the Act, which stipulates that, as soon as possible, an employee who has made an invention to which the provisions of section 5 are applicable shall inform the employer in this respect including all information on the invention, which enables the employer to evaluate the significance of the invention. Where the employer demands the right of an invention transferred to him/her, the employer shall notify the employee to that effect at the latest four months after

354. Cf. Schovsbo, Rosenmeier & Petersen (2024), 725 f.
355. Cf. s. 63 paras 1 and 4 of the Act.
356. Consolidated Act. No. 104 of 24 Jan. 2012.
357. Cf. s. 3 of the Act.
358. Cf. s. 8 para. 1 of the Act.

the employer has been informed of the creation of the invention according to the provision of section 6.[359] In the absence of the consent of the employer in writing within the said four-month term, the employee is not entitled to make arrangements regarding the invention or disclose it to others in a manner that makes it available to the public or enables others to exploit it. This does not apply where the employer has declared in writing that he/she has no interest in the invention.[360]

194. From a practical point of view, the problems stemming from the Act are primarily connected to the computation of a reasonable remuneration to the employee. In order to be entitled to remuneration, presumably, the employee shall have created something out of the normal; for example, he/she may have found a clearly unexpected solution to a technical problem.[361] The remuneration shall be computed in consideration of the value of the invention, the significance of the invention to the employer, the terms of the employment contract and the contribution of the employee to the creation of the invention.[362] Accordingly, the Act does not provide very precise guidelines for the computation of remuneration, but the built-in flexibility makes it possible to adjust the methods of computation in the long run in accordance with changes in the actual circumstances.[363] In practice, the amounts of remuneration are relatively small. It appears that the amounts of remuneration are considerably smaller than remuneration for similar inventions exploited in an efficient market, for example, by way of voluntary licence agreements.[364] In a Supreme Court decision, the employee claimed DKK 500,000 (approx. EUR 66,667) in addition to a 5% royalty depending on sales volume but was awarded a lump sum of DKK 50,000.[365]

The Act on Inventions of Employees applies to all inventions patentable in Denmark and to all creations that are protectable subject matter under the Act on Utility Models.[366]

Employees, no matter whether they are employed in the private or public sector, are subject to the Act. However, teachers and other scientific scholars employed by universities or similar educational institutions are excluded from the provisions of the Act.[367] Previously, the rights to inventions of such persons remained with the inventors. In 1999, that situation changed with the adoption of the Act on Inventions at Public Research Institutions.[368] The Act applies to teachers and other scientific scholars employed by universities, etc., and is somewhat similar to the Act

359. Cf. s. 7 para. 1 of the Act.
360. Cf. s. 7 para. 2 of the Act.
361. Cf. M.B. Andersen, *Lov om arbejdstageres opfindelser med kommentarer* (Copenhagen: Akademikernes Centralorganisation, 1995), 98.
362. Cf. s. 8 para. 2 of the Act.
363. *See also* s. 8 para. 4 of the Act.
364. In general, *see* Andersen (1995), 104 ff.
365. *Ugeskrift for Retsvæsen* 2004.1018 H.
366. *See* s. 1 para. 1 of the Act.
367. Cf. s. 1 para. 3 of the Act.
368. Now consolidated Act No. 210 of 17 Mar. 2009. In general on the Act, *see* J. Schovsbo, *Lov om opfindelser ved offentlige forskningsinstitutioner* (Copenhagen: Jurist- og Økonomforbundets Forlag, 2001).

on Inventions of Employees. However, according to this Act, the rights to inventions of the employee may be transferred to the employer to a larger extent than transfer of rights under the Act on Inventions of Employees.

§6. Scope of Exclusive Rights

195. Section 1 of the Patents Act expressly states that the patent right is an exclusive right to exploit the invention commercially. Patent protection consists of national rights; therefore, the geographical scope of the exclusive rights is limited to the territory of Denmark, including Greenland and the Faroe islands. Nevertheless, a limited exception to this fundamental principle is found in section 3 paragraph 1 subparagraph (iii) as described *infra.*

196. The patent claim is the decisive factor in determining the extent of protection. Thus, according to section 39 of the Act, the extent of protection conferred by a patent shall be determined by the claims. For interpretation of the claims, the description may serve as a guide. Issues concerning the patent claims and the extent of protection are elaborated *infra* paragraph 233 f. regarding infringement.

197. Various forms of exploitation covered by the exclusive right are enumerated in section 3 paragraph 1 of the Act: The exclusive right conferred by a patent shall imply that no one, except the owner of the patent, may without permission exploit the invention: (i) by making, offering, putting on the market or using a product that is the subject matter of the patent, or by importing or possessing the product for these purposes; or (ii) by using a process that is the subject matter of the patent or by offering the process for use in this country, if the person offering the process knows, or it is obvious in the circumstances that the use of the process is prohibited without the consent of the owner of the patent; or (iii) by offering, putting on the market or using a product obtained by a process that is the subject matter of the patent or by importing or possessing the product for these purposes.[369]

In principle, the exclusive right covers any kind of commercial exploitation of the invention. The various forms of exploitation enumerated in section 3 paragraph 1 must be understood as specifications of the exclusive right. However, section 3 paragraph 1 appears as an exhaustive list of the restricted acts since it is difficult to identify forms of commercial exploitation that are not covered by the wording of that provision.

I. Product and Apparatus

198. The essential restricted acts in relation to a patented product and apparatus are the exploitation of the invention by making, offering, putting on the market or using the product or apparatus. Protection against the unauthorized making of an invention is obviously a very important part of patent protection. In most cases, it

369. Section 3 para. 1 of the Act is similar to Art. 25 of the CPC.

is quite clear what constitutes unlawful making of a product. In some cases, however, where another person without permission has not made the invention in the whole but only in parts, for example, by repairs or reconditioning of the patented product, the scope of the right may create some doubts. As a main rule, if a patented product is repaired to such an extent that the invention is actually reconstructed, then permission from the patent owner is required.

By 'offering a product' is meant not only offering a product for sale but also offering a product for lending, rental, as a gift, etc. Unlawful offering of a patented product comprises situations where the product is offered for sale, etc., during the effective term of protection even though the product is to be delivered after the expiry of patent protection. Offering of a product takes place before the product is put on the market. When a product is put on the market, it is placed at the disposal of the person who demands the product, for example, by the actual delivery of the product. Enabling the patent owner to control the offering of a product and putting it on the market provides an important supplementary protection to the protection against unauthorized making of the invention since patent protection is not solely confined to potential infringers' actual manufacture of the patented product, but protection extends to subsequent acts related to the product. The importation and possession of a patented product is only prohibited to the extent that it enables an unauthorized person to conduct one of the restricted acts. The prohibition also applies in cases where the patented product has been manufactured in a country in which the invention is not protected by patent.

II. Process

199. Obviously, a patented process is infringed by using the process. Furthermore, the offering of the process for use in Denmark is prohibited. The prohibition is only effective if the potential infringer is in bad faith and the offering of the process is aimed at use in Denmark. Consequently, it must be assumed that the offering of a patented process in Denmark for use in countries other than Denmark is not a restricted act. It is not a condition for the prohibition that the protected process actually is infringed by a third person.

200. Section 3 paragraph 1 subparagraph (iii) of the Act provides indirect protection of products and strengthens patent protection granted for processes by extending protection of a process to the products obtained directly by the patented process. The provision is similar to Article 25(c) of the CPC and should be understood in the same way. Not all types of patentable processes are covered by section 3 paragraph 1 subparagraph (iii) of the Act; they are only processes that result in a product of some sort of a physical nature. This means that a patented process of, for example, examination, signalling, measuring and manoeuvring falls outside the scope of the provision. The provision deviates from the general principles of patent law, which delimit the scope of patent rights to the territory of a specific country. Naturally, the provision applies to products obtained from processes that take place in Denmark, but it also applies to products obtained from processes that take place in other countries, even if the process is not the subject matter of a patent in those countries. The need for this special rule is obvious. A process patent obtained in Denmark does not exclude other people from using the process in other countries, and since the products obtained from the process may be exported to Denmark, the protection of the Danish process patent is undermined in case of exports to Denmark. In the absence of this rule, the patent owner should obtain patent protection for the process in a large number of countries in order to ensure real and effective protection of the process patent, and, in practice, for many patent owners, that is not a realistic option. The protection against a product obtained by a process that is the subject matter of a patent is not conditioned on the product being a new product. In contrast, the patent owner is not protected against identical products being offered, put on the market or used, if they are obtained by a process other than the patented process.

201. In practice, it is often difficult for the patent owner to prove infringement of a patented process. To a certain extent, this problem is solved by section 64a paragraphs 1–2 of the Act that stipulates that if the subject matter of a patent is a process for the manufacture of a new product, the same product shall, when manufactured by any person other than the owner of the patent, be deemed to be manufactured on the basis of the patented process, unless evidence to the contrary is submitted. In connection with the submission of evidence to the contrary, the defendant's justified interest in protecting his/her manufacturing and business secrets shall be considered.[370] This special rule on the burden of proof is only applicable to new products; if the product is not new, the burden of proof regarding infringement of a patented process lies with the patent owner.

§7. Limitations and Exceptions to the Scope of Patent Protection

202. Patent protection confers on the owner an exclusive right, which enables the owner to prohibit any form of commercial exploitation of the invention. This extensive protection may in certain situations hinder technological progress or in other ways prove harmful to the society at large. In order to ensure a reasonable balance between the interests of the owner of the patent and the interests of the society at large, the Act includes a number of important limitations and exceptions to exclusive rights. In relation to this general balancing of interests, it must be borne in mind that the duration of patent protection is limited (*see infra* paragraph 225 ff.).

I. Non-commercial Purposes

203. By virtue of section 3 paragraph 3 subparagraph (i), the exclusive right shall not extend to acts done for non-commercial purposes.[371] Comprised by the term 'non-commercial purposes' are acts done in relation to research and teaching

370. The provision is similar to Art. 35 of the CPC. The provisions in the Danish Act was included in 1992 but was not considered a change in valid law compared to the time prior to 1992.
371. The provision is similar to Art. 27(a) of the CPC.

and acts done by individuals in their capacity as private persons. In most cases, section 3 paragraph 3 subparagraph (i) does not have large practical importance because in cases where the use of a protected invention takes place outside a business context, typically, the patent right has been exhausted.

II. Exhaustion

204. The exclusive patent right shall not extend to acts concerning products put on the market in Denmark or in a country within the EEA by the patent owner or with his/her consent, cf. section 3 paragraph 3 subparagraph (ii) of the Act. A product put on the market with the consent of the patent owner is, for example, a product put on the market by a licensee. The provision states the principle of exhaustion and ensures that patent protection does not constitute an unreasonable burden on users of patented products. Thus, a person buying a patented television set shall not acquire authorization from the patent owner every time he/she turns the television set on; the right to this kind of use of the patented product has been exhausted. The lawful first sale of a patented product implies that the patent right is exhausted. The exhaustion is comprehensive including rights to all subsequent acts relating to the patented product, for example, use, resale, rental and lending.

205. The patent right is exhausted only when products are put on the market in Denmark or in a country within the EEA.[372] If the product is put on the market outside the EEA, the patent owner may exercise his/her exclusive right to prevent importation of the product to Denmark. In a case before the Western Court of Appeal,[373] a Swiss company producing a patented chemical compound for protection of plants sought an injunction preventing a Danish company from parallel importing the product from countries outside the EU. The court held that the preparatory works of the Patents Act in certain cases did not exclude international exhaustion of patent rights (international exhaustion means that the patent right is exhausted when the product has been lawfully put on the market anywhere in the world); however, the fact that no production of the product took place in Denmark and the existence of price differentials between Denmark and the exporting countries did not provide sufficient grounds to conclude that the patent right had been exhausted. Hence, the Swiss company succeeded in preventing parallel import of the product. It was emphasized by the court that the principle of international exhaustion had not previously been applied in reported case law, and it was natural to assume that the business environment expected that international exhaustion only applied in situations where special market constellations have priority.

206. The main rule is that a patent owner cannot prevent importation of a patented product if the product has been put on the market in a country within the EEA by the patent owner or with his/her consent. When a patented product has been put on the market in a country due to a compulsory licence, the exclusive right is not

372. *See also* Order No. 238 of 30 Mar. 1994.
373. *Ugeskrift for Retsvæsen* 1994.488 V.

exhausted and the patent owner can prevent importation. This is in accordance with the decision of the European Court of Justice case 19/84 *Pharmon v. Hoechst.* However, the exclusive right is exhausted if the product is put on the market by the patent owner in a country where the invention is not patentable, cf. the decision of the European Court of Justice case 187/80 *Merck v. Stephar.*

III. Experimental Purposes

207. The exclusive patent right shall not extend to acts done for experimental purposes relating to the subject matter of the patented invention, cf. section 3 paragraph 3 subparagraph (iii).[374] The provision is not confined to non-commercial purposes. It is permitted to use a patented invention in a commercial context as part of a company's research, for example, in order to examine the prospects for elaborating and improving the invention. Accordingly, a competitor to the patent owner may reverse engineer a patented invention in order to reveal the technical idea of the invention and apply that idea in creating a new invention. In this respect the limitation on the exclusive patent right regarding use of a patented invention for experimental purposes is often valuable to the industry. Obviously, the provision does not permit production of the patented invention without authorization from the patent owner. The results of reverse engineering and other techniques of analysis may only be used to create a new invention independent of the existing patented invention.

IV. Prior Exploitation

208. The person first in time to file a patent application for a specific invention is granted the patent, provided the claimed invention is patentable; such follows from the first-to-file principle in patent law. The first-to-file principle may create unreasonable results. For example, in cases where two separate companies are engaged in a patent race – that is, where two companies are working in the same line of business and are controlling the same technologies and both companies' research and development activities are aimed at reaching a specific invention. In such a case, it may be incident which of the two companies is first in time to make the invention and subsequently applies for patent. According to the general principle, the loser of the patent race is excluded from using the invention if it is identical to the patented invention even if the invention has been made independently of the patented invention. Consequently, the investments in research and development made by the loser of the patent race have been lost. *Inter alia*, in order to avoid this inexpedient result it is stated in section 4 paragraph 1 of the Act that any person who, at the time when the patent application was filed, was exploiting the invention commercially in this country may, notwithstanding the grant of a patent, continue such exploitation retaining its general character, provided the exploitation does not constitute an evident abuse in relation to the applicant or his/her legal predecessor. Such a right of exploitation shall also, under similar conditions, be enjoyed by any

374. The provision is similar to Art. 27(b) of the CPC.

person who had made substantial preparations for commercial exploitation of the invention in this country. It is not possible to state precise criteria of what amounts to substantial preparations for commercial exploitation but a practical example of this is the construction of a production plant.

It is a condition for section 4 paragraph 1 to be applied that the invention was exploited or substantial preparations were made for exploitation for commercial purposes. If the invention was only used for private purposes, it is not possible to claim a right to prior exploitation in case later on the use of the invention is expanded into commercial exploitation. The right of prior exploitation is not an exclusive right and it is limited to future exploitation retaining the general character of the prior exploitation. This limitation shall be construed as a qualitative limitation not a quantitative limitation. Thus, a person owing a right of prior exploitation is permitted to expand the production volume of the patented product but he/she is not permitted to change his/her activities in relation to the patented product, for example, from producing the patented product to imports of the product.[375]

209. A person who claims a right of prior exploitation shall prove his/her prior activities in relation to the invention, and case law suggests a relatively heavy burden of proof on that person. In the Supreme Court decision reported in *Ugeskrift for Retsvæsen* 1964.628 H, the defendant claimed a right of prior exploitation in relation to a patented device for a threshing machine and substantiated this claim by a solemn declaration signed by six persons stating that the defendant had exploited the disputed invention before the priority date. The Supreme Court held that the declaration was not sufficient proof for prior exploitation, partly due to the fact that the said declaration came into existence two and a half years after the alleged prior exploitation.

Section 4 paragraph 1 does not require good faith on the person entitled to a right of prior exploitation; however, it is a condition of acquiring a right under section 4 paragraph 1 that the prior exploitation does not constitute an evident abuse in relation to the applicant or his/her predecessor. This means that a person who has taken the idea constituting the invention from the applicant is not entitled to a right of prior exploitation.

210. The transferability of the right of prior exploitation provided for in section 4 paragraph 1 of the Act is subject to substantial limitations since the right to prior exploitation shall only be transferred to others together with the business in which it has arisen or in which the exploitation was intended.[376] The term 'business' does not mean that the right of prior exploitation shall only be transferred together with the whole company, probably, the right may be transferred together with a single department of the company. The right may also be transferred by the way of inheritance or legal execution.

375. Cf. Schovsbo, Rosenmeier & Petersen (2024), 405 f and Lindgreen, Schovsbo & Thorsen (2024), 262 ff.
376. Cf. s. 4 para. 2 of the Act.

V. Compulsory Licence

211. Sections 45–50 of the Patents Act are concerned with compulsory licences. The Act states four different situations where compulsory licence may be granted: insufficient exploitation of the invention (section 45), dependency between several patents, etc. (section 46 and 46a), important public interests (section 47) and prior exploitation (section 48).

Various conditions and rules apply to all types of compulsory licences. Compulsory licences shall only be granted to persons who by agreement have not been able to obtain licence on reasonable terms and who may be regarded as being able to make use of the invention in a reasonable and proper manner.[377] The person seeking compulsory licence shall demonstrate a previous real and effective attempt to obtain a voluntary licence agreements; additionally, he/she shall be able to make use of the invention in a reasonable and proper manner. The latter condition means that the said person shall have sufficiently economic, organizational and technological resources to ensure that the resulting product meets a reasonable standard of quality and that he/she is able to pay the stipulated licence fees. In this way, the patent owner is not exposed to the risk that the market for the patented product is distorted by low-quality products.

212. It is not a condition for obtaining a compulsory licence that the person seeking the licence has clean hands in a strict sense. In the Supreme Court decision reported in *Ugeskrift for Retsvæsen* 1966.566 H, the defendant obtained a compulsory licence on a patented process of production of a chemical compound, irrespective of the fact that the defendant previously had infringed the patent in question.[378] From the decision, it must be concluded that compulsory licence is only denied in cases where the person applying for compulsory licence has exercised flagrant unlawful conduct.[379]

213. A right granted under a compulsory licence is not an exclusive right, thus, a compulsory licence does not prevent the owner of the patent from exploiting the invention himself/herself or from granting licences to others.[380] The right granted under a compulsory licence is only to a limited extent transferable. By virtue of section 49 paragraph 3 of the Act, compulsory licence can only be transferred to others together with the establishment in which it is used or in which the utilization was intended.[381] Moreover, for compulsory licences filed in accordance with section 46 paragraph 1 (dependency between several patents), the transfer of such a compulsory licence shall take place together with the patent the use of which is dependent on a patent or a registered utility model that belongs to another person.[382]

377. Cf. s. 49 para. 1 of the Act. The provision complies with Art. 31(b) of the TRIPs Agreement.
378. *See Ugeskrift for Retsvæsen* 1964.498 H.
379. Cf. J. Trolle in *Ugeskrift for Retsvæsen* 1966.B, 277.
380. Cf. s. 49 para. 2 of the Act. The provision is similar to Art. 31(d) of the TRIPs Agreement.
381. Cf. Art. 31(e) of the TRIPs Agreement.
382. Cf. Art. 31(l)(iii) of the TRIPs Agreement.

214. Pursuant to Article 31(c) of the TRIPs Agreement, a special provision regarding compulsory licences on semiconductor technology has been included into section 49 paragraph 4 of the Act. Compulsory licence concerning semiconductor technology can only be filed for public, non-commercial use or for terminating an anticompetitive practice that has been established after judicial or administrative process.

215. Compulsory licence under the Patents Act shall only be granted by the courts and, since decisions regarding compulsory licences are relatively rare and often have technical properties, it is stipulated in section 50 of the Act that the Maritime and Commercial Court in Copenhagen shall decide as the Court of First Instance whether a compulsory licence shall be granted; an appeal may be lodged to the Court of Appeal. Moreover, the Maritime and Commercial Court shall determine the extent to which the invention may be exploited, fix the compensation and lay down the terms of the compulsory licence. If circumstances should change considerably, the Court may, at the request of either party, cancel the licence or lay down new terms of the licence. The possibility, on request, of cancelling or changing the terms of the compulsory licence shall be construed as a narrow exception aiming at situation where a compulsory licence proves to be unreasonable on one of the parties.

216. Turning to the specific types of compulsory licences, section 45 paragraph 1 of the Act states that if a patented invention is not worked to a reasonable extent in this country when three years have elapsed from the grant of the patent and four years have elapsed from the filing of the patent application any person, wishing to work the invention in Denmark, may obtain a compulsory licence to do so unless there are legitimate reasons for failure to work the invention. The purpose of the compulsory licence in section 45 paragraph 1 has traditionally been to promote real production related to the patented invention in Denmark. Accordingly, imports of a patented product is not sufficient to prevent the grant of compulsory licence. The patented invention shall be worked to a reasonable extent in Denmark, but by virtue of section 45 paragraph 2 the Minister Industry, Business and Financial Affairs in this respect may direct that working of the invention in another country shall be equivalent to working in this country. Such a provision may be made subject to reciprocity. *Inter alia*, the provision was needed to fulfil obligations under EU law. Section 98 paragraph 1 of Order No. 2111 of 24 November 2021 stipulates that in assessing the conditions of obtaining compulsory licence pursuant to section 45 paragraph 1 of the Act, the working of the invention in the EU or in a country that has ratified or acceded to the EEA Agreement or the WTO Agreement shall be considered equivalent to the working of the invention in Denmark.

The patent owner has a reasonable period of time in which he/she can decide whether he/she wants to work the invention in Denmark or enter into voluntary licence agreements, or expose himself/herself to the risk of a compulsory licence: either three years from the grant of the patent or four years from the filing date, the longest of the two terms applies. Legitimate reasons for the patent owner's failure to work the invention may be legislation and other public restrictions preventing the exploitation of the invention. If the patent owner does not work the invention due to the lack of economic resources or due to the fact that the patent owner considers exploitation of the invention unprofitable, there are no legitimate reasons for failure to work the invention.[383]

217. By virtue of section 46 paragraph 1 of the Act the owner of a patent for an invention (the second patent), the use of which is dependent on a patent (the first patent) or a registered utility model that belongs to another person may obtain compulsory licence for use of the protected invention of the first patent or the protected model of the utility-model registration if the invention related to the second patent makes up an essential technical progress of substantial economic importance. Moreover, it is stated in section 46 paragraph 2 that the owner of the first patent or of the registered utility model for which use of compulsory licence has been granted pursuant to the provision in section 46 paragraph 1 shall on reasonable terms be able to obtain compulsory licence for use of the other invention related to the second patent.[384] Thus, the owner of the first patent may on reasonable terms obtain a cross-licence to use the invention claimed in the second patent. In deciding whether compulsory licence shall be granted under section 46, presumably, the court will take into consideration the market competition between the patented inventions. In casc the two inventions can be used in the same line of business and are close substitutes on the market, the court will be more reluctant to grant a compulsory licence. The scope of compulsory licence under section 46 is strictly limited to what is necessary in order to use the second patent.

Similar provisions on compulsory licence in respect of plant variety rights are found in section 46a of the Patents Act. The provisions implement Article 12 of the Biotech Directive. Thus, where a breeder cannot acquire or exploit a plant variety right without infringing a prior patent, he/she may apply for a compulsory licence for non-exclusive use of the invention protected by the patent inasmuch as the licence is necessary for the exploitation of the plant variety to be protected, subject to payment of an appropriate royalty. A compulsory licence is granted only when the breeder demonstrates that the plant variety makes up an essential technical progress of substantial economic importance compared with the invention claimed in the patent.[385] Where the patent owner has been granted compulsory licence pursuant to the Act on Plant Variety Protection in respect of a protected plant variety, the holder of the variety right will be entitled to a cross-licence on reasonable terms to use the protected invention.[386]

218. When required by important public interests, any person who wishes to exploit an invention commercially for which another person holds a patent may obtain a compulsory licence to do so, cf. section 47 of the Act. 'Important public interests' within the meaning of the Act shall be interpreted narrowly. Compulsory licence under section 47 can be granted on reasons of public safety or in order to

383. Cf. Koktvedgaard & Østerborg (1979), 241 ff.
384. Section 46 complies with Art. 31(l)(i) and (ii) of the TRIPs Agreement. A similar provision is included into s. 42 of the Act on Utility Models.
385. Cf. s. 46 a para. 1.
386. Cf. s. 46 a para. 2.

ensure the general supply to the public of pharmaceuticals, foodstuffs, power, communication facilities, etc. Private interests of any kind cannot justify compulsory licence under section 47. It is disputable whether section 47 can be applied as a means of price control. A patent owner may exploit his/her exclusive right by demanding exorbitant prices on the patented product, and if the product is of vital importance to the public at large, it may be argued that another person should be able to obtain compulsory licence on grounds of important public interests. On the one hand, parts of the preparatory works of the Act support this view; on the other hand, the Competition Authority has been given the powers to monitor and eventually intervene in harmful monopolistic pricing behaviour.[387]

In the somewhat peculiar case reported in *Ugeskrift for Retsvæsen* 1972.325 H, the Danish Ministry of Defence had bought forty-six fighter planes from the Swedish company SAAB; the fighter planes were equipped with ejection seats. An English manufacturer claimed that the ejection seats infringed patents he/she had been granted in Sweden and Denmark. In Sweden, the State had expropriated the patent. The Danish Ministry of Defence and SAAB applied for compulsory licence under section 47 regarding the use of fifty-two seats in the forty-six planes in Denmark. A majority of the judges in the Supreme Court held that importing and using the fighter planes without being required to make alterations in the equipment of the planes was of significant importance to the Danish Ministry of Defence, and, accordingly, delivery of the planes was considered an important public interest satisfying the conditions of compulsory licence according to section 47.

219. By virtue of section 48 paragraph 1 of the Act, any person who, in this country at the time when a patent application was made available to the public, was commercially exploiting the invention for which a patent is applied for, may, if the application results in a patent, obtain a compulsory licence to exploit the invention if very special circumstances make it desirable, and he/she had no knowledge and could not reasonably have obtained any knowledge of the application. Such a right shall also, under similar conditions, be enjoyed by any person who had made substantial preparations for commercial exploitation of the invention in this country.

As a limitation on the exclusive right, section 48 paragraph 1 is somewhat similar to the right of prior exploitation in section 4 of the Act. A right of prior exploitation under section 4 can be acquired only on the basis of acts that take place before the filing date (priority date); compulsory licence under section 48 paragraph 1 may be obtained on the basis of acts that take place after the filing data but before the date on which the patent application shall be made available to the public. The person who acquires a right to use a patented invention on the basis of prior exploitation has a more narrow right under section 48 paragraph 1 than under section 4. If compulsory licence is granted, the licensee cannot expand the exploitation of the invention neither quantitatively nor qualitatively, contrary to the person acquiring a right of prior exploitation under section 4 who is not restricted in respect of quantitatively expansion. The conditions of acquiring rights are stricter under section 48

387. *See* T. Riis, *Enerettigheder og vederlagsrettigheder. Håndhævelse af immaterialrettigheder i økonomisk perspektiv* (Copenhagen: Jurist- og Økonomforbundets Forlag, 2005), 397 ff; and Koktvedgaard & Østerborg (1979), 246 ff.

paragraph 1 than under section 4. Thus, obtaining compulsory licence requires that very special circumstances make it desirable; no such condition is contained in section 4. In addition, section 48 requires that the person applying for compulsory licence shall be in good faith; in section 4, it is just stipulated that the prior exploitation shall not constitute an evident abuse in relation to the applicant or his/her legal predecessor.

Compulsory licence under section 48 paragraph 1 may include the time preceding the grant of patent. Contrary to the other provisions of the Act on compulsory licence, compulsory licence under section 48 paragraph 1 may be applied retroactively. The reason for this is to avoid proceedings on patent infringement regarding prior exploitation where compulsory licence is permissible.

Section 48 paragraph 1 states that commercial exploitation or substantial preparations for commercial exploitation shall take place in this country. The Minister of Industry, Business and Financial Affairs may direct that exploitation of the invention in another country shall be equivalent to exploitation in this country. Such a provision may be made subject to reciprocity.[388] Section 98 paragraph 1 of Order No. 2111 of 24 November 2021 stipulates that in assessing the conditions of obtaining compulsory licence pursuant to section 48 paragraph 1, the exploitation of the invention in the EU or in a country that has ratified or acceded to the EEA Agreement or the WTO shall be considered equivalent to the exploitation of the invention in Denmark. This means that exploitation of the invention or substantial preparations for commercial exploitation in one of these countries may provide the basis for compulsory licence under section 48 paragraph 1 effective in Denmark.

220. If a patent has been granted to another person than the one entitled thereto, the court shall transfer the patent to the entitled person if he/she so claims. However, the person who is deprived of the patent shall, if he/she in good faith exploits the invention commercially in this country or has made substantial preparations for such exploitation, be entitled to a reasonable compensation and, on reasonable conditions in other respects, to continue the exploitation already commenced or to implement the planned exploitation retaining its general character. Such a right shall also, under the same conditions, be enjoyed by holders of registered licences. Such rights may only be transferred to others together with the business in which they are exploited or in which exploitation was intended.[389]

221. Apparently, the provisions regarding compulsory licences under section 46 and 46a (dependency between several patents, etc.) and section 48 (prior exploitation) have never been applied in practice.[390]

---

388. Cf. s. 48 para. 3. The provision is similar to s. 45 para. 2 of the Act.
389. Cf. s. 53 paras 1–3 of the Act.
390. Cf. Schovsbo, Rosenmeier & Petersen (2024), 411.

VI. Other Exceptions

222. The exclusive patent right shall not extend to acts necessary for the grant of a marketing authorization for pharmaceutical products for human use or veterinary pharmaceutical products.[391] When a patent on a pharmaceutical product expires, generic drug companies can produce and market a similar generic/imitation pharmaceutical product. However, the marketing of a pharmaceutical product requires a marketing authorization from the health authority. In order to be granted a marketing authorization for an imitation pharmaceutical product, the producer shall prove that the product has the same qualitative and quantitative composition in active substances and the same pharmaceutical form as the original pharmaceutical product. The provision allows others, in particular generic drug companies, to study, test, analyse, etc., patented pharmaceutical products and has the effect of reducing the period of time from the expiration of the patent on a pharmaceutical product and the marketing of an imitation product. The provision is related to the exception for experimental use in section 3 paragraph 3 subparagraph 3 of the Act.

223. The exclusive patent right shall not extend to the preparation in a pharmacy of a medicine in accordance with a medical prescription nor acts concerning the medicine so prepared.[392] The inclusion of chemical compounds as patentable subject matter in 1967, and, additionally, the inclusion of pharmaceutical products as patentable subject matter in 1983 necessitated this special provision enabling pharmacies to continue the practice of preparing medicine at pharmacies without infringing patent rights. The provision is limited to specific acts of preparation in accordance with a medical prescription; hence, it does not allow the preparation of a medicine with the purpose of stockpiling. Due to modern forms of production where pharmaceuticals primarily are produced as final products at a pharmaceutical company and rarely at a pharmacy, the provision has only minor practical importance.

224. In order to maintain the effectiveness in various forms of international transportation, it is stated in section 5 paragraph 1 of the Act that notwithstanding a patent having been granted for an invention, persons other than the owner of the patent may exploit the invention by the use of a foreign vehicle, vessel or aircraft when it temporarily or accidentally enters this country.[393] Only the use of the patented invention is covered by this provision contrary to, for example, the sale of the invention. Additionally, the Minister of Industry, Business and Financial Affairs is empowered to direct that notwithstanding the grant of a patent, spare parts and accessories for aircraft may be imported into and used in this country for the repair of aircraft belonging to a foreign State that grants similar rights in respect of Danish aircraft.[394] The Minister has used the authority under this provision to direct that spare parts and accessories for aircraft may be imported into and used in Denmark

391. Cf. s. 3 para. 3 subpara. 4 of the Act.
392. Cf. s. 3 para. 3 subpara. 5 of the Act. The provision is similar to Art. 27(c) of the CPC.
393. Cf. Art. 5*ter* of the Paris Convention.
394. Cf. s. 5 para. 2 of the Act.

for the repair of aircraft belonging to a foreign State that has acceded to the Convention on International Civil Aviation drawn up at Chicago on 7 December 1944 and that has either acceded to the Paris Convention or has adopted patent law recognizing inventions made by citizens of a State that has acceded to the former convention and grants protection of such inventions to an extent in the main conforming to the requirements of the Paris Convention.[395]

§8. Duration of Protection: Maintaining and Termination of Patent Protection

225. A granted patent may be maintained until twenty years have elapsed from the date of filing of the patent application. In order to maintain the patent, a renewal fee shall be paid for the patent in respect of each fee year beginning after the grant of the patent.[396] The term of protection corresponds with Article 63 of the EPC. Prior to the 1978 Patents Act the maximum duration of protection was seventeen years.

If the owner of a patent renounces the patent in writing to the Patent Authority, the Patent Authority shall declare the patent to have ceased to have effect.[397] If the patent owner has renounced the patent and the Patent Authority has published a notice to that effect, the patent cannot be revived.

I. Renewal Fee

226. For the patent application, the prescribed renewal fee in respect of each year beginning before the application is finally decided upon shall also be paid.[398] However, the renewal fee in respect of the first two fee years shall only fall due at the same time as the fee in respect of the third year.[399] Thus, the renewal fee is postponed for two years while the application is being processed. This is based on a view that it is not reasonable to impose on the applicant the duty to pay renewal fees until the applicant is able to assess the value of the application. Renewal fees shall not be paid if the application is revoked or repealed within two years from the filing date.

Any renewal fee may, together with the prescribed additional fee, be paid within six months after its due date.[400] If the inventor is the applicant or the owner of the patent, and if it is deemed to involve great difficulties for him/her to pay the renewal fees, the Patent Authority may grant him/her a respite for the payment thereof, provided that a request to that effect is submitted not later than on the date on which the renewal fees fall due for the first time. Respites may be granted for up to three years at a time but no longer than until three years have elapsed from the grant of

395. Cf. s. 94 of Order No. 2111 of 24 Nov. 2021.
396. Cf. ss 40 and 8 para. 5 of the Act.
397. Cf. s. 54 para. 1 of the Act.
398. Cf. s. 8 para. 5 of the Act.
399. Cf. s. 41 para. 1 of the Act.
400. Cf. s. 41 para. 3 of the Act. *See* Art. 5*bis*(1) of the Paris Convention.

the patent. Any request for a prolongation of a respite shall be submitted not later than on the date on which the granted respite expires.[401] If any renewal fee is not paid in accordance with the rules laid down in sections 40–42 of the Act, the patent shall lapse as from the beginning of the fee year in respect of which the fee has not been paid.[402]

227. Section 72 of the Act provides for the restoration of patents that have lapsed by reason of non-observance of a time limit vis-à-vis the Patent Authority prescribed by or provided for in the Act – including time limits for payment of renewal fees.[403] Restoration of a patent requires that the non-observance has caused a loss of right to the applicant and that the applicant has taken all due care reasonably required. The request shall be filed in writing with the Patent Authority within two months from the removal of the obstacle causing non-observance of the time limit though not later than one year after the expiry of the time limit. The omitted act shall be completed and the fee prescribed for the re-establishment of rights shall be paid within the same time limits. The provisions on restoration of patents have been interpreted rigorously requiring that extraordinary circumstances have caused non-observance of the time limit.[404]

II. Supplementary Protection Certificates

228. Various types of products cannot be introduced on the market until the product has been thoroughly tested and approved by the relevant public authority. The process of testing and approval can take several years and that means that the owner of a patent on such a product after the patent has been granted must wait until he/she gets the prescribed approval before he/she can exploit the invention on the market. Thus, of the twenty-year term of patent protection, the patent owner can exploit the patent for perhaps only thirteen years. To compensate the owners of certain kinds of patents for this loss of time, in which the patents can actually be exploited, they have the opportunity of applying for supplementary protection certificates which prolong the term of patent protection.

Supplementary protection certificates in Danish patent law are based on Council Regulation EEC No. 469/2009 of 6 May 2009 concerning the supplementary protection certificate for medicinal products (Codified version) and Regulation (EC) No. 1610/96 of the European Parliament and of the Council of 23 July 1996 concerning the creation of a supplementary protection certificate for plant protection products with later amendments. Pursuant to section 91 of the Act, the Minister of Industry, Business and Financial Affairs may lay down rules that are necessary for the application in Denmark of the EC's regulations concerning the implementation

401. Cf. s. 42 para. 1 of the Act.
402. Cf. s. 51 of the Act.
403. *See* Art. 5*bis*(2) of the Paris Convention.
404. *See* the Supreme Court cases reported in *Ugeskrift for Retsvæsen* 2006.612 H and *Ugeskrift for Retsvæsen* 2006.190/2 H.

of supplementary protection certificates. The authorization conferred on the Minister by virtue of section 91 extends to prospective regulations on supplementary protection certificates adopted by the European Parliament and the Council.

229. Protection under the regulations applies to any product protected by a patent in the territory of a Member State and subject, prior to being placed on the market as a medicinal product or as a plant protection product, to an administrative authorization procedure.[405] The basic patent can be a patent on a product as well as other kinds of inventions, for example, processes. Supplementary protection certificates prolong the term of protection by a period equal to the period that elapsed between the date on which the application for the basic patent was lodged and the date of the first authorization to place the product on the market in the Community reduced by a period of five years. The protection takes effect at the end of the lawful term of the basic patent. The duration of the certificates may not exceed five years from the date on which it takes effect.[406] Thus, in most cases, the Regulations ensure the owner an effective term of protection of fifteen years. Supplementary protection certificates confer the same rights as conferred by the basic patent and shall be subject to the same limitations and the same obligations.[407] Applications for supplementary protection certificates shall be lodged with the Patent and Trademark Office.[408] The provisions in section 72 of the Act on restoration of rights also apply to supplementary protection certificates.[409]

III. Provisional Protection

230. The period of time from the filing date to the actual grant of the patent may extend to several years. Pursuant to section 22 of the Act, the files shall be available to the public when eighteen months have elapsed from the filing date. The patent owner is given a provisional protection of the claimed invention prior to the date that the patent is granted. Accordingly, it is stated in section 60 paragraph 1 of the Act that if any person exploits an invention commercially without permission after the files of the application have been made available to the public, and the application results in a patent, the provision concerning patent infringement, with the exception of section 57 (on criminal liability) of the Act, shall apply *mutatis mutandis*. The protection conferred prior to grant of patent shall, however, only extend to subject matter disclosed both in the claims as worded at the time when the application was made available to the public and in the patent as granted or maintained in amended form under section 23 paragraph 3 of the Act. The scope of the provisional protection can never be broader than what follows from the patent claims at the time when the files were made available to the public. If the patent claims have

405. Cf. Art. 2 of the Regulations.
406. Cf. Art. 13 paras 1 and 2 of the Regulations.
407. Cf. Art. 5 of the Regulations.
408. Cf. s. 70 of Order No. 25 of 18 Jan. 2013.
409. Cf. s. 85 of Order No. 25 of 18 Jan. 2013.

not been worded at the time when the files were made available to the public – which occasionally occurs – the patent owner cannot benefit from provisional protection.

IV. Revocation

231. Various reasons may lead to the revocation of a patent. By virtue of section 52 paragraph 1 of the Act, a patent may be revoked by a court decision if: (i) it has been granted notwithstanding that the conditions of patentability in sections 1 and 2 of the Act are not satisfied; (ii) it relates to an invention that is not disclosed in a manner sufficiently clear to enable a person skilled in the art to carry out the invention; (iii) its subject matter extends beyond the contents of the application as filed; or (iv) the protection conferred by the patent has been extended after the Patent Authority has notified the applicant that the patent will be granted.[410] Questions concerning the conditions of patentability and insufficient description of the patent can at any time be brought before the courts. Whether the courts may amend the patent claims is not clear. The reasons for the revocation of patents listed in section 52 paragraph 1 are exhaustive.

A patent can be partially revoked as well as revoked in its entirety.[411] It is stated in section 52 paragraph 2 that a patent may not be revoked in its entirety on the ground that the owner of the patent was only partially entitled to the patent.

232. The amendment of the Patents Act in 1992 provided that a patent can be revoked by administrative procedure and not only by a court decision. Any person may file a written request with the Patent Authority to the effect that a patent granted by the Patent Authority or granted with effect for Denmark by the EPO be re-examined.[412] The patent owner himself/herself may request that his/her patent be restricted by amending the description, claims or drawings on the conditions referred to in section 53b, paragraph 1.[413] A request for re-examination by persons other than the patent owner shall only be filed on the grounds for revocation referred to in section 52 paragraph 1. As the result of a re-examination, the Patent Authority may revoke the patent or maintain it, amended or unamended.[414] If a request from persons other than the owner of the patent cannot be met, the request shall be refused and the patent shall be maintained unamended. If the request is met, but the patent cannot be maintained as amended, the Patent Authority shall revoke the patent. If the patent may be maintained as amended, the patent shall be amended accordingly if the owner of the patent approves the amended wording of the Patent Authority. If the owner of the patent does not approve the amended wording, the patent shall be revoked.[415] Administrative re-examination is conducted solely on the basis of the information substantiating the request for re-examination in addition to

410. The provision is in conformity with Art. 138 of the EPC.
411. *See*, for example, *Ugeskrift for Retsvæsen* 1935.104 H.
412. Cf. s. 53 b of the Act.
413. Cf. s. 53 e, para. 1 of the Act.
414. Cf. s. 53 c, paras 1 and 2 of the Act.
415. Cf. 53 d, paras 1 and 2 of the Act.

the information that was available when the patent was granted.[416] Hence, a new examination of novelty is not conducted by the Patent and Trademark Office.

If a patent is revoked wholly or partially, the patent shall, to the extent that it has been revoked, be considered not to have had the effects referred to in section 3 of the Act already from the date of filing of the patent application. If a patent is restricted at the request of the patent owner, the amendment shall only take effect from the date when a notice to that effect is advertised.[417] The effects of the revocation of a patent on licence agreements have to be decided on the basis of contract law.

The possibility of administrative re-examination is assumed to have great practical importance since it is a much cheaper way to challenge a patent than legal proceedings through the courts. A request for re-examination filed by the patent owner may prove a useful means for the patent owner because, on the basis of information obtained after the filing date, he/she can restrict the patent in various respects, and by doing this, he/she can prevent other persons from initiating proceedings with the purpose of revoking the patent.

§9. Infringement and Remedies

I. Infringement

233. The production of a patented invention requires the authorization of the patent owner; otherwise, the patent is infringed. However, in practice, it is often very difficult to determine the scope of the specific patent. The scope of protection conferred by a patent shall be determined by the claims. For the interpretation of the claims, the description may serve as a guide.[418] According to the preparatory works, it must be ensured that the patent owner does not avail himself/herself of ambiguities in the patent claims to extend the scope of protection. The Protocol on the interpretation of Article 69 of the EPC is probably in conformity with Danish patent law. An alleged infringing product shall be compared to the patented invention as it is stated in the patent claims. If the result of this comparison is that the alleged infringing product wholly or partially is perceived as identical to the patented invention, the patent has been infringed. More precisely, how to conduct the comparison and what is meant by identity between the alleged infringing product and the patented invention is not stated in the Act. Instead, one must look into the relevant case law. The courts have a certain amount of discretion in this respect, and at the end of the day, it turns on a specific assessment in each case. As the main rule, all amendments and modifications that are obvious to a man skilled in the art – that is amendments and modifications that are considered technically equivalent

416. Cf. s. 58 para. 3 of Order No. 2111 of 24 Nov. 2021.
417. Cf. s. 55 a of the Act.
418. Cf. s. 39 of the Act. The provision is similar to Art. 69 of the EPC.

to the patented invention – are within the scope of protection. Additionally, significant inventions are allowed a broader scope of protection than mediocre inventions.[419] The interpretation of the patent claims in Danish case law has been pragmatic and not particularly rigorous.

234. Situations may occur where means in the form of, for example, products are supplied and the supply of the products as such does not constitute patent infringement; however, the products may be used in a way that facilitates patent infringement. Section 3 paragraph 2 deals with this kind of contributory infringement and stipulates that the exclusive patent right shall also imply that no one, except the owner of the patent, may without authorization exploit the invention by supplying or offering to supply any person who is not entitled to exploit the invention with means for working it in this country, if these means relate to an essential element of the invention and the person supplying or offering to supply the means knows, or it is obvious in the circumstances, that these means are suitable and intended for such use. The provision does not apply when the means are staple commodities, except when the person supplying or offering to supply the means induces the person supplied to commit acts as referred to in section 3 paragraph 1 of the Act.[420] Irrespective of the potentially wide scope of the provision, it has not proven to be of great practical significance.

II. Remedies

235. Section 65b of the Patents Act confers the power to the Patents and Trademark Office to establish a specific unit for the enforcement of patent rights and the combating of piracy. Consumers, companies and public authorities shall be able to address this unit and receive information and guidance. The unit can also provide guidance to consumers and small- and medium-sized companies in individual cases. In addition, the unit can, on request and against a fee, submit a written informative statement. The unit shall furthermore assist the police and the prosecuting authority in their efforts against piracy. The Minister of Industry, Business and Financial Affairs has laid down specific rules on the functioning of the unit in Order No. 1578 of 14 December 2016 on a special unit in the Patent and Trademark Office on enforcement and piracy.

A. *Injunctions*[421]

419. Cf. Østerborg & Koktvedgaard (1979), 280 ff.
420. The provision is elaborated on the basis of Art. 26 of the CPC.
421. In general on injunctions in respect of intellectual property law, *see* C.S. Petersen, P. Møgelvang-Hansen & Thomas Riis, *Judicielle forbud/påbud og immaterialretsproces* (Copenhagen: Karnov Group 2015); C.S. Petersen, *Immaterialrettigheder og foreløbige forbud* (Copenhagen: Jurist- og Økonomforbundets Forlag, Copenhagen 2008); Andersen, Carlquist & Rubinstein (2006), 265–340; and T. Riis, *Enerettigheder og vederlagsrettigheder. Håndhævelse af immaterialrettigheder i økonomisk perspektiv* (Copenhagen: Jurist- og Økonomforbundets Forlag, 2005), 119–157.

236. In practice, the most important remedy available to the patent owner is injunctions. The Patents Act does not include provisions to that effect; hence, the legal basis for injunctions is the general rules in Chapter 40 of the Act on Civil Proceedings (sections 411–430). An interim injunction can be rescinded if the party applying for the injunction proves on a balance of probabilities or by clear and convincing evidence: (1) that the party holds the right for which protection by way of an injunction is sought; (2) that the conduct of the opposing party necessitates the granting of the injunction; and (3) that the ability of the party to enforce his right will be lost if the party has to await a full trial.[422] In addition, it is stated in section 414 of the Act on Civil Proceedings that no injunction may be granted if the general provisions on penalty and compensation and any security offered by the opposing party are deemed to provide adequate protection to the party and, furthermore, that the grant of an injunction can be refused if such injunction would cause the opposing party to suffer a detriment or disadvantage which is clearly disproportionate to the party's interest in obtaining the injunction.

237. Normally, adequate security is required in order to rescind an interim injunction.[423] The required security may prove a significant impediment for the patent owner in enforcing his/her rights since the demanded security occasionally is very large. Besides, the patent owner is liable for the loss of the alleged infringer if it turns out that the interim injunction was illegal and the patent owner ought not to have claimed the injunction.[424] To a limited extent, the alleged infringer may prevent an interim injunction by providing adequate security;[425] it appears that this opportunity has never been used in patent infringement cases. The crux of the problem in deciding whether an interim injunction shall be rescinded or not is related to the standard of proof. The burden of proof lies with the patent owner, and as the main rule, the patent owner shall produce a reasonable corroborated presumption.[426] An injunction does not require negligent or intentional acts on part of the alleged infringer. The patent owner shall within two weeks take action to confirm the interim injunction.[427]

B. Liability[428]

238. Pursuant to section 58 paragraph 1, any person who intentionally or negligently commits patent infringement shall pay: (i) reasonable remuneration to the infringed party for the exploitation and (ii) damages to the infringed party for any

422. Cf. s. 413 of the Act on Civil Proceedings.
423. Cf. s. 415 of the Act on Civil Proceedings.
424. Cf. s 428 of the Act on Civil Proceedings.
425. Cf. s. 414 para. 1 of the Act on Civil Proceedings.
426. *See* A. Jacobi, 'Fogedforbud, særlig i patenttvister', in *Ugeskrift for Retsvæsen* (1968.B), 51 ff.
427. Cf. s. 425 para. 1 of the Act on Civil Proceedings.
428. In general on liability in respect of intellectual property law, *see* Andersen, Carlquist & Rubinstein (2006), 419–495; and T. Riis, *Enerettigheder og vederlagsrettigheder. Håndhævelse af immaterialrettigheder i økonomisk perspektiv* (Copenhagen: Jurist- og Økonomforbundets Forlag, 2005), 225–367.

additional damage caused by the violation. Liability under the Patents Act conforms to the general principles of liability in tort law, and it requires negligence, causality and adequacy. Due to the registration system, a patent infringer cannot claim ignorance of the patent right; hence, bona fide infringements very seldom occur.

Typically, in patent infringement cases, damages are computed at the discretion of the court and, in general, awarded damages are small. The last part of section 58 paragraph 1 ('… damages to the infringed party for any additional damage') conforms to the basic rule of tort law, according to which the claimant is entitled to damages for the full loss that the tortious act has caused. The most important element in the computation of damages is often the lost market sales of the patent owner. Lost sales are computed as the number of products that have not been sold due to the infringement multiplied by the loss connected to each product. It cannot be assumed that the computation of lost market sales equates to the infringer's profits.[429] Another element in the computation of damages may be compensation for the distortion of the market for the patent owner's product. The market for the patent owner's product may be distorted if the infringer's product that is put on the market is similar to the patent owner's product but of poor quality. The result may be that the goodwill connected to the patent owner's product is significantly reduced, and consequently, it requires large investments in marketing measures to re-establish that goodwill. However, it can be rather difficult for the patent owner to provide sufficient evidence to be awarded compensation for distortion of the market.

As a consequence of the implementation of the Directive 2004/48/EC on the enforcement of intellectual property rights (The Enforcement Directive), it is now stated in the Act that when setting the damages, consideration shall be given to such matters as the infringed party's loss of profits and the offender's unfair profits.[430] Computation of damages in consideration of the offender's unfair profits is an innovation in Danish law. This new provision provides the courts with the legal basis for the award of damages at higher level than previously; however, it is doubtful whether this will happen to any significant extent.

According to section 24 paragraph 1 of the Damages Liability Act,[431] liability may be mitigated or may lapse where liability would involve an unreasonable burden on the party liable or where very special circumstances otherwise make it reasonable. Patent infringements take place in a commercial context, and reducing the award of damages pursuant to section 24 of the Damages Liability Act is not likely to occur.[432]

239. As indicated, it is difficult to determine the actual loss of the patent owner caused by the infringement and often the result is small damages. In order to ensure

429. In the Supreme Court case reported in *Ugeskrift for Retsvæsen* 1964.628 H the majority stated that the infringer's profits were not decisive in determining the lost sales of the patent owner.
430. Cf. s. 58 para. 2 of the Act.
431. Consolidated Act No. 1070 of 24 Aug. 2018.
432. Cf. Schovsbo, Rosenmeier & Petersen (2024), 718.

the patent owner a kind of minimum compensation, according to the first part of section 58 paragraph 1, he/she is entitled to a reasonable compensation for the exploitation of his/her invention. The provision implies that the patent owner in all cases at a minimum is entitled to 'a reasonable royalty', notwithstanding that he/she cannot prove an actual loss caused by the infringement.[433]

In cases of intentional or negligent infringement, compensation can also be set to the infringed party for non-financial damage.[434] The provision on non-financial damage was introduced in the Patents Act in 2005 when the Enforcement Directive was implemented and yet it has not resulted in any reported case law.

The remedies available to an applicant who benefits from provisional protection pursuant to section 60 of the Act are restricted in certain respects. For example, this kind of infringement is not sanctioned by punitive measures.[435] The person concerned (i.e., the infringer) shall only be liable to pay compensation and damages if and to the extent this is found reasonable.[436] Claims for damages under section 60 shall not be statute-barred earlier than one year after the grant of the patent.[437] This provision deviates from the general rule according to which claims for damages are estopped after three years from the time of the infringement.

C. Destruction, Seizure and Recall

240. The risk of further infringements can justify destruction, seizure, etc., of existing infringing products. It is stipulated in section 59 paragraph 1 of the Act that in the case of patent infringement and in order to prevent further infringement, the court may, when so claimed, by sentence decide that infringing products shall:

- be recalled from the channels of commerce;
- be definitively removed from the channels of commerce;
- be destroyed;
- be handed over to the infringed party; or
- be altered in a specified way.

The remedies are not confined to infringing products since they also may apply to apparatuses, articles, tools, etc., that primarily have been used for unauthorized production of a patented invention.[438] Destruction, etc., according to these provisions, shall be undertaken without any form of compensation to the offender and does not have any effect on any possible compensation to the infringed party. Furthermore, such measures shall be undertaken at the offender's expense, unless special reasons dictate otherwise.[439]

433. *See* Koktvedgaard & Østerborg (1979), 290 ff.
434. Cf. s. 58 para. 3 of the Act.
435. Cf. s. 60 para. 1 of the Act. Regarding punitive measures in general *see infra* para. 243.
436. Cf. ss 60 paras 2 and 58 para. 2 of the Act.
437. Cf. s. 60 para. 3 of the Act.
438. Cf. s. 59 para. 2 of the Act.
439. Cf. s. 59 para. 3 of the Act.

A principle of proportionality applies to these remedial measures. Thus, in considering a request for corrective measures, the need for proportionality between the seriousness of the infringement and the remedies ordered as well as the interests of third parties shall be taken into account by the court.[440]

Additionally, it is stated in section 59 paragraph 5 that on request, the court may grant the infringer permission to dispose freely of the said products, apparatuses, articles, tools, etc. during the term of the patent or part of that term provided: (i) the infringement is not intentional or negligent; (ii) the measures referred to in section 59 paragraph 1 will cause disproportionate harm on the infringer; and (iii) a reasonable compensation for the infringed party is considered sufficient.

D. Search[441]

241. Measures for preserving evidence in cases of infringement of intellectual property rights were included into Danish legislation in 2001 in order to satisfy the national obligations under the TRIPs Agreement. Subsequently, in 2006, the provisions were amended in conformity to Article 7 of the Enforcement Directive (2004/48/EC). The provisions are placed in the Chapter 57a in the Act on Civil Proceedings (section 653–653d); nevertheless, they only apply in cases of infringement of intellectual property rights. In conformity with Article 7 of The Enforcement Directive, the purpose of such interim measures is to preserve relevant evidence in respect of an alleged infringement. On the request of the patent holder, the bailiff's court can decide to search the premises of an alleged infringer in order to preserve evidence on the infringement or the extent of the infringement. The claimant shall produce a reasonable corroborated presumption that an infringement has taken place or will take place and that it is likely that the evidence for the infringement or the extent of the infringement can be found on the pertinent premises.[442] The search may involve, for example, the detailed description, with or without the taking of samples, or the physical seizure of the infringing goods, the materials and implements used in the production and/or distribution of these goods, and the documents (including digitally stored information) relating thereto. The claimant's request may be denied in consideration of the privacy or trade secrets of the alleged infringer or if the interest of the claimant in the search is disproportionate to the harm the search is likely to cause on the alleged infringer.[443] The bailiff's court can decide to search the premises of the alleged infringer without the alleged infringer having been heard where there is a demonstrable risk of evidence being

440. Cf. s. 59 para. 4 of the Act.
441. In general, on measures for preserving evidence, *see* Petersen, C.S., P.M. Hansen & T. Riis. Judicielle forbud/påbud og immaterialretsproces. Copenhagen: 2015, Chs 7 and 8.
442. Cf. s. 653 para. 1 of the Act on Civil Proceedings.
443. Cf. s. 653 para. 4 of the Act on Civil Proceedings.

destroyed, removed or amended.[444] The search is an interim measure, and the claimant shall, within four weeks after the bailiff's court decision on a search, initiate a civil proceeding in respect of the alleged infringement of the search concern.[445]

E. *Right of Information*[446]

242. The provisions in Chapter 29a (sections 306–307) of the Act on Civil Proceedings were adopted in 2006 and implement Article 8 of the Enforcement Directive. This 'right of information' is an innovation in Danish law and, similar to the provisions in Chapter 57a of the Act on Civil Proceedings on Search, the provisions in Chapter 29a only apply in cases of infringement of intellectual property rights. On the request of the claimant, the court can order that the infringer and/or any other person provides information on goods or services that infringe an intellectual property right, provided the person in question:

(a) was found in possession of the infringing goods on a commercial scale;
(b) was found to be using the infringing services on a commercial scale;
(c) was found to be providing on a commercial scale services used in infringing activities; or
(d) was indicated by the person referred to in point (a), (b) or (c) as being involved in the production, manufacture, or distribution of the goods or the provision of the services.[447]

The information that shall be provided includes:

(a) the names and addresses of the producers, manufacturers, distributors, suppliers and other previous holders of the goods or services, as well as the intended wholesalers and retailers the goods or services in question were aimed at, and
(b) information on the quantities produced, manufactured, delivered, received, or ordered, as well as the price obtained for the goods or services in question.[448]

The provisions on the right of information enable that in a court case between A and B, C can be ordered to provide information on D, even though the information is of no relevance in the conflict between A and B. In this way, the right of information departs from the tradition of the Danish law on civil procedure because according to the general principle of the law on civil procedure the courts shall deny all requests and evidence that bear no relevance to the litigated conflict. The right of information creates a risk of abuse of the procedural system; however, as the main safeguard against abuse, the court may deny a request if it must be assumed

444. Cf. s. 653a, para. 2 of the Act on Civil Proceedings.
445. Cf. s. 653c, para. 1 of the Act on Civil Proceedings.
446. In general on the right of information, *see* Petersen, C.S., P.M. Hansen & T. Riis. Judicielle forbud/påbud og immaterialretsproces. Copenhagen: 2015, Ch. 9.
447. Cf. s. 306 para. 1 of the Act on Civil Proceedings.
448. Cf. s. 306 para. 2 of the Act on Civil Proceedings.

that the interest of the claimant in the information is disproportionate to the harm the provision of the information may cause on the person providing the information or on other persons.[449]

F. Penalties

243. Patent infringement may involve criminal liability. If any person infringes the exclusive right conferred by a patent, and the infringement is committed intentionally, he/she shall be punished by a fine. Under aggravating circumstances, including in particular if by the infringement an appreciable and clearly wrongful gain is intended, the punishment may be increased to simple detention or imprisonment up to one year and six months.[450] What constitutes aggravating circumstances may be repeating infringements, continued infringement in spite of warnings from the patent owner or flagrant exploitation of the patented invention combined with a low probability of detection by the patent owner. Legal persons, for example, a company with limited liability, can be penalized according to the provisions in Chapter 5 of the Civil Penal Code.[451] Criminal liability under the Civil Penal Code requires, among other things, that the infringement can be imputed to a natural person who is associated with the legal person. The penalty provisions are seldom used in patent infringement cases.

G. Publication of Judgments

244. When The Enforcement Directive (2004/48/EC) was implemented, a new provision on publication of judgments was included in the Act. In a judgment in which someone is sentenced according to sections 58–60 (liability and destruction, etc.), the court may upon request decide that the judgment shall be published in full or in part. The obligation to publish rests with the offender. Publication shall be arranged at the offender's expense and in as prominent a way as can reasonably be expected.[452]

§10. Overlapping and Relation to Other Intellectual Property Laws

245. In the preparatory works to the Utility Models Act, it is stated that the purpose of the Act is to provide a fast and inexpensive form of protection, which in addition may serve as an alternative or supplement to patent and design protection.[453] Patent protection and utility-model protection are cumulative, and due to the

449. Cf. s. 306 para. 3 of the Act on Civil Proceedings.
450. Cf. s. 57 para. 1 of the Patents Act.
451. Cf. s. 57 para. 2.
452. Cf. s. 60 a, paras 1–2.
453. Cf. FT 1991–1992, A, col. 2513.

less rigorous conditions of protection in the Utility Models Act, a patentable invention is, in principle, also eligible for utility-model protection. However, protectable subject matter under the Utility Models Act is restricted in certain respects compared to protectable subject matter under the Patents Act. Often, it is possible for the inventor to decide whether he/she wants patent or utility-model protection of his/her invention. That decision depends on economic and strategic considerations. On the one hand, by choosing utility-model protection, the inventor avoids a long period of uncertainty while the patent application is being processed, and furthermore, the costs of obtaining utility-model protection are insignificant compared to those of patent protection. On the other hand, utility-model protection is only half the term of patent protection. The inventor may file applications for patent and utility models simultaneously. This solution can be beneficial to the inventor who in the long run wants patent protection, but in the short run, needs protection of his/her invention based on a registered right. If the inventor has filed an application for patent protection, he/she can subsequently amend it to an application for utility-model protection and vice versa. In the assessment of the conditions of protectability, the filing date of the first application applies.

246. Traditionally, patent law and copyright law are aimed at fundamentally different subject matters. Computer software is protectable subject matter under the Copyright Act and, as the main rule, is excluded from patent protection. The existing uncertainty as to what constitutes a patentable software-related invention suggests that computer software to a certain extent may obtain patent protection in addition to copyright protection.

247. If a patented invention is protected by trademark rights, the termination of the patent does not terminate the trademark right.

248. When the patent right is terminated for one reason or the other, as the main rule, the invention enters the public domain. However, according to the circumstances, the owner of the invention may obtain a certain narrow protection pursuant to section 3 of the Marketing Practice Act. Section 3 of the Marketing Practice Act provides no protection of the technical idea. Protection under the Marketing Practice Act requires that the competing product has been marketed in an unfair manner or by unfair means; for example, this may be the case if the competing product is a slavish imitation of the original product.[454]

454. *See*, for example, the Supreme Court case reported in *Ugeskrift for Retsvæsen* 1994.72 H.

Chapter 3. Utility Models

§1. Sources – Legislation

249. Utility models were included in Danish intellectual property law as late as 1992 when Act No. 130 of 26 February 1992 on Utility Models, etc., was passed. The Danish Act is essentially based on the German '*Gebrauchmustergesetz*' of 1891, but contrary to German law, the term 'utility model' was chosen instead of 'utility design' to emphasize that legal protection under the Act is not related to design law. The Utility Models Act is at present consolidated Act No. 91 of 29 January 2019.[455] Utility-model law is one area of intellectual property law where large discrepancies between the Nordic countries exist.

In the main, the Utility Models Act is in conformity with the Commission's amended proposal for a directive approximating the legal arrangements for the protection of inventions by utility model.[456]

§2. The Protection of Utility Models

250. In the preparatory works to the Utility Models Act, it is stated that the purpose of the Act is to provide a fast and inexpensive form of protection for minor inventions, which in addition may serve as an alternative or supplement to patent and design protection.[457] Utility model protection does not preclude patent protection since the two forms of protection are cumulative. To a large extent, the Utility Models Act is organized in conformity to the corresponding provisions of the Patents Act, which underline the close relationship between the two forms of protection and create a certain degree of similarity in the substantive provisions of the two Acts.

I. Subject Matter of Protection

251. Any creation that is susceptible of industrial application or that provides a solution to a technical problem may, on application, in accordance with the Utility Models Act, be registered as a utility model.[458] The second criterion for protectable subject matter is 'a solution to a technical problem', among other things, which

455. Under the provisions of the Act various regulations have been issued: Order No. 518 of 18 Jun. 1992 on How to Construe 'War Matériel' within the Meaning of the Utility Models Act; Order No. 892 of 21 Sep. 2009 on the Patent and Trademark Board of Appeal (*Ankenævnet for patenter og varemærker*); Order No. 12 of 12 Jan. 2012 on the remuneration of the Patent and Trademark Office for the performance of tasks, specific transactions and transcripts, etc. Order. No. 1605 of 19 Jun. 2006 of 8 December on Utility Model Applications and the Procedure for Registration of Utility Models, and Order No. 1578 of 14 Dec. 2016 on a special unit in the Patent and Trademark Office on enforcement and piracy.

456. COM(1999) 309 final/2, Brussels, 12 Jul. 1999.

457. Cf. FT 1991–1992, A, col. 2513.

458. Cf. s. 1 para. 1 of the Act.

serves the purpose of delimiting the scope of the Act in relation to the Designs Act. Examples of protectable subject matter are listed in the preparatory works instruments, apparatuses, tools, mechanical devices and parts thereof, electric circuits, chemical compounds, foodstuffs and pharmaceuticals.[459] Accordingly, protectable subject matters of utility model law and patent law to a large extent overlap.

252. Excluded from protection under the Act are items referred to in section 1 paragraph 2 of the Patents Act,[460] that is, discoveries, scientific theories, mathematical methods; artistic creations; plans, rules or methods for intellectual activity, games or business activity or computer programs; and presentation of information.[461] Moreover, by virtue of section 2 paragraph 2 subparagraphs (ii) and (iii) of the Act, methods and war material are excluded subject matter. The purpose of excluding war materiel is to prevent evasion of the provisions of the Act on Secret Patents.[462]

On the exclusion of methods from protection, it is said in the preparatory works that it is found most expedient to copy German law in this respect.[463] The exclusion on methods covers methods for surgical or therapeutic treatment or for determination of diagnoses practised on human beings and animals; however, products, including substances and compositions, for use in any of these methods are not excluded.[464]

Plant and animal varieties are not protectable subject matter. However, creations that concern plants or animals are protectable if the technical feasibility of the creation is not confined to a particular plant or animal variety.[465] Creations are not excluded from protection on the sole ground that they contain biological material. Biological material that is isolated from its natural environment or produced by means of a technical process may be the subject of a creation even if it previously occurred in nature. Within the meaning of the Act, 'biological material' means any material containing genetic information that is capable of reproducing itself or being reproduced in a biological system.[466]

The human body, at the various stages of its formation and development, and the simple discovery of one of its elements, including the sequence or partial sequence of a gene, cannot constitute protectable creations; but an element isolated from the human body or otherwise produced by means of a technical process, including the sequence or partial sequence of a gene, may constitute a protectable creation, even if the structure of that element is identical to that of a natural element.[467]

459. Cf. FT 1991–1992, A, col. 2518.
460. Cf. s. 2 para. 1 of the Act.
461. Cf. s. 2 para. 1 subpara. (i) of the Act.
462. The term 'war materiel' is defined in the Order No. 518 of 18 Jun. 1992.
463. Cf. FT 1991–1992, A, col. 2519.
464. Cf. s. 2 para. 3 of the Act.
465. The concept of 'plant variety' shall be construed in conformity with the definition in Art. 5 of Regulation (EC) No. 2100/94, cf. s. 2 para. 4 of the Act.
466. Cf. s. 2 para. 5 of the Act.
467. Cf. s. 3 paras 1 and 2 of the Act.

Creations, the commercial exploitation of which would be contrary to law and order or morality, are not protectable under the Act. One type of creation excluded under this provision is the use of human embryos for industrial or commercial purposes.[468]

II. Conditions of Protection

253. As a condition of protection, the creation shall be new in relation to the state of the art and shall differ distinctly therefrom, cf. section 5 paragraph 1 of the Act. The novelty requirement is specified in section 5 paragraph 2 of the Act: The state of the art shall be held to comprise everything made available to the public by means of a written or oral description, lectures, exhibition, offer for sale, use, representation or in any other way. Additionally, the contents of patent applications or utility-model applications filed with effect for Denmark before the said date of filing shall be regarded as comprised in the state of the art, if such applications are made available to the public. However, the requirement in section 5 paragraph 1 of the Act, that the creation shall differ distinctly from the state of the art, does not apply in relation to the contents of such applications. Prima facie, the novelty requirement is identical to the novelty requirement of patent law, and accordingly, the Act requires objective and global novelty. However, it is stated in the preparatory works that the novelty requirement of the Utility Models Act is not as comprehensive as the patent law novelty requirement. Under the Utility Models Act, in order to qualify for protection, a creation shall deviate to a certain extent from solutions to a technical problem that is obvious to a person skilled in the art. This difference compared to patent law is indicated by using the term 'differ distinctly' instead of the patent law term 'differ essentially'.[469] The decisions of the Patent and Trademark Office indicate that the novelty requirement of the Utility Models Act has been interpreted very leniently.[470] The interpretation of the novelty requirement conforms to the general purpose of the Act, which is described as providing an opportunity for legal protection of certain technical creations that do not relate to the state of the art in a way that implies an inventive step within the meaning of the Patents Act.[471] Nonetheless, the Patent and Trademark Board of Appeal held that a combined screw cap of plastic and bottle opener was a creation obvious to a person skilled in the art, and thus, the creation did not satisfy the conditions of protection under the Act. In reaching its decision, the Board referred to a Danish design application, a German-published document and an American patent document concerning similar subject matter.[472]

468. Cf. s. 4 paras 1 and 3 of the Act.
469. Cf. FT 1991–1992, A, col. 2520.
470. *See* Schovsbo, Rosenmeier & Petersen (2024), 439.
471. Cf. FT 1991–1992, A, col. 2513. *See* E. Roth & N.H. Svendsen, 'Lov om brugsmodeller m.v.', *Ugeskrift for Retsvæsen* (1992 B), 223, 227.
472. B 2/94, decision of 17 Mar. 1997.

254. The provisions in section 2 paragraph 6 of the Patents Act relating to exceptions from the novelty requirement (i.e., the provisions on disclosure of an invention as a consequence of evident abuse or of display of the invention at an official or officially recognized international exhibition) also apply to utility model applications[473] (*see supra* paragraph 166.

255. Section 11 of the Act stipulates a right of priority. On request, an application for utility-model registration of a creation, which has been disclosed not earlier than twelve months before the date of filing in an application for a utility model or a patent in Denmark or a utility model, a patent or an inventor's certificate in another country party to the Paris Convention for the Protection of Industrial Property of 20 March 1883, shall, for the purpose of section 5 paragraphs 1 and 2 and section 9 (prior right of exploitation), be regarded as filed at the same time as the earlier application. The same right of priority shall be enjoyed where the earlier application for protection is filed in a country that is not a party to the Paris Convention, provided an equivalent right of priority is granted on the basis of a Danish utility model application by the country in which the earlier application was filed and that the legislation of that country in principle is in conformity with the Convention.[474]

III. Formalities

256. A utility model right is conditioned on registration.[475] The provisions of the procedure for application and registration are contained in Order No. 1605 of 8 December 2006. No formal requirements apply to the application; however, application forms may be requested from the Patent and Trademark Office free of charge.[476] An application for the registration of a utility model shall be filed with the Patent and Trademark Office that is the registration authority. The application shall include a statement of the matter for which protection is sought (the utility model claims), and the prescribed fee shall accompany the application.[477]

257. The creation shall be described or shown sufficiently in the application to enable a person skilled in the art to carry out the creation.[478] The requirements for the contents of the application shall as far as possible be reasonably proportional to the economic potential of the utility model. Hence, the applicant for a utility-model registration is not required to respect the same rigorous requirements as to the wording and description of the claimed subject matter as the applicant for a patent. As

473. Cf. s. 5 para. 3 of the Act.
474. Cf. s. 11 para. 1 of the Act. The provision is similar to s. 6 of the Patents Act (*see supra* para. 168) and meets the obligations under Art. 4 of the Paris Convention. *See also* Ch. 2 of Order No. 1605 of 8 Dec. 2006.
475. Cf. s. 1 paras 1 and 2 of the Act.
476. Cf. s. 1 para. 1 Order No. 1605 of 8 Dec. 2006.
477. Cf. s. 14 para. 1 of the Act.
478. Cf. s. 14 para. 2 of the Act.

regards very simple creations, a simple wording of the claimed subject matter, including a reference to the description and drawings, suffices.[479]

258. An application for registration of a utility model may not be amended in such a way that protection is claimed for subject matter that was not disclosed in the application at the time when it was filed, cf. section 18 of the Act.[480]

259. The Act differs from the Patents Act in one important respect since the Patent and Trademark Office does not conduct an examination of the substantive conditions of protection under the Utility Models Act. By virtue of section 19 paragraph 1 of the Act, the Patent and Trademark Office solely shall ensure that the application satisfies the requirements of sections 1, 2, 3, 4 (the provisions on protectable subject matter), 16[481] and 18 of the Act. Accordingly, the Office does not examine whether the creation is new in relation to the state of the art and differs distinctly therefrom. The insubstantial examination of utility model applications has been necessary in order to ensure a fast and relatively inexpensive registration procedure.[482] The application and registration procedure creates a substantial risk of invalid registrations. From the right owner's point of view, the uncertainty as to the validity of the registration may be reduced by requesting the Patent and Trademark Office to extend the examination. By virtue of section 19 paragraph 2 of the Act, the applicant may request the Patent and Trademark Office to examine that the requirements of section 5 of the Act (i.e., whether the creation is new in relation to the state of the art and differs distinctly therefrom) are satisfied.[483] Such a request shall be accompanied by a fee.[484] Persons other than the applicant cannot request an extended examination prior to the registration pursuant to section 19 paragraph 2. However, one should note the provisions of section 50 of the Act on administrative revocation that involve extended examination by the Patent and Trademark Office. By virtue of section 50 of the Act after registration, any person is entitled, without specific documentation (unless the Patent and Trademark Office demands otherwise) and against payment of a fee, to request that the Patent Office examine whether the requirements of registration have been met.

260. If the Patent and Trademark Office finds that the application does not comply with the requirements, the applicant shall be notified accordingly and be invited to file his/her observations or to correct the application within a time limit to be specified.[485] The application shall be shelved if the applicant fails to file the required observations or to take steps to correct the application before expiry of the time

479. Cf. FT 1991–1992, A, col. 2522.
480. *See also* Ch. 5 of Order No. 1605 of 8 Dec. 2006.
481. Section 16 stipulates that in the same application, utility model registration may not be applied for in respect of two or more mutually independent creations. The provision is based on procedural considerations related to the classification of utility model applications. Registration of a utility model in contravention of s. 9 does not invalidate the registration.
482. Cf. FT 1991–1992, A, col. 2522 f.
483. On the extended examination *see* Ch. 6 of Order No. 1605 of 8 Dec. 2006.
484. *See also* s. 5 paras 2 and 4 of Order No. 1605 of 8 Dec. 2006.
485. Cf. s. 20 para. 1 of the Act.

limit.[486] The proceedings for grant shall be resumed if the applicant submits his/her observations or takes steps to correct the application within two months after expiry of the specified time limit and pays a resumption fee.[487] If the application is found to comply with the requirements, the creation is registered. Notification of utility model registration shall be published by the Patent and Trademark Office.[488] If the Patent and Trademark Office still has objections to the acceptance of the application, and the applicant has had an opportunity to file his/her observations in respect of the objections, the application is refused, unless the Patent and Trademark Office considers it necessary once more to invite the applicant under section 20 of the Act.[489] If the applicant has requested extended examination under section 19 paragraph 2 of the Act and the Patent and Trademark Office finds that the conditions have not been met, the application is refused.[490] An appeal from the final decision of the Patent and Trademark Office concerning a utility model application may be filed by the applicant with the Patent and Trademark Board of Appeal.[491]

261. The earliest date the creation can be registered is fifteen months from the date of application or, if priority has been claimed, from the date of priority according to section 11 of the Act.[492] When fifteen months have elapsed from the date of filing or, if priority has been claimed, from the date of priority, the files shall be available to the public, even if the creation has not been registered.[493] However, if a document contains business secrets that do not concern the creation, the Patent and Trademark Office on request may decide that the document shall not be available or only available in part.[494] At the request of the applicant, the creation may be registered and the files may be made available to the public before fifteen months have elapsed from the date of filing or, if priority has been claimed, from the date of priority.[495]

262. If the applicant has filed a previous patent application for Denmark, the applicant may use the patent application, in whole or in part, as a basis for a utility model application in respect of the same creation. The applicant may request that the date of filing of the patent application shall apply to the utility-model application. If priority has been requested in the patent application, according to section 6 of the Patents Act, such request also applies to the utility-model application.[496] The use of a patent application as a basis for a utility model application shall be requested at the latest ten years after the filing date of the patent application and no later than two months after a final decision has been made to shelve or refuse the

486. Cf. s. 20 para. 2 of the Act.
487. Cf. s. 20 para. 3 of the Act.
488. Cf. s. 21 para. 1 of the Act.
489. Cf. s. 21 para. 2 of the Act.
490. Cf. FT 1991–1992, A, col. 2525.
491. Cf. s. 25 para. 1 of the Act.
492. Cf. s. 24 para. 1 of the Act.
493. Cf. s. 24 para. 3 of the Act.
494. Cf. s. 24 para. 5 of the Act.
495. Cf. s. 24 para. 2 of the Act.
496. Cf. s. 12 para. 1 of the Act.

patent application.[497] The provision may prove particularly useful to the applicant in situations where the patent application is refused on the ground that the creation does not involve an inventive step; but it may as well be applied in cases where the applicant wants to maintain the patent application.

263. Oppositions cannot be filed prior to registration. After registration, the provisions of sections 50–52 on revocation of registrations apply.

264. An 'International utility model application' within the meaning of the Act is an application under the PCT.[498] An international utility model application shall be filed with a patent authority or an international organization that is competent under the Treaty and the Regulations to receive such application (receiving Office). An international utility model application may be filed with the Danish Patent and Trademark Office in accordance with the rules laid down in Chapter 8 (sections 40–44) of the Order No. 1605 of 8 December 2006.[499] The specific rules on international utility-model application are contained in Chapter 3 (sections 26–35) of the Act.

IV. Ownership and Transfer

265. Like most kinds of intellectual property rights, the exclusive right under the Utility Models Act originates in natural persons but may be transferred to legal persons. As to ownership and transfer of utility model rights, utility model law closely parallels patent law. Any person who has created a utility model, or his/her successor in title, shall obtain an exclusive right to exploit the creation commercially upon registration.[500] The right to apply for utility model registrations as well as the utility model registration may freely be transferred to other persons, and the transfer is not contingent on formalities.

If any person claims before the Patent and Trademark Office that he/she, and not the applicant, is entitled to the invention, the Patent and Trademark Office may, if it finds the question doubtful, invite him/her to bring it before the courts within a time limit to be specified. If the invitation is not complied with, the Patent and Trademark Office may disregard the claim when deciding on the application.[501] If any person proves to the Patent and Trademark Office that he/she and not the applicant is entitled to the creation, the Patent and Trademark Office shall on request transfer the application to the said person.[502]

497. Cf. s. 13 paras 1 and 3 of Order No. 1605 of 8 Dec. 2006.
498. Cf. s. 26 para. 1 of the Act.
499. Cf. s. 26 para. 2 of the Act.
500. Cf. s. 1 para. 2 of the Act.
501. Cf. s. 22 para. 1 of the Act. The provision resembles s. 17 para. 1 of the Patents Act.
502. Cf. s. 23 para. 1 of the Act. The provision resembles s. 18 para. 1 of the Patents Act.

266. The Act on Inventions of Employees and the Act on Inventions at Public Research Institutions apply to all creations that are protectable subject matter under the Utility Models Act[503] (*see supra* paragraph 193 f.).

267. The transfer of a right to a registered utility model, the grant of a licence (including compulsory licence), pledging or execution proceedings shall on request be recorded in the Register. If a registered licence has terminated, the licence shall be deleted from the Register.[504] The provision corresponds to section 44 paragraphs 1–3 of the Patents Act and accordingly does not imply any requirements for the validity of a transfer or a licence.

V. Scope of Exclusive Rights and Limitations on the Scope of Protection

268. According to section 1 paragraph 2 of the Act, a utility model registration involves an exclusive right to exploit the creation commercially. The extent of protection conferred by the utility model registration is determined by the claims. For the interpretation of the claims, the description and drawing may serve as a guide.[505]

The extent of protection under the Utility Models Act is delimited on the same lines as the scope of patent rights, which in the main implies that all kinds of commercial exploitation require the consent of the right owner. Thus, pursuant to section 6 paragraph 1 of the Act, the exclusive right conferred by a utility model registration shall imply that no one, except the owner of the utility model, may without permission exploit the invention by making, offering, putting on the market, or using a product that is the subject matter of the utility model, or by importing or possessing the product for these purposes. In principle, the exclusive right covers any kind of commercial exploitation of the utility model. The various forms of exploitation enumerated in section 6 paragraph 1 must be understood as specifications of the exclusive right. In addition, section 6 paragraph 2 stipulates that the exclusive utility model right also implies that no one, except the owner of the utility model, may, without authorization, exploit the utility model by supplying or offering to supply any person who is not entitled to exploit the utility model with means for working it in Denmark, if these means relate to an essential element of the invention and the person supplying or offering to supply the means knows, or it is obvious in the circumstances, that these means are suitable and intended for such use. The provision does not apply when the means are staple commodities, except when the person supplying or offering to supply the means induces the person supplied to commit acts as referred to in section 6 paragraph 1 of the Act.

269. The exclusive right does not extend to: (i) acts done for non-commercial purposes; (ii) acts concerning products put on the market in this country or in a

503. *See* s. 1 para. 1 of the Consolidated Act No. 104 of 24 Jan. 2012 and s. 3 in the Consolidated Act No. 210 of 17 Mar. 2009.
504. Cf. s. 40 paras 1–3 of the Act.
505. Cf. s. 37 para. 1 of the Act.

country within the EEA by the owner of the utility model or with his/her consent; (iii) acts done for experimental purposes relating to the subject matter of the registered creation; and (iv) specific acts of preparation in a pharmacy of a medicine in accordance with a medical prescription nor acts concerning the medicine so prepared.[506]

The provisions of sections 9 and 10 of the Utility Models Act are similar to section 4 of the Patents Act relating to a prior right of exploitation and section 5 of the Patents Act relating to the right of exploitation.

A. Compulsory Licence

270. The Utility Models Act contains the same types of compulsory licences as the Patents Act:

> If a registered creation is not worked to a reasonable extent when 3 years have elapsed from the registration of the utility model and 4 years have elapsed from the filing of the utility model application, any person wishing to work the invention in this country may obtain a compulsory license to do so, unless there are legitimate reasons for failure to work the invention.[507]

The owner of a registered utility model, the use of which is dependent on a patent or a registered utility model that belongs to another person, may obtain compulsory licence for use of the patent-protected invention or the protected creation of the utility model registration if the former creation makes up an essential technical progress of substantial economic importance.[508] Moreover, it is stated that the owner of the patent or of the registered utility model for which use compulsory licence has been granted pursuant to the provision in section 42 paragraph 1 shall on reasonable terms be able to obtain compulsory licence for use of the other creation (cross-licence).[509]

When required by important public interests, any person who wishes to exploit an invention commercially for which another person holds a registered utility model may obtain a compulsory licence to do so.[510]

Any person who, in this country, at the time when a utility model application was made available to the public, was commercially exploiting the creation for which a utility-model registration is applied for, may, if the application results in a utility model registration, obtain a compulsory licence to exploit the creation, if very special circumstances make it desirable, and he/she had no knowledge and could not reasonably have obtained any knowledge of the application. Such a right shall also,

506. Cf. s. 6 para. 3 of the Act. The provision resembles s. 3 para. 3 of the Patents Act.
507. Cf. s. 41 para. 1 of the Act. The provision resembles s. 45 para. 1 of the Patents Act.
508. Cf. s. 42 para. 1 of the Act. The provision resembles s. 46 para. 1 of the Patents Act.
509. Cf. s. 42 para. 2 of the Act. The provision resembles s. 46 para. 2 of the Patents Act.
510. Cf. s. 43 of the Act. The provision resembles s. 47 of the Patents Act.

under similar conditions, be enjoyed by any person who had made substantial preparations for commercial exploitation of the creation in this country.[511] Compulsory licence under section 44 paragraph 1 may include the time preceding the registration of the utility model.[512]

Various conditions and rules apply to all types of compulsory licences. Compulsory licences shall only be granted to persons who by agreement have not been able to obtain licence on reasonable terms and who may be regarded as being able to make use of the creation in a reasonable and proper manner.[513] A compulsory licence does not prevent the proprietor of the utility model from exploiting the creation himself/herself or from granting licences to others.[514] Compulsory licence can only be transferred to others together with the establishment in which it is used or in which the utilization was intended. For compulsory licence filed in accordance with section 42 paragraph 1, it shall moreover be applicable that transfer of compulsory licence shall take place together with the registered utility model, the use of which is dependent on a patent or a registered utility model that belongs to another person.[515] The Copenhagen Maritime and Commercial Court shall decide as The Court of First Instance whether a compulsory licence shall be granted and shall also determine the extent to which the creation may be exploited, fix the compensation and lay down the other terms of the compulsory licence. If circumstances should change considerably, the Court may, at the request of either party, cancel the licence or lay down new terms of the licence.[516]

VI. Duration of Protection

271. The utility model registration applies until three years have elapsed from the date of filing of the application for registration and may be renewed for an additional two periods of three and four years, respectively, against payment of the prescribed fees.[517] If the registration is not renewed in accordance with the prescribed rules – for example, if the renewal fee is not paid before the expiry of the prescribed period – the registration is lost since the Act provides no opportunity for restoration of utility model registrations.

If the owner of a registered utility model renounces the registration in writing to the Patent and Trademark Office, the Patent and Trademark Office declares the registration to have ceased to have effect.[518]

511. Cf. s. 44 para. 1 of the Act. The provision resembles s. 48 para. 1 of the Patents Act.
512. Cf. s. 44 para. 2 of the Act. The provision resembles s. 48 para. 2 of the Patents Act.
513. Cf. s. 45 para. 1 of the Act. The provision resembles s. 49 para. 1 of the Patents Act.
514. Cf. s. 45 para. 2 of the Act. The provision resembles s. 49 para. 2 of the Patents Act.
515. Cf. s. 45 para. 3 of the Act. The provision resembles s. 49 para. 3 of the Patents Act.
516. Cf. s. 46 of the Act. The provision resembles s. 50 of the Patents Act.
517. Cf. s. 38 para. 1 of the Act.
518. Cf. s. 49 para. 1. The provision resembles s. 54 para. 1 of the Patents Act.

A. Revocation

272. A utility model registration may be revoked either by a court decision or by an administrative decision.

Regarding administrative revocation, section 50 of the Act stipulates that when a utility model registration has taken place any person may, without specific documentation (unless the Patent and Trademark Office demands otherwise) and against payment of a fee, request that the Patent and Trademark Office examines whether the requirements of registration have been met. The proprietor of the utility model registration shall be notified accordingly and be invited to file his/her observations.[519]

If, after the submission of a request according to section 50 of the Act, the Patent and Trademark Office establishes any objections to registration, the registration is deleted.[520] If the registration can be maintained in amended form, the Patent and Trademark Office decides to amend it correspondingly. The registration is deleted if the proprietor does not agree to the amended registration or does not pay the prescribed fee related to the amendment.[521]

An appeal from the final decision of the Patent and Trademark Office concerning a utility model application may be filed by the applicant with the Patent and Trademark Board of Appeal. The same applies to the proprietor of the utility model registration when a utility model registration is deleted in whole or in part on request under section 50.[522] The decisions of the Patent and Trademark Office, which may be brought before the Patent and Trademark Board of Appeal, may not be brought before the courts of law before the Patent and Trademark Board of Appeal has made its decision. If it is desired to bring a decision of the Patent and Trademark Board of Appeal before the courts of law, proceedings shall be instituted not later than two months from the date when the party concerned was notified of the Patent and Trademark Board of Appeal's decision.[523]

273. A utility model registration may be revoked by a court decision if: (i) registration has not been made according to sections 1–5 of the Act; (ii) registration relates to a creation that is not disclosed in a manner sufficiently clear to enable a person skilled in the art to carry out the creation; (iii) the scope of protection has been amended contrary to section 18 of the Act; or (iv) the protection has been extended after registration.[524]

519. Cf. s. 51 of the Act.
520. Cf. s. 52 para. 1 of the Act.
521. Cf. s. 52 paras 2 and 3 of the Act.
522. Cf. s. 25 para. 1 of the Act.
523. Cf. s. 25 para. 5 of the Act.
524. Cf. s. 47 para. 1 of the Act.

VII. Infringement and Remedies

274. The extent of protection conferred by the utility model registration is determined by the claims. It is stated in the preparatory works that if the utility model registration relates to a very simple product with only a modest inventive step, the extent of protection is relatively narrow. This is similar to patent protection of mediocre inventions. However, it is emphasized that the extent of protection even for mediocre creations in addition to identical creations comprises creations that do not distinctly differ from the registered utility model. The precise extent of protection and, consequently, the interpretation of the utility model claims have to be determined by the courts. Patent case law may serve as a guide until an independent utility model case law has been established.[525]

The approach to determining the extent of protection under utility model law and patent law, respectively, appears to be identical, but it differs in one respect. Contrary to patent law, the claims under utility model law are not necessarily stated by precise wording in the registration. The utility model claims shall be specified in accordance with the provisions of section 19 of Order No. 1605 of 8 December 2006, in particular section 19 paragraph 1. However, by virtue of section 19 paragraph 2 of the Order, the claims may be specified by a reference to the description of the creation, including prospective drawings and photographs. As a consequence, the interpretation of the utility model claims is not as formalistic as the interpretation of patent claims.

A. Remedies

275. The competence of the specific unit established by the Patents and Trademark Office for the enforcement of patent rights and the combating of piracy is extended to utility model rights pursuant to section 61b of the Utility Models Act (*see supra* paragraph 235).

276. Like the other intellectual property acts, the Utility Models Act does not contain provisions for injunction. In case of infringement, an interim injunction may be rescinded according to the provisions of the Act on Civil Proceedings (*see supra* paragraphs 134 f. and 236 f). The registration of the utility model as such forms the legal basis for an injunction, but since, in most cases, a substantial examination of the utility model has not been conducted prior to registration; a significant risk exists that the registration is invalid and consequently that the interim injunction is illegal.

The provisions relating to remedies in Chapter 10 (sections 54–60) of the Act are not applicable if the registration of a utility model is revoked, deleted or declared invalid.

According to section 55 of the Act, any person who with intent or negligence infringes another person's exclusive right under the Utility Models Act shall pay a

525. Cf. FT 1991–1992, A, col. 2528.

reasonable compensation for the exploitation of the utility model as well as damages for the further injury that the infringement may have caused. Section 55 is identical to section 58 of the Patents Act (*see supra* paragraph 238 f.).[526]

Section 54 of the Act on penalties is identical to section 57 of the Patents Act (*see supra* paragraph 243).

Section 56 of the Act on destruction, seizure and recall is identical to section 59 of the Patents Act (*see supra* paragraph 240).

Section 58 of the Act on the publication of judgments is identical to section 60a of the Patents Act (*see supra* paragraph 244).

The provisions of the Act on Civil Proceedings on search and right of information (*see supra* paragraphs 139-140 and 241-242 apply to utility-model rights.

VIII. Overlapping and Relation to Other Intellectual Property Laws

277. A creation eligible for protection under the Utility Models Act is not precluded from protection under the Patents Act and the Designs Act. In principle, protection under all three Acts may be applied for and granted if the pertinent conditions of protection are satisfied.

On the overlapping and relation to patent law, *see supra* paragraph 245.

526. Section 57 of the Utility Models Act contains a provision identical to s. 60 of the Patents Act concerning provisional protection (*see supra* para. 230).

Chapter 4. Trademarks

§1. Sources – Legislation

278. Danish trademark law is statutory and based on the Trademarks Act. The first Trademark Act was adopted in 1880 but prior to that, legal protection of trademarks was available under other headings. A major revision of the Act took place in 1991 and was based on the Council Directive 89/104 to approximate the laws of the Member States relating to trademarks.[527] The Report No. 199, Copenhagen 1958, '*En ny dansk lov om varemærker*', which was prepared for the previous revision of the Trademarks Act in 1959, is still an important contribution to the interpretation of the valid Act. The latest major amendment of the Act took place in 2018 by the implementation of the new Trademarks Directive, Directive (EU) 2015/2436 of 16 December 2015.

279. Denmark has been a party to the Paris Convention for the Protection of Industrial Property since 1894. Denmark has acceded to the Nice Agreement Concerning the International Classification of Goods and Services for the Purposes of the Registration of Marks and the Trademark Law Treaty and, moreover, Denmark has ratified the TRIPs Agreement, which resulted in minor amendments to the Trademarks Act. The provisions of the TRIPs Agreement and the Trademark Law Treaty were implemented by Act No. 1201 of 27 December 1996 on certain amendments to the Trademarks Act. As late as 1996, Denmark became a party to the Madrid Agreement Concerning the International Registration of Marks and the Protocol Relating to the Madrid Agreement Concerning the International Registration of Marks. Denmark is not a party to the Trade Mark Registration Treaty (the Vienna Treaty) and the Vienna Agreement Establishing an International Classification of the Figurative Elements of Marks (the Vienna Agreement). Nevertheless, the Patent and Trademark Office is using the classification system of the Vienna Agreement to facilitate the computer-based process of examination of marks.

280. The Consolidated Act is, at present, Act No. 88 of 29 January 2019. The Act is administered by the Patent and Trademark Office (*Patent-og Varemærkestyrelsen*).[528] Previously, an Act on Collective Marks, originally from 1913, supplemented the Trademark Act. By the 2018 amendment, the provisions on collective marks were integrated into the Trademark Act.

527. Now codified version 2008/95/EC.

528. Under the provisions of the Act various orders have been issued: Order No. 1685 of 18 Dec. 2018 on the Application and Registration, etc. of Trademarks; Order No. 238 of 30 Mar. 1994 on Amendments of the Rules of Exhaustion of the Patents Act, the Trademarks Act and the Act on Protection of Topographies of Semiconductor Products; Order No. 892 of 21 Sep. 2009 on the Patent and Trademark Board of Appeal (*Ankenævnet for patenter og varemærker*); Order No. 12 of 12 Jan. 2012 on the remuneration of the Patent and Trademark Office for the performance of tasks, specific transactions and transcripts, etc. and Order No. 1578 of 14 Dec. 2016 on a special unit in the Patent and Trademark Office on enforcement and piracy.

§2. Subject Matter of Protection

281. The Act confers exclusive rights to owners of trademarks. The Act defines the following concepts:

- 'Trademark': A business sign that fulfils the conditions to constitute a trademark under this Act as an individual trademark, a guarantee or certification mark or a collective mark.
- 'An individual trademark': A business sign registered or applied for as a trademark or used as such when the sign is used or intended to be used for specific goods or services and is capable of distinguishing the goods or services of one undertaking from those of other undertakings.
- 'Guarantee or certification mark': A trademark registered or applied for as a guarantee or certification mark where the sign is capable of distinguishing goods or services certified by the proprietor as to the material, method of manufacture of goods or provision of services, quality, accuracy or other characteristics of the goods or services from other goods or services not so certified.
- 'Collective mark': A trademark registered or applied for as a collective mark where the sign is capable of distinguishing the goods or services of the members of an association which is the proprietor of the collective mark from those of other undertakings.[529]

I. Signs that May Serve as Trademarks

282. A registered trade mark may consist of any signs, particularly words, including personal names, designs, letters, numerals, colours, the shape of goods or of their packaging, or sounds, provided that they are capable of:

(1) distinguish the goods or services of one undertaking from those of other undertakings; and
(2) be reproduced in the trade mark register in such a way as to enable the competent authorities and the public to determine the clear and precise subject matter of the protection afforded to its proprietor.[530]

Thus, all kinds of signs may serve as trademarks, provided they are distinctive. The fact that some symbols may be perceived by other senses than the eye – for example, smells and sounds – does not exclude the symbols from protectable subject matter per se. Presumably, Danish law is in conformity with the Sieckmann decision[531] of the European Court of Justice in respect of trademark registration of smells leaving a very narrow scope of protectable subject matter, if any. The Patent and Trademark Office has in a number of cases accepted the trademark registrations

529. Cf. s. 1 a nos 1–4 of the Act.
530. Cf. s. 2 of the Act.
531. Case C-273/00 (Sieckmann).

of sounds; the legal situation should be construed in conformity with Case C-283/01 (Shield Mark) of the European Court of Justice.

283. A trademark right shall not be acquired for signs that consist exclusively signs which consist exclusively of the shape or other characteristic inherent in the nature of the goods; the shape or other characteristic of goods which is necessary to obtain a technical result; or the shape or other characteristic which gives substantial value to the goods.[532]

A trademark shall be a specific symbol that is distinctive for goods. The symbol shall not necessarily be connected to an inherent feature of the good, and in all circumstances, it shall not be in a shape that gives substantial value to the good. Presumably, the good as such cannot be its own trademark; however, the shape of the good is eligible for trademark protection. The distinction between the good as such and the shape of the good may be blurred. In the case reported in *Ugeskrift for Retsvæsen* 1995.92 SH, the Maritime and Commercial Court held that the form of the famous Danish toy bricks LEGO did not comprise such characteristic or independent element of signs that the basic LEGO toy brick as such constituted a trademark within the meaning of the Act.[533] In an older case, an ink bottle in a form that made the bottle more user-friendly was excluded from trademark protection.[534]

II. Different Categories of Marks

284. The enumeration in section 2 of the Act of signs that may serve as a trademark is not exhaustive. Section 3 in Order No. 1685 of 18 December 2018 stipulates requirements for the representation in the trademark application of the following eleven categories of trademarks: word mark, figurative mark, three-dimensional mark, position mark, pattern mark, colour mark, colour combination mark, sound marks, movement mark, multimedia mark and hologram mark.

Approximately two-thirds of all trademarks registered in Denmark consist of words or word combinations. Letters and numerals such as 4711 and IBM are eligible for trademark protection. Obviously, such signs often are not inherently distinctive; not quite as obviously, such signs may also be descriptive – for example, WWW and PVC. The shape, equipment or packaging of the goods have been accepted as trademarks under the Act since 1936.

In *Ugeskrift for Retsvæsen* 1974.287 SH, the court held that the Johnnie Walker whisky bottle, including the labels, in particular, the placement of the top label at an oblique angle, was protected under the Trademarks Act. This kind of protectable subject matter is delimited by section s. 14 no. 1 of the Act. A German producer of chocolate had for a long period marketed chocolate bars of 100 g in a square form packed by way of the flowpack method under the name 'Ritter Sport'. The Supreme

532. Cf. s. 14 no. 1 of the Act.
533. *See* J. Schovsbo, 'Passer til LEGO?', *Ugeskrift for Retsvæsen* (1996.B): 33–38; and J. Schovsbo, 'Varemærkeretlig beskyttelse af industrielt design?', *Nordiskt Immateriellt Rättsskydd* (1996): 53–68.
534. Cf. *Ugeskrift for Retsvæsen* 1941.574 SH.

Court held that the square form of the chocolate bar was not protectable subject matter under the Trademarks Act and added that the square form could not acquire distinctive character (secondary meaning) by extensive use of the square form. Furthermore, the Court stated that the part of the packaging that was a result of using the flow pack method was not protected by trademark rights pursuant to section 14 no. 1 of the Act because the shape of the goods was necessary to obtain a technical result.[535]

§3. Conditions of Protection

285. A trademark right may be established either by registration of a trademark in accordance with the rules of the Trademarks Act or by commencement of use of a trademark in Denmark for the goods and services for which the trademark has commenced to be used and for which it is continuously used, provided the extent of use is of a more than of a local nature.[536] Thus, trademark rights may come into existence in two different ways; either way the conditions of protection and the scope of protection are identical.

As regards trademark rights established by commencement of use, the Act does not specify conditions as to the intensity or duration of the use of the mark. A trademark right may be established when the trademark is applied on a good that is available from shops, etc., and the good is advertised using the trademark. Internal acts of preparation for putting a good on the market under a particular trademark that does not include advertising involving the trademark – for example, the mere decision of applying the trademark on a good that has not yet been put on the market – is not sufficient to establish a trademark right. Acts of preparation for putting a good on the market under a particular trademark may suffice if the acts are aimed at the general public or the commercial partners of the trademark owner, provided the good is available on the market within a short period of time.[537] In the case reported in *Ugeskrift for Retsvæsen* 1995.14 H, a few invoiced sales of goods under a particular mark had taken place; however, subsequently, the sales had stopped. The Supreme Court held that a trademark right had not been established by commencement of use. In another case, the Supreme Court held that advertising in an international journal (*Nature*) did not suffice to establish a trademark right by commencement, although the journal had between 250 and 375 subscribers in Denmark.[538]

535. Cf. *Ugeskrift for Retsvæsen* 1996.848 H. *See* J. Schovsbo, *Nordiskt Immateriellt Rättsskydd* (1996): 527 ff.
536. Cf. s. 3 para. 1 of the Act.
537. Cf. Report No. 199, *En ny dansk lov om varemærker* (Copenhagen, 1958), 96 ff; and K. Wallberg & M.F. Ravn, *Varemærkeloven* (Copenhagen: Jurist- og Økonomforbundets Forlag, 2021), 157 ff.
538. *Ugeskrift for Retsvæsen* 2006.480 H.

I. Distinctiveness

286. For a trademark to be registered, it shall be of the nature referred to in section 2 of the Act, including a distinctive character.[539] The same condition applies to trademark rights established by commencement of use; thus, section 3 paragraph 3 of the Act stipulates that use of a trademark, which according to its nature is excluded from registration, shall not establish any trademark right. A trademark consisting of ordinary words may not be distinctive when the evaluation of the trademark exclusively is based on the words; however, the words may be formed and arranged graphically in a way that may impart distinctiveness to the trademark. The scope of protection of such a trademark is confined to the particular graphical form and arrangement of the words. The requirement of distinctiveness applied to figurative trademarks is relatively modest since most such trademarks are often of a distinctive nature. Even rather simple geometric figures may be distinctive. The requirement of distinctiveness has resulted in comprehensive case law. In *Ugeskrift for Retsvæsen* 1996.468 Ø, a group of real estate agencies used the trademark *'Real Erhverv'* (Real Industry) in advertising real estate for industrial purposes. The court held that the trademark had a sufficient degree of distinctive character to be granted trademark protection. Normally, where a trademark is devoid of distinctive character, it is due to the fact that the trademark is considered a descriptive mark (on descriptive trademarks, *see infra* paragraph 288–289).

287. In the absence of distinctiveness, a trademark right is not established. Section 3 paragraph 3 of the Act stipulates that if the trademark is devoid of the required distinctive character on commencement of use, the right shall not be established until a distinctive character is created by the use of the mark.[540] In other words, a trademark right can be established when the trademark has acquired a secondary meaning. A soft drink manufacturer used for one of its products the trademark 'Kondi' ('Kondi' is used colloquially as a synonym with '*kondition*', which is a predicate indicating whether a person is in good or bad condition). Originally, the trademark was found not to be distinctive. Extensive advertising of the soft drink under the trademark 'Kondi', for a period of more than ten years involving advertising expenses of approximately DKK 18 million in total, imparted distinctiveness on the trademark.[541]

Single letters and numerals often are not distinctive signs within the meaning of trademark law. In the case reported in *Ugeskrift for Retsvæsen* 2003.1020 H, coffee filters were marketed under the numbers '202', '206' and '220'. The Supreme Court found that the purpose of the numbers primarily was to indicate the size of the coffee filters and that it was ordinary industry practice to indicate the size of coffee filters by a three-digit number. The numbers were devoid of distinctiveness and the numbers had not acquired secondary meaning by intensive use.

---

539. Cf. s. 13 para. 1 of the Act.
540. *See also* s. 13 para. 2 of the Act regarding conditions of registration of trademarks.
541. Cf. *Ugeskrift for Retsvæsen* 1987.230 SH.

II. Descriptive Trademarks

288. The requirement of distinctiveness prevents the grant of exclusive rights in a trademark consisting of ordinary words when the trademark is understood in compliance with the primary meaning of the words. As a main rule, trademark rights cannot be established in descriptive trademarks. According to section 13 paragraph 2 no. 3 of the Act, trademarks that consist exclusively of signs or indications that may serve, in trade, to designate the kind, quality, quantity, intended purpose, value, geographical origin, or the time of production of the goods or of rendering the services or other characteristics of the goods or services shall not be registrable. The same applies to trademarks that consist exclusively of signs or indications that are customarily used to designate the goods or services in the current language or in the established practices of trade. The Maritime and Commercial Court has held that the trademark '*Præcisionsskum*' (precision foam) was not protected under the Trademarks Act because the trademark consisted of two ordinary words '*præcision*' (precision) and '*skum*' (foam), which also in combination were descriptive to the product and devoid of distinctiveness. The product in question was polyurethane foam, which is used as a building material.[542] In *Ugeskrift for Retsvæsen* 1982.656 SH, a company had registered the trademark 'Top Twenty' for thread. The fineness of threads is indicated by numbers, and the number twenty was found to refer to the fineness of the threads supplied by the trademark owner. The court held that 'Twenty' was descriptive for the threads irrespective of the fact that the trademark consisted of numerals and not of numbers. The fact that the trademark included English numerals and not Danish numerals (*tyve*) did not devoid the trademark of its descriptive character because also, in Denmark, 'Twenty' will be perceived as a numeral. According to the practice of the Patent and Trademark Board of Appeal, the following trademarks were held to be descriptive and thereby did not satisfy the requirement of distinctiveness: 'Datamanager' for certain technical instruments and apparatuses,[543] 'Turbodrill' for machines and tools,[544] 'After Dinner Sweet' for chocolate,[545] 'Wonderlotion' for a product for personal care,[546] 'Pure Premium' for beer[547] and 'Sport 2000' for sportswear.[548]

289. Rights may be established in a trademark partly consisting of descriptive signs, provided the trademark in total is distinctive. In that case, the trademark right does not extend to the parts of the trademark that are descriptive or otherwise devoid of distinctiveness. Accordingly, a trademark right acquired by registration shall not include such elements of the trademark that cannot be registered separately. If elements of the trademark that have been exempted from the protection appear later on to have become registrable, a new registration may be made of these elements or of the actual trademark without the limitations.

542. Cf. *Ugeskrift for Retsvæsen* 1993.643 SH.
543. Case No. V 13/89.
544. Case No. V 4/90.
545. Case No. V 43/91.
546. Case No. V 17/91.
547. Case No. V 27/92.
548. Case No. V 41/92.

III. Other Impediments to Establishing Trademark Rights

290. Various kinds of trademarks are excluded from protection under the Trademarks Act – for example, trademarks that are contrary to law, public order or morality.[549]

Trademarks that are liable to mislead the public, for instance, as to the nature, quality or geographical origin of the goods and services cannot be registered.[550] A roofer used the trademark '*Autoriseret Tagmester*' (authorized roofer). Since no public authorization of the roofer was present, the Maritime and Commercial Court held that the trademark was deceptive according to section 14 paragraph (iii) of the Act.[551] In a case before the Patent and Trademark Board of Appeal, the trademark '*Scan Advokater*' (Scan Law Firm) used by a Danish law firm was held to be deceptive because 'Scan' referred to Scandinavia and the law firm only operated in Denmark.

A. *Personal Names*

291. Trademarks that without permission consist of or contain an element that can be construed as a personal name to which another party has a legal title or as a portrayal provided allusion is not made to persons long dead are excluded from registration as trademarks provided that the party with legal title has a right to prevent the use of the name as a trademark.[552] In this connection, the crucial point is to decide who has a legal title to a personal name. Provisions on legal title to personal names are included in the Act on Names.[553] The Act on Names distinguishes between protected and non-protected family names. According to section 2 of the Act, family names used by more than 2,000 people in this country are not protected and can be taken by anyone, which means that family names used by less than 2,000 are protected and cannot be taken by others.

The primary purpose of the provisions of the Act on Names combined with the provision of section 15 paragraph 3 (vi) of the Trademarks Act is to protect the integrity of individuals; hence, if a name refers to an individual or a small group of individuals, as the main rule, it cannot be used as a trademark. Usually, Christian names refer to a large group of individuals, and therefore, they can be used as trademarks. Similarly, very common family names may lawfully be used as trademarks.

The Patent and Trademark Office denied registration as a trademark of the personal name 'Rambo' (used for a weed killer product) on the grounds that bearers of that personal name existed abroad.[554] Probably, the denial was influenced by the existence of a number of famous feature films in which the lead character was called Rambo, and using the trademark for a weed killer would involve misappropriation

549. Cf. s. 14 para. (ii) of the Act.
550. Cf. s. 14 para. (iii) of the Act.
551. Cf. *Ugeskrift for Retsvæsen* 1997.584 SH.
552. Cf. s. 15 para. 3 (vi) of the Act.
553. Consolidated Act No. 1074 of 9 Aug. 2023.
554. Case No. V 36/92.

of goodwill from those films. In comparison, in a previous case, the Supreme Court held that a Danish citizen bearing the family name Bogart could not prevent a gentlemen's outfitting shop from using the trademark 'Bogart'. The Supreme Court argued that the use of a trademark consisting of the name Bogart in inverted commas in combination with a portrayal of the American actor Humphrey Bogart must be perceived as a reference to the actor and not to the Danish citizen bearing the same name and the use of the name in this way was in conformity with the provisions of the Act on Names. However, the shop was not entitled to use as a trademark the name Bogart in inverted commas followed by the sentence 'by Erling Skjødt' (the name of the owner of the shop) because it could be perceived as a reference to the Danish citizen named Bogart and thereby violate the provisions of the Act on Names.[555] In a controversial judgment from 2020, the Supreme Court held that the protection of names under the Danish Names Act only concerns infringements consisting of the unauthorized use of another person's name as a personal name or equivalent and not as a trademark or company name.[556] The Court reached its conclusion contrary to earlier case law that assumed that the Names Act actually protected against the use of a personal name as a trademark. Following the judgment, it is unclear whether there might be some specific cases where the provisions of the Names Act can be invoked against the use of a personal name as a trademark because the Court states that the protection is not restricted to the use as a personal name but extends to the equivalent of such use. The Patent and Trademark Office had in its practice interpreted the provision that is now found in section 15 paragraph 3 (vi) of the Act in a way that it only prevented the registration of other's names if they were very rare. According to the Patent and Trademark Office, a name is very rare if it is used by less than thirty persons. The Office's interpretation of section 15 paragraph 3 (vi) of the Trademark Act was confirmed by the Supreme Court.

It follows from the above that, to a certain extent, rights in trademarks consisting of personal names of others may be established. When rights in such trademarks have been established a conflict may arise if a person having legal title to the name wants to use his/her name as a trademark. According to section 10 paragraph 1 (i), the owner of a trademark right is not entitled to prohibit others from using, in the course of trade and in accordance with honest practices[557] in industrial or commercial matters, his/her own name and address. Accordingly, an individual has a relatively broad right of using his/her name to which he/she has legal title as a trademark. According to the Supreme Court, the owner of an art gallery named Louise Lego was entitled to market her art gallery under the name of 'Galleri Lego' and use the domain name louiselego.dk. In reaching its decision, the Supreme Court found that LEGO is a particularly well-known and distinctive trademark to such a degree that the public inevitably has associations with the toy manufacturer who owns the trademark LEGO. However, pursuant to the Trademarks Act, the gallery

555. Cf. *Ugeskrift for Retsvæsen* 1984.1103 H.
556. *Ugeskrift for Retsvæsen* 2021.958 H. For a critical view on the judgement, *see* T. Riis & J. Schovsbo, 'Kommentar til Højesterets dom i Ørsted-sagen', *Nordiskt Immateriellt Rättsskydd* (2021): 61- 71.
557. 'Honest practices' is evaluated on the basis of the general norm of s. 3 of the Marketing Practice Act.

owner is entitled to use her own name in accordance with honest practices, and since the gallery owner and the toy manufacturer use the sign for goods of very different descriptions, there was not found to be a real risk of confusion on part of the public, and hence the gallery owner's use of LEGO was held to be in accordance with honest practices.[558]

292. A company had registered the trademark 'Hunter' for, among other things, dental products. That trademark registration did not preclude an individual named Ruth Hunter from using the trademark 'Hunter' for toothpaste. The Supreme Court noted that the company did not actually use the trademark in relation to dental products (at that time, the Danish Trademarks Act did not include a use requirement), and that supported the notion that Ruth Hunter's use of her name as a trademark was not in violation of honest practices.[559] In the case reported in *Ugeskrift for Retsvæsen* 1967.371 V, a well borer's use of the trademark 'Vandfoss' infringed the well-known and strong trademark 'Danfoss'. The well borer who originally was named Petersen changed his name to Vandfoss, but his new name did not entitle him to use the trademark 'Vandfoss' in relation to his business.

B. Company Names

293. Provisions on legal title to company names are contained in the Danish Companies Act,[560] the Danish Act on Undertakings Carrying on Business for Profit[561] and the Act on Commercial Foundations[562] (In general, on the protection of trade names, see infra Chapter 5). The owner of a company name is protected against others' use of the company name as a trademark, cf. section 15 paragraph 3 (iv) of the Trademarks Act. According to this provision, a trademark may infringe a right to a company name if the name is registered in the Central Business Register (CVR). Furthermore, infringement of a right to a company name requires that the business name has more than a localised character and that:

(a) the name and the trademark are similar, and the goods or services for which the company name has been used as a business sign prior to the application for registration of the trademark are the same as or similar to those covered by the trademark and the use of the trademark would create a likelihood of confusion, including a likelihood of association between them; or
(b) the use of the trademark without due cause would take unfair advantage of, or be detrimental to, the distinctive character or the repute of the company name, where the company name has been used in connection with goods or services and such use has led to the name becoming well-known in this country prior to the application for registration.

558. Cf. *Ugeskrift for Retsvæsen* 2008.372 H.
559. Cf. *Ugeskrift for Retsvæsen* 1955.99 H.
560. Consolidated Act No. 1168 of 1 Sep. 2023.
561. Consolidated Act No. 249 of 1 Feb. 2021.
562. Consolidated Act No. 984 of 20 Sep. 2019.

C. Literary and Artistic Works, Etc.

294. A trade mark will infringe someone else's copyright or industrial property rights when a right to prohibit the use of the trade mark is attached to these rights, cf. section 15, paragraph 3 (viii).

The Commercial and Maritime Court has refused the registration of the trademark 'Flipper' used for toys because 'Flipper', when used for toys, makes strong associations to the feature film and the television show *Flipper*; however, 'Flipper' was registered for food products because associations to the feature film and the television show were not found to exist.[563]

295. Trademarks that have not been authorized by the competent authorities and are to be refused pursuant to Article 6*ter* of the Paris Convention for the protection of Industrial Property and trademarks that indulge badges, emblems and escutcheons that are of public interest, unless the consent of the appropriate authority to their registration has been given, cannot be registered.[564]

§4. Formalities

296. No formalities apply to trademark rights established by commencement of use. Registration of trademarks is subject to the provisions of the Act and to the provisions of Order No. 1685 of 18 December 2018 issued under various provisions of the Act[565] (the Order).

297. An application for the registration of a trademark shall be filed with the Patent and Trademark Office. The application shall contain a reproduction of the trademark and state the applicant's name or company. Furthermore, the goods or services for which registration of the trademark is applied shall be stated.[566] Stating the pertinent goods or services shall be in conformity with the classification of the Nice Agreement of 1957 with later amendments. Within each class, it shall be stated for which goods or services registration is applied. Accordingly, it is not possible to apply for registration for a whole class of goods or services without further specifications. Forms for the registration of trademarks can be obtained from the Patent and Trademark Office free of charge, but they are not mandatory. The application shall be written in Danish. The prescribed fee shall accompany the application. Presently, a basic fee of DKK 2,000 shall accompany the application and, additionally, a fee of DKK 200 for the first additional class of goods or services and of DKK 600 for further additional classes are required.[567]

563. Decision of 29 Oct. 1999 (V-0090-98).
564. Cf. s. 14 para. 1 (iii) of the Act.
565. *See* s. 48 of the Act.
566. Cf. ss 11–12 of the Act, and ss 1–2 of the Order.
567. Cf. s. 60 a of the Act.

298. A fundamental change in the way the Patent and Trademark Office examines an application took effect on 1 January 1999 in order to make the examination process similar to that of the EUIPO. Prior to 1 January 1999, the Patent and Trademark Office conducted a thorough examination of the application, resulting in a large degree of certainty as to the validity of the registration. According to the present examination process, the Patent and Trademark Office ensures that there are no impediments to registration; according to section 2, paragraphs 1 and 5–8 and sections 13–14 of the Act, in particular, the Patent and Trademark Office ensures that the trademark is distinctive, not descriptive, not contrary to law or public order and not deceptive. If the Office finds that there is an impediment to approving the application, the Office may set a deadline for rectification of the application or reject the application.

299. Moreover, the Patent and Trademark Office conducts a search for earlier applied for and registered trademarks and prepares a search report that is sent for information to the applicant with a deadline for comments.[568] In the examination report, the Patent and Trademark Office is only communicating the result of the examination and does not make any conclusions as to thc validity of the subsequent registration; not even if the result points to a prospective registration almost with certainty will be invalid. The existence of older colliding rights is communicated to the applicant, and the applicant must decide whether he/she wants to proceed with the application. The Patent and Trademark Office cannot refuse an application on the grounds mentioned in section 15 of the Act.

300. If the application does not comply with the Act or the provisions laid down pursuant to the Act, or if the Patent and Trademark Office has other objections to the acceptance of the application, the Patent and Trademark Office shall notify the applicant accordingly and invite him/her to file his/her observations within a specified time limit.

301. The changes in the examination process of 1 January 1999 create a substantial risk of invalid registrations. Hence, the owners of existing trademark rights must at their own initiatives ensure against infringing registrations by filling oppositions. To facilitate this process, against a prescribed fee, an owner of a registered trademark can request the Patent and Trademark Office, currently, to notify him/her whenever a trademark registration is published and his/her trademark has been mentioned in the examination report connected to the published registration. The service is available to owners of national trademark rights and Community trademark rights and to persons who have filed an application for registration of such a trademark.

568. Cf. s. 17 of the Act and s. 12 of the Order.

I. Oppositions

302. When the application has been accepted, the trademark is registered and the registration is published.[569] When the registration has been published, opposition may be filed against the validity of the registration. The opposition, which shall be reasoned, shall be filed with the Patent and Trademark Office within two months from the date of publication. The prescribed fee shall accompany the opposition. When an opposition has been filed, the Patent and Trademark Office takes the registration up for renewed treatment, according to the provisions of section 19 of the Act. The owner of the registered trademark right is notified of the opposition and is granted the right to file his/her observations. If the registration is sustained, this is communicated to the opponent and the owner of the right. If the registration is revoked in full or in part, the decision to that effect is published when it is final.[570] Thus, the Patent and Trademark Office has the possibility of administrative revocation of a registration on the basis of an opposition.

II. The Trademark Register

303. The Patent and Trademark Office keeps a Register of Trademarks and publishes registrations, etc.[571] (*see* section 26 of the Order on the contents of the Register). The Patent and Trademark Office registers international trademarks as well, and thus, it registers information on international registrations received from the International Bureau; in addition, certain other information concerning international trademark registrations may be entered into the register.[572]

304. Deletion from the Register is made if: (i) the registration is not renewed; (ii) the owner of the trademark requests deletion of the trademark; (iii) the registration is declared invalid; or (iv) if a decision or judgment is issued cancelling the registration.[573]

Where a company closes down, often the trademarks of the company are up with no significant commercial value. In case such a company does not request deletion of its trademarks, trademark registrations with no practical significance will be the result. With a view to such cases, it is stipulated in section 36 paragraphs 1 and 2 of the Act that if there is reasoned doubt as to the existence of an owner of a trademark or if his/her address is unknown, any person with a legal interest therein may request that the trademark be deleted from the Register. Prior to any deletion, the Patent and Trademark Office requests the owner to come forward within a time limit fixed by the Patent and Trademark Office. Notification of the time limit is given by registered letter or a similar, satisfactory method. If the address of the owner is

569. Cf. s. 18 of the Act, and s. 13 of the Order.
570. Cf. s. 19 of the Act, and s. 22 of the Order.
571. Cf. s. 1 para. 1 a(v) of the Act.
572. Cf. s. 25 of the Order.
573. Cf. s. 37 of the Act.

unknown, the time limit will be communicated by public notification. If, thereafter, the owner has not come forward, the trademark is deleted from the Register.

III. Revocation

305. If a trademark is registered contrary to the provisions of the Act, the registration may be revoked. In practice, one of the most common reasons for revocation is conflicting rights. The fact that oppositions previously have not been filed does not preclude subsequent revocation of a registration due to conflicting rights. Prior to the completion of the registration procedure, registration can only be revoked by a court decision in pursuance of section 33.

By virtue of section 25 paragraph 1,[574] the proprietor of a registered trade mark may forfeit his rights where no genuine use has been made of the trade mark in this country for the goods or services for which it is registered within a continuous period of five years and there is no reasonable cause for non-use. No application for revocation of a registered trademark may be filed if genuine use of the trademark commences or resumes between the expiry of the five-year period and the filing of the application for revocation.[575] Commencement or resumption of use within the three months preceding the filing of the application for revocation shall not be taken into account if the preparations for the commencement or resumption of use do not begin until the proprietor has become aware that an application for revocation may be filed. This three-month period shall begin at the earliest at the end of the continuous five-year period.[576] Genuine use of a mark includes the following situations:

- the mark is used in a form which does not affect the distinctiveness of the mark;
- the mark is used in a form which does not differ from the form in which it was registered;
- where the trade mark right is established by use, the form to which the trade mark right was originally attached;
- affixing the trade mark to goods or their packaging in this country for the sole purpose of export.[577]

306. Section 26 paragraph 1 subparagraph (i) covers situations where a trademark has become generic. When a trademark has become generic, it is devoid of distinctive character and the trademark right is forfeited. It is a condition for forfeiture that genericism has happened as a consequence of acts or inactivity of the proprietor. Contrary to English, there is in the Danish language no strong propensity to use trademarks as generic terms. Consequently, the practical problem of the Danish trademark owners is relatively small in this respect. However, for example, the famous Danish toy manufacturer Lego takes a lot of effort to ensure that its

574. *See also* s. 10 c of the Act.
575. Cf. s 25 para. 2 of the Act.
576. Cf. s 25 para. 3 of the Act.
577. Cf. s 10 c, para. 4 of the Act.

trademark does not become generic. To facilitate the rightholder in this regard, it is stated in section 7 of the Act that where the representation of a trade mark in a dictionary, encyclopaedia or similar printed or electronic reference work gives the impression that it constitutes the generic name of the goods or services for which the trade mark is registered, the publisher of the work shall, at the request of the proprietor of the trade mark, ensure that the representation of the trade mark is accompanied by an indication that it is a registered trade mark (e.g., by adding 'Reg. VM' or ®). If any party fails to comply with this provision, he/she shall be liable to pay the costs of publishing a correcting notice in the manner deemed reasonable.

Registrations of deceptive trademarks may be revoked pursuant to section 26 paragraph 1 subparagraph (ii). The provision corresponds to section 14 paragraph 1 subparagraph (iii) of the Act and has no great practical importance.

307. Revocation of a registration can be made by a court decision. Court proceedings shall be instituted against the rightholder and may be instituted by any person with a legal interest therein. Proceedings pursuant to the provisions of sections 13 and 14 may also be instituted by the Patent and Trademark Office.[578] The provision contains no time limits and, hence, proceeding can be instituted any time. A trademark registration may be revoked by administrative procedure as well; however, only after the completion of the registration procedure, provided the conditions for revocation in Chapter 3 of the Act are fulfilled.[579] The prescribed fee shall accompany the request. The owner of the registered trademark right is notified on the request and is granted the right to file his/her observations.[580]

308. The decision of the Patent and Trademark Office (on administrative revocation) may be brought before the Patent and Trademark Board of Appeal and the courts in accordance with section 46 of the Act. However, any of the parties may at any time institute proceedings against the other party concerning issues that have been raised in the case irrespective of whether the Patent and Trademark Office has made a decision in the case.[581] The decision of the Patent and Trademark Board of Appeal may not be brought before any higher administrative authority.[582] Proceedings for the trial of decisions of the Patent and Trademark Office, which may be appealed to the Patent and Trademark Board of Appeal, may not be brought before the courts until the decision of the Patent and Trademark Board of Appeal has been given.[583]

IV. Amendments of Trademarks

309. Pursuant to section 40 paragraph 1 of the Act, at the request of the rightholder, insignificant amendments of a registered trademark may be made, provided

578. Cf. s. 33 of the Act.
579. Cf. s. 34 para. 1 of the Act. *See also* ss 27–28 of the Order.
580. Cf. s. 27 of the Order.
581. Cf. s. 34 para. 6.
582. Cf. s. 46 para. 2 of the Act.
583. Cf. s. 46 para. 3 of the Act.

the general impression of the trademark is not influenced by the amendment. Amendments of registered trademarks are entered in the Register and published.

V. International Trademark Registration

310. An international trademark registration means a registration under the agreement adopted in Madrid on 14 April 1891 concerning the international registration of marks as subsequently revised (the Madrid Agreement) or under the protocol relating to the Madrid Agreement (the Protocol) adopted in Madrid on 27 June 1989. Denmark acceded to the Protocol in 1996. From the date of registration or from the date of a subsequent designation, an international trademark registration that designates Denmark shall have the same legal effect as if the trademark was registered in Denmark.[584] When the Patent and Trademark Office is informed by the International Bureau that Denmark is designated in an international registration, the Patent and Trademark Office examines the validity of the registration on the same lines that apply to national registrations. If an international registration under the Protocol is deleted at the request of the original registration authority, or as a consequence of a contracting State withdrawing from the Protocol (central attack), the owner of an international trademark registration may file a Danish trademark application with the same effect as if the application had been filed on the filing date of the application for the international registration or the date of a subsequent designation provided: (i) the application is filed within three months after the date of deletion; (ii) the Danish trademark application does not comprise other goods or services than the international trademark application; and (iii) the application, moreover, complies with the requirements of a trademark application and (iv) the applicant pays the prescribed fees.[585] In the case where, at the request of the owner of the trademark, a trademark registered in Denmark is also the object of an international trademark registration, the international trademark registration shall replace the Danish registration if: (i) Denmark is designated either originally or subsequently; (ii) the goods or services comprised by the Danish registration are also comprised by the international registration; and (iii) Denmark is designated later than the date of application for the Danish registration.[586]

311. As regards application for international trademark registration on the basis of an application or registration in Denmark, it is stated in section 50 paragraph 1 of the Act that international trademark applications may be filed by Danish subjects and legal and physical persons who are residing in Denmark or who have real industrial or commercial activities in Denmark. International trademark applications on the basis of an application or registration in Denmark shall be filed with the Patent and Trademark Office.[587] An international trademark application can only comprise

584. Cf. s. 57 of the Act.
585. Cf. s. 58 of the Act.
586. Cf. s. 60 of the Act.
587. Cf. s. 51, para. 1 of the Act.

the goods or services comprised by the Danish application or registration.[588] On filing an international trademark application, priority may be claimed pursuant to the Paris Convention.[589] The rules laid down in the Madrid Agreement and the Protocol shall apply to renewal.[590]

§5. Ownership and Transfer

312. Natural persons as well as enterprises and public authorities may obtain an exclusive right to trademarks (trademark rights), *see* section 1 b paragraph of the Act. The owner of a trademark right is the natural or legal person who has obtained a trademark registration or who has obtained the trademark right by commencement of use of the trademark in Denmark. By the death of the rightholder, the ordinary principles of inheritance law apply.

I. Coexisting Trademark Rights

313. If two or more parties individually claim a trademark right in the same or similar signs, the right that has come into existence first shall have priority, unless otherwise provided for in Chapter 1 B of the Act.[591]

The proprietor of an earlier right to prohibit the use or registration of a trade mark who has tolerated and been aware of the use of a later registered trade mark for five consecutive years shall no longer be entitled, on the basis of the earlier right, to apply for a declaration that the later trade mark is invalid for goods or services for which the later trade mark has been used, unless the application for the later trade mark was made in bad faith, cf. section 10 b paragraph 1 of the Act.[592] It is a condition for the coexistence of the two rights that the later mark has been used for five years continuously. Section 10 b paragraph 1 applies only to later registered trademarks. Later trademark rights established by commencement of use are subject to section 10 b paragraph 2 of the Act, which, however, also applies to registered trademarks. Pursuant to 10 b paragraph 2, a later right to a trademark may also exist alongside an earlier right which includes a right to prohibit the use of the trade mark if the proprietor of the earlier right has not taken the necessary steps to prevent the use of the later trademark within a reasonable time. If it is considered reasonable, a judgment may order that one or both of the signs may only be used in a particular way, for example, in a certain form or with the addition of an indication of location. Typically, such a court decision stipulates that the legitimate use of the later trademark is confined to the extent to which the trademark previously has been used.[593]

---

588. Cf. s. 50 para. 3 of the Act.
589. Cf. s. 50 para. 4 of the Act.
590. Cf. s. 53 of the Act.
591. Cf. s. 6 of the Act.
592. The provision is in conformity with Art. 9 para. 1 of the Trademark Directive (2015/2436/EU).
593. *See for example*, *Ugeskrift for Retsvæsen* 1990.782 SH.

In the main, the provision conforms to the basic principle of acquiescence in Danish law and under certain conditions it entitles the owner of a later right to maintain the right in more situations than covered by section 10 b paragraph 1.[594]

In the cases referred to in sections 10 b paragraphs 1 and 2 of the Act, the owner of a later trademark shall not be entitled to oppose the use of an earlier trademark, even if the owner of the earlier trademark may no longer invoke his/her right against the later trademark.[595]

II. Transfer and Licence

314. Trademark rights may be transferred in full or in part. In case of partial transfer of a trademark right, the rightholder can decide to divide the registration according to the provisions of section 34 of Order No. 1685 of 18 December 2018. A separated registration cannot be extended to goods or services that were not comprised in the original registration at the date when the division was requested. Moreover, the original registration and the separated registration cannot cover the same goods or services.

315. No formal requirements apply to agreements on the transfer of trademark rights; hence, oral agreements to that effect are valid.

316. By virtue of section 38 paragraph 1 of the Act, the right to a trademark may be transferred in or without connection to the enterprise in which it is used. The transfer of a business in its entirety involves the transfer of the trademark, unless there is an agreement to the contrary or the contrary is clear from the circumstances.[596] The provision in section 38 paragraph 1 is significant, especially in relation to strong and valuable trademarks that can be exploited detached from the enterprise or the product line in which the trademark has been built, for example, by way of trademark merchandising. However, if the transfer results in a use of the trademark that is deceptive to the consumers, the registration may be revoked pursuant to section 26 paragraph 1 (ii) of the Act.

317. In the case reported in *Ugeskrift for Retsvæsen* 1985.642 SH, two accountants had obtained rights to the same trademark under the Trademarks Act. The court stated that in such a case where more persons have obtained rights to the same trademark, each rightholder's right to transfer the trademark right freely is limited by considerations to the other rightholder. Accordingly, transfer of the trademark to a certain extent requires consent from the other rightholder. In determining the suitable limitations on the right to transfer the trademark, the court held that each rightholder was only entitled to expand his/her business by way of admitting one or more

594. Cf. FT 1990–1991, A, col. 1913 ff.
595. Cf. s. 10 b para. 3 of the Act. The provision is in conformity with Art. 9 para. 3 of the Trademark Directive (2015/2436/EU).
596. Cf. s. 38 para. 2 of the Act.

additional partners to his/her accountant firm and to transfer the trademark in connection with the firm. Additional forms of transfer of the trademark required consent from the other rightholder.

318. The transfer of the right to a registered trademark shall on request be entered in the Register of Trademarks, cf. section 38 paragraph 3 of the Act. A trademark right established by commencement of use of the trademark cannot be entered in the Register. Section 38 paragraph 3 does not form part of the substantive law. Hence, a transfer of a registered trademark right which has not been entered in the Register can be enforced in relation to a bona fide third party who is seeking to acquire the trademark right.[597]

319. A trademark may be licensed for some or all of the goods or services for which it is registered and for the whole or part of the country. A licence may be exclusive or non-exclusive.[598] At the request of the owner of the trademark or the licensee, the licence shall be entered into the Register of Trademarks. It shall also be entered in the Register when it is later established that the licence has terminated.[599] Similar to section 38 b paragraph 3, it is not a condition of validity for the licence that has been entered in the Register. If a licence has been granted to use a trademark, the licensor as well as the licensee are deemed to be entitled to bring proceedings in cases of infringement of the trademark right, unless otherwise has been agreed upon. A licensee who wishes to institute proceedings shall inform the licensor thereof.[600]

320. The owner of a trademark may invoke the rights conferred by the trademark against a licensee who contravenes any provision in the licencing contract with regard to its duration, the form in which the trademark may be used according to the registration, the nature of the goods or services for which the licence is granted, the territory within which the trademark may be used or the quality of the goods manufactured or the services provided by the licensee.[601]

321. Trademarks can be mortgaged according to the ordinary principles of mortgage on personal property. If a right to a registered trademark has been mortgaged or a writ of *fieri facias* has been executed therein, the Patent and Trademark Office shall at the request of the owner of the trademark, the mortgagee or the execution creditor enter a note to that effect in the Register of Trademarks.[602] Entering a note to that effect in the Register is not a condition of validity of the mortgage.

597. Cf. Schovsbo, Rosenmeier & Petersen (2024), 573.
598. Cf. s. 38 b para. 1 of the Act.
599. Cf. s. 38 b para. 3 of the Act.
600. Cf. s. 45 paras 1 and 2 of the Act.
601. Cf. s. 38 b para. 2 of the Act. The provision implements Art. 25 para. 2 of the Trademark Directive (2015/2436/EU).
602. Cf. s. 38 a of the Act.

§6. Scope of Exclusive Rights

322. Section 4 paragraph 1 of the Act stipulates that the establishment of a trademark right provides the owner with an exclusive right. By virtue of section 4 paragraph 2 subparagraphs (i) and (ii), the owner of a trademark is entitled to prohibit all persons not having his/her consent from using in the course of trade any sign: (i) if the sign is identical with the trademark and the use of the sign relates to goods or services that are of the same description as those comprised by the trademark and (ii) if the sign is identical with or similar to the trademark and the use of the sign relates to goods or services that are of the same or a similar description as those comprised by the trademark, provided there exists a likelihood of confusion including the likelihood of assuming a connection between the trademarks.[603]

323. As the main rule, the crucial criterion in delimiting the scope of trademark rights is the likelihood of confusion about the trademark and other signs used in the course of trade. The assessment of 'likelihood of confusion' within the meaning of the Act is based on two elements: partly, the similarity between the marks and partly, the similarity between the goods or services for which the marks are used. According to case law, a certain inherent connection exists between these two elements. If there is a high degree of similarity between two marks, a relatively low degree of similarity between the goods or services for which the marks are used may suffice to establish likelihood of confusion between the two marks and vice versa.[604] In principle, the division of goods and services into various classes according to the Nice Agreement used in the registration process and in the Trademark Register does not influence the assessment of similarity between the goods or services. Case law on the issue of similarity between goods or services within the meaning of the Trademarks Act is rather sparse and not very informative because it has to be understood in connection to the similarity between the marks. Therefore, it is difficult to extract more general principles in this respect. When the conflict arises, the result closely depends on a general assessment of the specific circumstances of the case. In relation to the previous Trademarks Act, it was stated that, primarily, similarity of goods or services depends on similarities in respect of composition, field of application and purpose. As examples of similar goods were mentioned, for example, footwear/galoshes and brassieres/corsets.[605] In the case reported in *Ugeskrift for Retsvæsen* 1977.993 SH, a company had registered the word '*Guldæg*' (golden egg) and a picture of a characteristic golden egg as a trademark for goods and services in various classes comprising, among many other things, saving boxes (at that time, there was no use requirement in Danish trademark law). A bank started to sell savings boxes, which were formed as eggs made of golden material. As advertising for the saving boxes, the bank put up posters at its business premises, including pictures of a golden egg and the word '*Guldæg*'. The court held that the bank had used the word '*Guldæg*' as a term for its saving

603. The provision implements Art. 10 para. 2 subparagraph (a9 and (b) of the EU Trademark Directive (2015/2436/EU).
604. Cf., for example, Wallberg & Ravn (2021), 193 ff.
605. Cf. Report No. 199, *En ny dansk lov om varemærker* (Copenhagen, 1958), 109.

boxes and had not used the word as a trademark for its business. Consequently, the use of the word did not constitute an infringement of the trademark right.

324. Section 4 paragraph 2 subparagraph 2 extends the scope of protection by including the use of a sign relating to goods or services that are of a similar description as those comprised by the trademark provided there is a likelihood of confusion, including the likelihood of assuming a connection between the trademarks. The provision shall be understood as extending the scope of protection to situations where there exists a likelihood of association between two marks, cf. the terms used in Article 10 paragraph 2 subparagraph b of the EU Trademark Directive. The provision was included in the Trademarks Act in 1991, implementing the 1989 EC Trademark Directive; however, presumably, it did not result in any changes in the substantive law. Contrary to section 4 paragraph 2 subparagraph (i), the provision is not aimed at confusion as to the origin of the goods or services as such but rather at other forms of confusion, for example, where the use of the infringing mark is likely to be perceived as being approved by the owner of the trademark right. In *Ugeskrift for Retsvæsen* 1994.147/2 SH, a producer of matches had since 1865 marketed matchboxes with a head-and-shoulder portrait in an oval frame of the famous Danish/Norwegian naval hero Tordenskjold affixed on the matchboxes. The picture was a registered trademark for, among other things, matches. A competitor applied for registration of a trademark in the form of a head-and-shoulder portrait of another Danish naval hero, Niels Juel; the applicant stated matches as the relevant class of goods. Otherwise, there were no similarities between the portraits of the two naval heroes. Nevertheless, the court found that the two marks were based on the same idea and choice of basic subject and held that it was likely for the consumers to assume a connection between the marks; hence, the Tordenskjold trademark was infringed.

Well-known trademarks are granted a broad scope of protection. This principle is included in section 4 paragraph 2 subparagraph (iii) of the Act, according to which the proprietor of an established trademark right may prohibit the commercial use of any sign in relation to goods or services by a third party who does not have the proprietor's consent where: the sign is identical with or similar to the trade mark, regardless of whether it is used in relation to goods or services which are identical, similar or dissimilar to those for which the trade mark is protected, where the trade mark is well known in this country, and the use of the sign without due cause takes unfair advantage of the distinctive character or the repute of the trade mark or is detrimental to that character or repute.

Accordingly, as regards well-known trademarks, the scope of protection may be independent of the kinds of goods for which the trademark is used. The Supreme Court has held that the owner of the 'Coca-Cola' trademark could prohibit the use of the mark 'Coca-Line' for footwear.[606] However, in another case, 'McDonald's' was found to be a well-known trademark in Denmark protected under section 4

606. *Ugeskrift for Retsvæsen* 1991.697 H.

paragraph 2 subparagraph (iii); nonetheless, the rightholder could not prohibit the owner of a local hot dog stand from using the trademark 'McAllan' for his business.[607]

325. Irrespective of the wording, the broad scope of protection of well-known trademarks under section 4 paragraph 2 subparagraph (iii) also applies to signs used for identical or similar goods or services. This is the conclusion of the case reported in *Ugeskrift for Retsvæsen* 1998.1029 SH. The famous trademark 'BMW' is registered for conveyances. An Italian company applied for registration of the mark 'AMW' for various automobile parts. The Patent and Trademark Office found that the two marks were used for goods of the same description but did not find similarity between the marks. However, the Maritime and Commercial Court stated that well-known marks within the meaning of section 4 paragraph 2 such as 'BMW' are granted a broad scope of protection not only in relation to other kinds of goods or services but also in relation to goods or services of the same or a similar description. Accordingly, the registration of the mark 'AMW' for various automobile parts was revoked.

326. How to construe 'use in the course of trade' is specified in section 4 paragraph 3 of the Act:

> The proprietor's right of prohibition under paragraph 2 includes the following:
> 1) Affixing the sign to the goods or their packaging.
> 2) Offering the goods for sale, marketing them, storing them for these purposes or offering or providing services under the sign.
> 3) Importing or exporting the goods under the sign.
> 4) Using the sign as a trade or business name or part of a trade or business name.
> 5) Using the sign on business papers and for advertising purposes.
> 6) Using the sign in comparative advertising in a way that is contrary to section 21 of the Danish Marketing Practices Act on comparative advertising.[608]

Section 4 paragraph 3 does not state an exhaustive list of the various forms of use of a trademark in the course of trade but only examples thereof. Other kinds of restricted uses of a trademark are, for example, oral presentation of the trademark included in speech to radio or television advertising.[609]

327. Private use of a trademark is not restricted by trademark law. Neither all forms of using another person's trademark commercially are prohibited by the Act. The consent of the rightholder is required only when the trademark is used as a

607. *Ugeskrift for Retsvæsen* 1997.253 H. In general on s. 4 para. 2, *see* T. Riis, 'Forretningskendetegn og varemærker med egenværdi', *Nordiskt Immateriellt Rättsskydd* (2000): 18–53.
608. The provision implements Art. 10 para. 3 of the Trademark Directive (2015/2436/EU).
609. Cf. Wallberg & Ravn (2021), 209 ff.

trademark; for example, a textbook on trademark law, including reproductions of various valid trademark registrations, does not require the consent of the rightholders.

§7. Limitations of the Scope of Trademark Protection

328. By virtue of section 10 paragraphs 1 and 2 of the Act, the owner of a trademark right is not entitled to prohibit others from using it in the course of trade and in accordance with honest practices in industrial or commercial matters: (i) his/her own name and address; (ii) indications concerning the kind, quality, quantity, intended purpose, value or geographical origin of the goods or services, the time of production of the goods or of rendering the service or other characteristics of the goods or services; or (iii) the trademark when it is necessary for the indication of the intended purpose of the goods or services, in particular as accessories or spare parts.[610]

'Honest practices in industrial or commercial matters' shall be understood in the light of sections 3[611] and 22[612] of the Marketing Practice Act. *Inter alia*, this implies that section 10 paragraphs 1 and 2 do not entitle a person in all situations to use his/her own name and address as a trademark in the course of trade. A person is not entitled to make use of his/her own name or address as a business mark in a manner likely to cause such mark to be confused with those of other traders (On trade names, *see infra* Chapter 5). However, according to section 10 paragraph 1 subparagraph (i), a person's use of his/ her own name and address in a fair manner in the course of trade, prima facie, cannot be prohibited by the owner of a trademark (*see supra* paragraph 291 on the trademark and personal name LEGO).

329. The limitations of the scope of trademark protection according to section 10 paragraph 1 subparagraph (ii) shall be seen in the light of the provisions of section 13 paragraph 1 subparagraph (iii) and section 13 paragraph 2 of the Act, according to which descriptive marks are excluded from registration unless they have acquired a secondary meaning. In a court decision, the name 'Budweiser' was not found to be an indication of geographical origin referring to the Czech city Budweis (Budejovice), which was considered unknown in Denmark. Therefore, section 10 paragraph 1 subparagraph (ii) was not applicable.[613]

610. The provision implements Art. 14 the Trademark Directive (2015/2436/EC).
611. Section 3 of the Marketing Practice Act: '(1) Traders shall exercise good marketing practice with reference to consumers, other traders and public interests....'
612. Section 22 of the Marketing Practice Act: 'Traders must not use business identifiers and similar devices that do not belong to them, nor use their own business identifiers in a manner that is likely to cause confusion with those of others.'
613. Cf. *Ugeskrift for Retsvæsen* 2002.612 SH.

330. Traditionally, the provision of section 10 paragraph 1 subparagraph (iii) has had great practical importance to spare parts.[614] From a practical point of view, non-original spare parts are unsaleable if it is not indicated on the packaging or the product itself that the spare parts fit and match the original product. This indication usually requires the use of the trademark for the original product. Pursuant to section 10 paragraph 1 subparagraph (iii), non-original spare parts marketed with a statement that they fit and match the original product cannot be prohibited by the rightholder. The requirement of honest practice implies that non-original spare parts must be marketed as non-original products; it is not in conformity with honest practices if the consumers are given the impression that the non-original spare parts have been supplied or approved by the original producer.

In modern times, the limitation of section 10 paragraph 1 subparagraph (iii) is an important prerequisite for the proper functioning of the market concerning computer products. In order to evaluate the applicability of most software and hardware products, it is necessary to know the technical conditions of interoperability with other computer and software components and the interoperability feature is communicated by use of trademarks, and thus, it is permitted for other traders than the owners of the trademarks to describe their products or services by using phrases such as 'Windows 11 Compatible', 'Works with Windows 11', 'Optimized for Mozilla Firefox', 'To view PDF files, you will need the Adobe Acrobat Reader.'

331. The limitations of the scope of trademark protection mentioned in section 10 paragraph 1 do not constitute an exhaustive list in this respect. *Inter alia*, it is accepted that a trademark can be used in comparative advertising without the consent of the rightholder. This notion is underlying the European Parliament and Council Directive 2006/114/EC of 12 December 2006 concerning misleading and comparative advertising (codified version).[615] Legitimate comparative advertising has to be in accordance with honest practices in industrial or commercial matters, and 'honest practices' shall be interpreted in conformity with the requirements in Article 4 of Directive 2006/114/EC. In particular, it is required that comparative advertising is accurate, fair and informative.

332. Contrary to the Patents Act and Copyright Act, the Trademarks Act does not contain any provisions on compulsory licences.

I. Exhaustion[616]

333. The principle of exhaustion of trademark rights is contained in section 10 a paragraph 1 of the Act:

---

614. In general, *see* J. Schovsbo, *Grænsefladespørgsmål mellem immaterialretten og konkurrenceretten* (Copenhagen: Jurist- og Økonomforbundets Forlag, 1996), 267 ff; and J. Schovsbo, 'Som skabt for hinanden. Immaterial- og konkurrenceretlig beskyttelse af kompatible produkter', *Nordiskt Immateriellt Rättsskydd* (1997): 16–47, 44 ff.

615. *See* the recitals of the Trademark Directive (2015/2436/EU) Nos 20.

616. In general on exhaustion of trademark rights, *see* Schovsbo (1996), Ch. III, 81–162.

> A trade mark shall not entitle the proprietor to prohibit its use in relation to goods which have been put on the market in this country or in the European Economic Area (EEA) under that trade mark by the proprietor himself or with his consent.[617]

334. According to the wording of section 10 a paragraph 1, the trademark right is exhausted only when products are put on the market in the EC. However, according to section 2 paragraph 1 of Order No. 238 of 30 March 1994, the principle of exhaustion in the Trademarks Act also applies to goods that have been put on the market under the trademark by the owner himself/herself or with his/her consent in a country that has ratified or acceded to the EEA Agreement.[618] Previously, it was debatable whether a trademark right was exhausted when goods were put on the market under the trademark in a country outside the EEA.[619] After the 'Silhouette' decision of the European Court of Justice,[620] it is clear that a principle of global exhaustion is not applicable.

335. Exhaustion under section 10 a paragraph 1 of the Act is almost complete. When the trademark right has been exhausted, anyone is entitled to use the good onto which the trademark is affixed by way of resale, rental, lending and other forms of commercial use. The practical significance of the principle of EEA exhaustion is primarily that the rightholder cannot use the trademark right to prevent parallel importation. However, the parallel importer must be cautious when using the trademark in a commercial context. In *Ugeskrift for Retsvæsen* 1983.923 H, distribution in Denmark of spare parts for 'British Leyland' automobiles was organized around an exclusive importer who authorized local distributors. A Danish company obtained original 'British Leyland' spare parts from a foreign distributor without using the national distribution system and sold the spare parts on the Danish market. In addition, the company advertised its products by using the 'British Leyland' trademark. The advertising contained the statement 'We are specialists in … ' followed by a reproduction of the 'British Leyland' trademark. The Supreme Court held that the parallel importer of spare parts was entitled to sell the spare parts on the Danish market, retaining the trademark when the trademark was affixed on the product or the packaging. But the use by the parallel importer of the trademark in the specific form of the advertising was not legitimate because the actual form of the advertising was likely to confer on the consumers the impression that the parallel importer was an authorized distributor. A somewhat similar result was reached in an unreported decision of 29 March 1994 of the Maritime and Commercial Court.[621] A parallel importer of 'Hugo Boss' suits had used the trademark 'Hugo Boss' in advertising. In the advertisement next to the trademark, the parallel

617. The provision implements Art. 15 of the Trademark Directive (2015/2436/EU) which codified a long established practice of the European Court of Justice.
618. The EEA.
619. *See*, for example, Cf. Report No. 199, *En ny dansk lov om varemærker* (Copenhagen 1958), 101.
620. Case 355/96 '*Silhouette v. Hartlauer*', [1998] ECR I-4799. The decision was anticipated by the Western Court of Appeal in *Ugeskrift for Retsvæsen* 1997.486 V.
621. *See* Schovsbo (1999) B.96.

importer added the term 'parallel imports'. Nevertheless, the court held that the parallel importer had infringed the trademark right because irrespective of the term 'parallel imports', according to the court, the 'Hugo Boss' trademark appeared as a trademark of the parallel importer's business. Apparently, the parallel importer could have escaped liability if the term 'parallel imports' had been placed in advertising in a more conspicuous way. The decision suggests that the right to use the trademark in advertising, as mentioned in section 4 paragraph 3 subparagraph (v) of the Act, is not exhausted. If that is so, one may consider whether this state of law is in conformity with Article 15 of the Trademark Directive. The issue is not explicitly dealt with in the Directive; however, the European Court of Justice considered the issue in its '*Dior*' decision,[622] which seems to allow the parallel importers relatively extensive use of the pertinent trademarks in advertising compared to the Danish decisions. The situation seems to be that as long as the parallel importer uses the trademark in advertising as a means of describing the goods offered for sale, the use is legitimate; however, the parallel importer is not entitled to use the trademark as a distinctive business sign referring to the business of the parallel importer.

336. As the main rule, the parallel importers and others are not entitled to affix the trademark on goods or packaging, including original goods and packaging, without the consent of the rightholders. Certain exceptions to this rule have resulted from decisions of the European Court of Justice on the repackaging of pharmaceuticals. In spite of the numerous decisions of the European Court of Justice on repackaging of pharmaceuticals and the relatively specific criteria stated in the Paranova decision,[623] various problems still need to be clarified. In a Supreme Court decision of March 1999,[624] a German producer of pharmaceuticals marketed particular tablets in Denmark in packages of ten blister packs, each containing ten tablets. A parallel importer, Paranova, bought the same pharmaceutical in Greece and Spain, where it was marketed in packages of thirty and sixty tablets, respectively. After importing the pharmaceutical into Denmark, the parallel importer repackaged the pharmaceutical into packages of 100 tablets and re-affixed the producer's trademark. The Supreme Court assumed that the size of the packages (100 tablets) was adapted to the therapeutic purpose of the pharmaceutical and the durability of the pharmaceutical, and furthermore, that the size of the packages was incorporated into the prescription practice of physicians. Irrespective that no legal obstacles existed to the marketing in Denmark by the parallel importer of packages of thirty and sixty tablets, the court held that it was necessary to repackage the pharmaceutical in order to create a real possibility of parallel import.[625] Hence, under the circumstances, repackaging and re-affixing the original trademark did not constitute trademark infringement.

622. Case C-337/95 '*Dior v. Evora*' [1997] ECR I-6013. *See also* case C-63/97 '*BMW v. Deenik*' [1999] ECR I-0905.

623. C-427, C-429 and C-436/93 '*Bristol-Myers Squibb v. Paranova*' [1996] ECR I-3457.

624. *Ugeskrift for Retsvæsen* 1999.952 H.

625. The Supreme Court relied on the cases 102/77 '*Hoffman la Roche v. Centrafarm*' and C-427, C-429 and C-436/93 '*Bristol-Myers Squibb v. Paranova*'. The case C-426/93 was referred to the European Court of Justice by the Danish Supreme Court in relation to this particular case reported in *Ugeskrift for Retsvæsen* 1999.952 H.

In another decision on repackaging of pharmaceuticals, once more involving the parallel importer Paranova,[626] the Supreme Court restated the criterion that the parallel importer shall have a real possibility of marketing the product in the state of importation. However, in this case, the parallel importer was found to infringe the trademark right. The Supreme Court emphasized that the parallel importer had not changed the size of the packages. Nevertheless, the parallel importer had repackaged the pharmaceuticals and subsequently re-affixed the trademark. It was undisputed that the parallel imported pharmaceuticals could be provided with labels and inserted notices containing the necessary information in Danish, and this could be done without breaking open the packaging. The parallel importer argued that packages plastered with labels create uncertainty on part of the pharmacists, physicians and consumers and, consequently, repackaging was necessary. However, on the evidence of the case, the Supreme Court held that repackaging was not necessary in order to create a real possibility of marketing the products in Denmark.[627]

337. Exhaustion is contingent on the goods that have been put on the market by the owner himself/herself or with his/her consent. Influenced by the EU case law, this is construed as a question of whether the owner of the trademark is in control of marketing the goods in relation to which the trademark is used. If the owner is in control of the marketing, the right is exhausted. In *Ugeskrift for Retsvæsen* 1997.462 SH, a Danish producer of garments had its goods produced by a Portuguese contractor. The Danish company provided the Portuguese company with labels with the Danish company's trademark, which were to be affixed on the garments. It was agreed upon between the parties that the Portuguese company could sell excess production and second-quality goods on the condition that the Danish trademark was removed. Somehow, a Danish parallel importer succeeded in acquiring from Portugal a consignment of second-quality goods with the Danish trademark affixed onto the goods. The rightholder tried to prevent the marketing of these goods in Denmark. However, the court held that the trademark right had been exhausted. Apparently, the court recognized that the sale of the goods in Portugal was in violation of the agreement with the Danish producer, but since the Danish company had not adopted any measures whatsoever to ensure compliance with the agreement, it had accepted the risk that such unwarranted sales could take place. In other words, the rightholder was considered de facto to have consented to the marketing of the goods in Portugal.

338. The principle of exhaustion is confined by section 10 a paragraph 2 of the Act:

626. *Ugeskrift for Retsvæsen* 1999.1678 H.

627. *See* the similar decisions in *Ugeskrift for Retsvæsen* 2003.1807 H; *Ugeskrift for Retsvæsen* 2003.1825 H; *Ugeskrift for Retsvæsen* 2003.1826 H; *Ugeskrift for Retsvæsen* 2003.1844 H; and *Ugeskrift for Retsvæsen* 2003.1845 H.

> [The principle of exhaustion in section 10 a paragraph 1 of the Act] shall not apply if the proprietor has reasonable grounds for opposing further commercialisation of the goods, in particular in cases where the condition of the goods has changed or deteriorated after they have been put on the market.[628]

The purpose of the provision is to protect the rightholder against goods of an inferior quality put on the market under the trademark, which will be detrimental to the reputation or the goodwill of the trademark. One field of application of the provision is durable consumer goods that are resold after extensive repairing. The crucial criterion of section 10 paragraph 2 is whether the owner has legitimate reasons to oppose further commercialization of the goods. Instances where the condition of the goods has been changed or impaired are examples and do not form an exhaustive list of which circumstances may constitute 'legitimate reasons'. In *Ugeskrift for Retsvæsen* 1979.593 SH, the Royal Copenhagen Porcelain Manufactory, which produces and sells various lines of primarily ornamented porcelain, offered for sale in its shop items of unornamented porcelain; the trademark of the Porcelain Manufactory was affixed to these items before the firing of the porcelain. An individual bought some of these unornamented porcelain items, decorated them and sold them from her own shop. The individual had stated her name on the items decorated by her. The court held that the Porcelain Manufactory had a reasonable need of protection against such commercial resale of porcelain items decorated by another party when the items were still carrying the trademark of the Porcelain Manufactory. Consequently, the court concluded that commercial resale in the specific case required that either: (i) the trademark of the Porcelain Manufactory was removed from the items or covered in a durable way or (ii) it was stated on the items in a durable way that the items were unornamented by the Porcelain Manufactory in addition to who had decorated the items.

§8. Use Requirements

339. 'The proprietor of a registered trade mark … may forfeit his rights if the trade mark has not been put to genuine use in this country for the goods or services for which it is registered within a continuous period of five years and there is no reasonable cause for non-use,' cf. section 25, paragraph 1 of the Act.[629] The use requirement of section 25 was introduced into Danish trademark law in 1991. According to the preparatory works, 'genuine use' shall be understood in accordance with normal marketing activities within the area.[630] 'Proper reasons' for non-use may be circumstances that affect the whole industry in question such as import prohibition or military operations, or circumstances that affect only the rightholder

628. The provision implements Art. 15 para. 2 of the Trademark Directive (2015/2436/EU).
629. *See also* s. 10 c of the Act. The provisions implements Art. 19 of the Trademark Directive (2015/2438/EU).
630. Cf. FT 1990–1991, A, col. 1918.

such as lack of marketing approval from the competent public authority or unanticipated obstacles to production due to fire at the production premises.[631] Obviously, in case of non-use, the owner of the trademark cannot prevent revocation of the registered trademark right by re-registering the trademark every five years.

The following shall constitute use within the meaning of section 25 paragraph 1: (i) Use of the trade mark in a form which differs from the form in which it was registered only in elements which do not alter the distinctive character of the mark, or, where the trade mark right is established by use, the form to which the trade mark right is originally attached, regardless of whether the trade mark is also registered by the proprietor in the form in which it is used. (ii) Affixing the trade mark to goods or their packaging in this country for the sole purpose of export.[632] Additionally, use of a trademark by, for example, a licensee constitutes use within the meaning of section 25 paragraph 1.[633] If the trademark is used simultaneously as a trade name for the rightholder's business, the use requirement of section 25 has been satisfied.

340. The use requirement as stipulated in sections 10 c and 25 does not imply that the trademark shall be used at the time of registration. Hence, within a period of five years, it is possible to maintain a formal registration of a trademark, and that possibility may be strategically valuable if the rightholder plans to extend a line of business under a specific trademark into new products or services.

The five-year period is calculated from the date of the completion of the registration procedure; it means the date of the final registration, which is two months after the publication of the registration, provided no oppositions are filed. When oppositions are filed, the date of the final registration is the date of the final decision on the opposition.

341. If the use requirement is not satisfied, the registration may be revoked according to the provisions of section 25 of the Act. Revocation of a trademark grounded on non-use of the mark may not be claimed where, in the interval between the expiry of the five-year period and the filing of the application for revocation, genuine use of the trademark has been commenced or resumed. The commencement or resumption of use within a period of three months preceding the filing of the application for revocation shall, however, be disregarded where preparations for the commencement or resumption occur only after the owner has become aware that an application for revocation may be filed.[634] Where grounds for revocation or invalidity of a trade mark registration exist in respect of only some of the goods or services for which a trade mark right has been registered, the trade mark right shall be revoked, or the registration declared invalid only in respect of those goods or services.[635] Accordingly, the registration can be maintained only in relation to goods for which the trademark has been used in conformity with the use requirement. It follows from the general principle of section 4 of the Act that the registration can

631. *Ibid.*
632. Cf. s. 10 c para. 4 of the Act.
633. Cf. s. 10 c para. 5 of the Act.
634. Cf. s. 25 para. 3 of the Act. The provision implements Art. 19 para. 3 of the Trademark Directive (2015/2436/EU).
635. Cf. s. 31 of the Act which implements Art. 21 of the Trademark Directive (2015/2436/EC).

be maintained, as well, in relation to goods similar to those for which the trademark has been used. More precisely, how to construe 'similar goods' in this respect has to be decided in case law.[636]

342. In cases on infringement, the proprietor of a trade mark shall only be entitled to prohibit the use of a sign to the extent that the proprietor's rights cannot be revoked under section 25 at the time when the trade mark infringement action is brought. If the defendant so requests, the proprietor of a registered trade mark shall prove that the trade mark has been put to genuine use as defined in section 10 c in connection with the goods or services for which it is registered and on which the action is based during the five-year period preceding the institution of proceedings, or that there are proper reasons for non-use if at least five years have elapsed since the registration procedure for the trade mark was completed on the date of institution of proceedings.[637] The provision thus establishes reverse burden of proof in respect of genuine use in infringement cases.

Regarding trademark rights established by commencement of use, that is, protected but not registered trademarks, the right lapses when the use is suspended. Incidental or short-term non-use of the trademark is not sufficient for the right to lapse.

§9. Duration of Protection: Renewal – Termination

343. The period of trademark protection may be infinite. The right obtained by registration of a trademark is effective from the date on which the application is filed and continues to be effective for ten years from the date of registration. The registration may be renewed for periods of ten years from the expiry of the period of registration concerned.[638] Application for renewal is made by payment to the Patent and Trademark Office of the prescribed fee not earlier than six months before and not later than six months after the expiry of the registration period. If the application is accepted, the renewal is entered into the Register.[639]

344. Trademark rights established by commencement of use do not expire automatically after a certain period of time. A non-registered trademark right continues as long as the trademark is used. Where a trademark has been used for various types of goods and the rightholder ceases to use the trademark for certain goods, protection expires for these goods – but only for these goods.[640]

345. A trademark registration may be revoked by court decision as well as by administrative procedure (on revocation, *see supra* paragraph 305 ff.).

636. Cf. FT 1990–1991, A, col. 1919.
637. Cf. s. 10 d, paras 1–2 of the Act.
638. Cf. s. 24 paras 1 and 2 of the Act.
639. Cf. s. 24 paras 3, 5 and 7 of the Act.
640. *See* Wallberg & Ravn (2021), 161.

§10. INFRINGEMENT AND REMEDIES

I. Infringement

346. The basic criterion in determining infringement is whether there exists a likelihood of confusion between two marks. As mentioned *supra* paragraph 323, the assessment of 'likelihood of confusion' within the meaning of the Act is based on two elements: partly, the similarity between the marks and partly, the similarity between the goods or services for which the marks are used.

347. The approach in infringement cases is to establish the general impressions of the two marks, including distinctive character, extent of actual use, and market and product characteristics. Strong trademarks are granted a broader scope of protection, and as a consequence, a later mark may constitute infringement, even though there is not a close similarity between the two marks. For example, the mark 'Solram' infringed the strong trademark 'Osram' where both marks were used for light bulbs.[641]

348. When a protected trademark is compared to an alleged infringing mark, it is recognized that the buying public may have a blurred memory image, implying that confusion between the two marks is more likely to occur when the two marks cannot be observed at the same time. The blurred memory image is most relevant in relation to low-cost consumer goods. Taken at face value, the recognition of the blurred memory image may lead to a broad and indeterminate scope of protection. The notion is used by the courts, however, cautiously. In *Ugeskrift for Retsvæsen* 1967.367 V, the court held that 'Stanmore' was likely to be confused with 'Starmount' (both marks were used for shirts) and emphasized that the consuming public would have a blurred memory image of the plaintiff's mark 'Starmount', *inter alia*, because purchases of shirts usually are not frequent.[642] It was a crucial element of the decision that the plaintiff was considered the owner of a relatively strong trademark. The test was not used in *Ugeskrift for Retsvæsen* 1981.501 SH, in which the court found that by simultaneous observation of the two trademarks, significant differences appeared, and hence, the plaintiff's trademark was not infringed.

349. Where the buyers of the goods on which the trademark is affixed are confined to a certain kind of professionals instead of laymen, a larger degree of similarity between the two marks is accepted. In *Ugeskrift for Retsvæsen* 1996.1309 H, according to the Supreme Court, 'Vibradox' was not likely to be confused with 'Vibramycin'. Both marks were used for antibiotics, and in reaching its decision, the court found that the likelihood of confusion was reduced because the goods were only obtainable from the doctors' prescription. Arguably, the two marks were likely to be confused if the goods concerned had not been prescriptive drugs.

Different channels of distribution of the goods may imply that two otherwise similar marks are not deemed likely to be confused. In an unreported decision, the

641. Cf. *Ugeskrift for Retsvæsen* 1979.497 H.
642. *See also Ugeskrift for Retsvæsen* 1992.319 SH.

Maritime and Commercial Court[643] held that the mark 'Multi-tabs' used for vitamin pills was not confused with 'Multimax' used for a herbal remedy. The court based its decision, *inter alia*, on the fact that the former product was exclusively sold by pharmacies (licensed to sell pharmaceuticals on prescription), whereas the latter product was distributed through drugstores. In *Ugeskrift for Retsvæsen* 1998.483 SH, the court held that the marks 'Nitromex' and 'Nitroven', which were used for similar pharmaceuticals, were not likely to be confused, *inter alia*, because 'Nitromex' exclusively were available at dispensaries in hospitals and not like 'Nitroven' at ordinary pharmacies.

350. As regards trademarks consisting of pictures or designs, prospective infringement will primarily rest on a comparison of the dominant parts of the pictures. Usually, such a trademark is not infringed on the sole ground that another trademark consists of the same motif. In assessing whether two trademarks are likely to be confused, the colours of the marks may play an important role; however, in principle, a trademark registered in black and white is protected against a similar mark in any colour combination.[644]

351. The associations evoked by a trademark may play a significant role in deciding whether two marks are likely to be confused. In *Ugeskrift for Retsvæsen* 1981.533 SH, the court held that the two marks 'Splendance' and 'Tendance' used for hair tonic were not likely to be confused partly because the former trademark connotes the term 'resplendence' and the latter trademark connotes the term 'tendency'. Similarly, the Patent and Trademark Board of Appeal held that the trademark 'Everlast' was not likely to be confused with the trademark 'Everest' because the former trademark refers to the English term 'everlasting' and the latter trademark refers to the highest mountain in the world.[645]

II. Remedies

352. The competence of the specific unit established by the Patents and Trademark Office for the enforcement of patent rights and the combating of piracy is extended to trademark rights pursuant to section 45b of the Trademarks Act (*see supra* paragraph 235).

A. *Jurisdiction*

353. The Maritime and Commercial Court in Copenhagen is the Community Trademark Court of First Instance, pursuant to Article 123(1) of Regulation (EU) 2017/1001 of the European Parliament and of the Council of 14 June 2017 on the EU trade mark (codification)

643. Decision of 10 Jun. 1991 (H 529/1989).
644. Cf. Schovsbo, Rosenmeier & Petersen (2024), 610.
645. Cf. V 17/94.

B. Injunctions[646]

354. Similar to copyright and patent infringement cases, in trademark infringement cases as a practical matter, an injunction is the primary remedy available to the rightholder. The Trademarks Act contains no provisions for injunctions. The pertinent legal basis in this respect is found in Chapter 40 of the Act on Civil Proceedings (sections 411–430). An interim injunction can be rescinded if the party applying for the injunction proves on a balance of probabilities or by clear and convincing evidence: (1) that the party holds the right for which protection by way of an injunction is sought; (2) that the conduct of the opposing party necessitates the granting of the injunction; and (3) that the ability of the party to enforce his right will be lost if the party has to await a full trial.[647] In addition, it is stated in section 414 of the Act on Civil Proceedings that no injunction may be granted if the general provisions on penalty and compensation and any security offered by the opposing party are deemed to provide adequate protection to the party and, furthermore, that the grant of an injunction can be refused if such injunction would cause the opposing party to suffer a detriment or disadvantage which is clearly disproportionate to the party's interest in obtaining the injunction.

355. Normally, adequate security is required in order to rescind an interim injunction.[648] The required security may prove a significant impediment for the rightholder to enforce his/her rights since the demanded security is occasionally very large. Besides, the rightholder is liable for the loss of the alleged infringer if it turns out that the interim injunction was illegal and the rightholder ought not to have claimed the injunction.[649] To a limited extent, the alleged infringer may prevent an interim injunction by providing adequate security;[650] it appears that this opportunity has never been used in trademark infringement cases. The crux of the problem in deciding whether an injunction shall be rescinded or not is related to the standard of proof. The burden of proof lies with the rightholder, and as the main rule, the rightholder shall produce a reasonable corroborated presumption.[651] An injunction does not require negligent or intentional acts on part of the alleged infringer. The rightholder shall within two weeks take action to confirm the interim injunction.[652]

In *Ugeskrift for Retsvæsen* 1993.158 H, the bailiff's court found that the trademark 'Mars Gold' infringed various strong marks including the word 'Guld' (the Danish term for gold). All marks were used for chocolate products. Accordingly, an

---

646. In general on injunctions in respect of intellectual property law, *see* C.S. Petersen, P. Møgelvang-Hansen & Thomas Riis, *Judicielle forbud/påbud og immaterialretsproces* (Copenhagen: Karnov Group 2015); C.S. Petersen, *Immaterialrettigheder og foreløbige forbud* (Copenhagen: Jurist-og Økonomforbundets Forlag, 2008); N.M. Andersen, A. Carlquist & A. Rubinstein, *Retshåndhævelse af immaterialrettigheder* (Copenhagen: Jurist- og Økonomforbundets Forlag, 2006), 265–340; and T. Riis, *Enerettigheder og vederlagsrettigheder. Håndhævelse af immaterialrettigheder i økonomisk perspektiv* (Copenhagen: Jurist- og Økonomforbundets Forlag, 2005), 119–157.
647. Cf. s. 413 of the Act on Civil Proceedings.
648. Cf. s. 415 of the Act on Civil Proceedings.
649. Cf. s. 428 of the Act on Civil Proceedings.
650. Cf. s. 414 para. 1 of the Act on Civil Proceedings.
651. *See* A. Jacobi, 'Fogedforbud, særlig i patenttvister', *Ugeskrift for Retsvæsen* (1968 B): 51 ff.
652. Cf. s. 425 of the Act on Civil Proceedings.

interim injunction was rescinded. The rightholder pledged the required DKK 2.7 million as security. Subsequently, the Supreme Court found that the injunction was illegal because the defendant did not infringe the right of the plaintiff. After the injunction was rescinded but before the Supreme Court's decision, the defendant destroyed a consignment of the disputed goods representing DKK 270,000 in production costs. The Supreme Court presumed that the destruction of the goods partly was a consequence of the interim injunction and awarded the defendant damages computed at the discretion of the court to DKK 150,000 as compensation for the destroyed goods. In *Ugeskrift for Retsvæsen* 1982.646 SH, an interim injunction was rescinded. Subsequently, the Maritime and Commercial Court held that the injunction was justified, but the actual injunction had too broad a scope. Accordingly, the injunction was maintained with a more narrow scope, but the defendant was not awarded damages.

356. Injunctions pursuant to Article 131(1) of Regulation (EU) No. 2017/1001 (the EU Trademark Regulation) (codification) are rescinded by the bailiff's court or the Maritime and Commercial Court; the provisions of Chapter 40 of the Act on Civil Proceedings apply *mutatis mutandis*. The Maritime and Commercial Court in Copenhagen has jurisdiction to rescind injunctions that are applicable in any Member State, in accordance with Article 131(2) of the EU Trademark Regulation. The provisions of Chapter 40 of the Act on Civil Proceedings apply *mutatis mutandis.*[653]

C. *Liability*[654]

357. Anyone who intentionally or negligently infringes the trademark right of another person shall pay: (i) reasonable remuneration to the infringed party for the exploitation and (ii) damages to the infringed party for any additional damage caused by the violation, cf. section 43 paragraph 1 of the Act. Liability under the Trademarks Act conforms to the general principles of liability in tort law; it requires negligence, causality and adequacy.

Typically, in trademark infringement cases, damages are computed at the discretion of the court[655] and awarded damages are in general small, primarily, because it is very difficult for the rightholder to provide sufficient evidence for all losses caused by the trademark infringement.

The provisions of the Act on damages conform to the basic rule of tort law according to which the claimant is entitled to damages for the full loss that the tortious act has caused. The most important element in the computation of damages is

653. Cf. s. 43b paras 1–3 of the Act.

654. In general on liability in respect of intellectual property law, *see* Andersen, Carlquist & Rubinstein (2006), 419–495; and T. Riis, *Enerettigheder og vederlagsrettigheder. Håndhævelse af immaterialrettigheder i økonomisk perspektiv* (Copenhagen: Jurist-og Økonomforbundets Forlag, 2005), 225–367.

655. *See*, for example, *Ugeskrift for Retsvæsen* 1994.147 SH.

often the lost market sales of the rightholder. Lost sales are computed as the number of products that have not been sold due to the infringement multiplied by the loss connected to each product. In general, it cannot be assumed that the computation of lost market sale equates the infringer's profits. Another element in the computation of damages may be compensation for the distortion of the market for the rightholder's product. The market for the rightholder's product may be distorted if the infringer's product, which is put on the market, is similar to the rightholder's product but of poor quality. The result may be that the goodwill connected to the rightholder's product is significantly reduced, and, consequently, it requires large investments in marketing measures to re-establish that goodwill. However, it can be difficult for the rightholder to provide sufficient evidence to be awarded compensation for distortion of the market.

As a consequence of the implementation of the Directive 2004/48/EC on the enforcement of intellectual property rights (The Enforcement Directive), it is now stated in the Act that when setting the damages, consideration shall be given to such matters as the infringed party's loss of profits and the offender's unfair profits.[656] Computation of damages in consideration of the offender's unfair profits is an innovation in Danish law. This new provision provides the courts with the legal basis for the award of damages at a higher level than was awarded previously; however, it is doubtful whether this will happen to any significant extent.

According to section 24 paragraph 1 of the Damages Liability Act,[657] liability may be mitigated or lapse where liability would involve an unreasonable burden on the party liable or where very special circumstances otherwise make it reasonable. Trademark infringement that leads to claims from the rightholder takes place in a commercial context, and therefore, reducing the award of damages pursuant to section 24 of the Damages Liability Act is not likely to occur.[658]

358. As indicated, it is difficult to determine the actual loss of the rightholder caused by the infringement and often the result is small damages. In order to ensure the rightholder a kind of minimum compensation, according to section 43 paragraph 1 subparagraph (i) of the Trademarks Act, he/she is entitled to a reasonable compensation for the exploitation of his/her trademark. The provision implies that the rightholder in all cases at a minimum is entitled to 'a reasonable royalty', notwithstanding that he/she cannot prove an actual loss caused by the infringement.

D. Destruction, Seizure and Recall

359. The risk of further infringements can justify destruction, seizure, etc., of existing infringing products. It is stipulated in section 44 paragraph 1 of the Act that in the case of infringement of trademark rights and in order to prevent further infringement, the court may, when so claimed, by sentence decide that infringing products shall:

656. Cf. s. 43 para. 2 of the Act.
657. Consolidated Act No. 1070 of 24 Aug. 2018.
658. Cf. Schovsbo, Rosenmeier & Petersen (2024), 794.

- be recalled from the channels of commerce;
- be definitively removed from the channels of commerce;
- be destroyed;
- be handed over to the infringed party; or
- the illegally affixed trademarks shall be removed from the goods.

The remedies are not confined to infringing products since they also may apply to articles, tools, etc., that primarily have been used for unauthorized production of the infringing goods.[659] Destruction, etc., according to these provisions, shall be undertaken without any form of compensation to the offender and does not have any effect on any possible compensation to the infringed party. Furthermore, such measures shall be undertaken at the offender's expense, unless special reasons dictate otherwise.[660]

A principle of proportionality applies to these remedial measures. Thus, in considering a request for corrective measures, the need for proportionality between the seriousness of the infringement and the remedies ordered as well as the interests of third parties shall be taken into account by the court.[661]

E. Search[662]

360. Measures for preserving evidence in cases of infringement of intellectual property rights were included in Danish legislation in 2001 in order to satisfy the national obligations under the TRIPs Agreement. Subsequently, in 2006, the provisions were amended in conformity with Article 7 of the Enforcement Directive (2004/48/EC). The provisions are placed in Chapter 57a of the Act on Civil Proceedings (section 653–653d); nevertheless, they only apply in cases of infringement of intellectual property rights. In conformity with Article 7 of the Enforcement Directive, the purpose of such interim measures is to preserve relevant evidence in respect of an alleged infringement. On the request of the rightholder, the bailiff's court can decide to search the premises of an alleged infringer in order to preserve evidence of the infringement or the extent of the infringement. The claimant shall produce a reasonable corroborated presumption that an infringement has taken place or will take place and that it is likely that the evidence for the infringement or the extent of the infringement can be found on the pertinent premises.[663] The search may involve, for example, the detailed description, with or without the taking of samples, or the physical seizure of the infringing goods, the materials and implements used in the production and/or distribution of these goods and the documents (including digitally stored information) relating thereto. The claimant's request may be denied in consideration of the privacy or trade secrets of the alleged infringer or

659. Cf. s. 44 para. 2 of the Act.
660. Cf. s. 44 para. 3 of the Act.
661. Cf. s. 44 para. 4 of the Act.
662. In general on measures for preserving evidence, *see* Petersen, C.S., P.M. Hansen & T. Riis. Judicielle forbud/påbud og immaterialretsproces. Copenhagen: 2015, Chs 7 and 8.
663. Cf. s. 653 para. 1 of the Act on Civil Proceedings.

if the interest of the claimant in the search is disproportionate to the harm the search is likely to cause on the alleged infringer.[664] The bailiff's court can decide to search the premises of the alleged infringer without the alleged infringer having been heard where there is a demonstrable risk of evidence being destroyed, removed or amended.[665] The search is an interim measure, and the claimant shall within four weeks after the bailiff's court decision on a search initiate a civil proceeding in respect of the alleged infringement of the search concern.[666]

F. Right of Information[667]

361. The provisions in Chapter 29a (sections 306–307) of the Act on Civil Proceedings were adopted in 2006 and implement Article 8 of the Enforcement Directive. This 'right of information' is an innovation in Danish law and, similar to the provisions in Chapter 57a of the Act on Civil Proceedings on Search, the provisions in Chapter 29a only apply in cases of infringement of intellectual property rights. On the request of the claimant, the court can order that the infringer and/or any other person provides information on goods or services that infringe an intellectual property right, provided the person in question:

(a) was found in possession of the infringing goods on a commercial scale;
(b) was found to be using the infringing services on a commercial scale;
(c) was found to be providing on a commercial scale services used in infringing activities; or
(d) was indicated by the person referred to in point (a), (b) or (c) as being involved in the production, manufacture or distribution of the goods or the provision of the services.[668]

The information that shall be provided includes:

(a) the names and addresses of the producers, manufacturers, distributors, suppliers and other previous holders of the goods or services, as well as the intended wholesalers and retailers the goods or services in question were aimed at, and
(b) information on the quantities produced, manufactured, delivered, received or ordered, as well as the price obtained for the goods or services in question.[669]

The provisions on the right of information enable that in a court case between A and B, C can be ordered to provide information on D, even though the information

664. Cf. s. 653 para. 4 of the Act on Civil Proceedings.
665. Cf. s. 653a para. 2 of the Act on Civil Proceedings.
666. Cf. s. 653c para. 1 of the Act on Civil Proceedings.
667. In general on the right of information, *see* Petersen, C.S., P.M. Hansen & T. Riis. Judicielle forbud/påbud og immaterialretsproces. Copenhagen: 2015, Ch. 9.
668. Cf. s. 306 para. 1 of the Act on Civil Proceedings.
669. Cf. s. 306 para. 2 of the Act on Civil Proceedings.

is of no relevance in the conflict between A and B. In this way, the right of information departs from the tradition of the Danish law on civil procedure because, according to the general principle of the law on civil procedure, the courts shall deny all requests and evidence that bear no relevance to the litigated conflict. The right of information creates a risk of abuse of the procedural system; however, as the main safeguard against abuse, the court may deny a request if it must be assumed that the interest of the claimant in the information is disproportionate to the harm the provision of the information may cause on the person providing the information or on other persons.[670]

G. *Penalties*

362. Trademark infringement may involve criminal liability. According to section 42 paragraph 1 of the Act, intentional infringement of a trademark established by registration or by commencement of use shall be punished by a fine. Under aggravating circumstances, including in particular if the purpose of the violation is a significant and obviously unlawful profit, punishment may increase to ordinary imprisonment of not more than one year and six months. Hence, grossly negligent acts do not incur criminal liability. Proceedings in respect of violations comprised by section 42 paragraph 1, first sentence, shall be brought by the injured party. Proceedings in respect of other violations (i.e., 'under aggravating circumstances') shall be brought by the State at the request of the injured party.[671] A company, etc. (legal persons) may be subject to criminal liability according to the rules of Chapter 5 of the Civil Penal Code.[672] Criminal liability under the Civil Penal Code requires, among other things, that the infringement can be imputed to a natural person who is associated with the legal person. The penalty provisions are seldom used in trademark infringement cases.

H. *Publication of Judgments*

363. When the Enforcement Directive (2004/48/EC) was implemented, a new provision on publication of judgments was included in the Act. In a judgment in which someone is sentenced according to section 43 or 44 (liability and destruction, etc.), the court may upon request decide that the judgment shall be published in full or in part. The obligation to publish rests with the offender. Publication shall be arranged at the offender's expense and in as prominent a way as can reasonably be expected.[673]

670. Cf. s. 306 para. 3 of the Act on Civil Proceedings.
671. Cf. s. 42 para. 4 of the Trademarks Act.
672. Cf. s. 42 para. 3 of the Trademarks Act.
673. Cf. s. 44a paras 1–2.

§11. Overlapping and Relation to Other Intellectual Property Laws

364. Protectable subject matter under the Trademarks Act is trademarks as such. Distinctive business emblems other than trademarks are protectable under various rules outside the scope of the Trademarks Act, in particular, section 22 of the Marketing Practice Act and the company law provisions concerning trade names (On the protection of trade names, *see infra* under Chapter 5).

365. Normally, signs that in a general way characterize the exterior visual appearance of a company – for example, shopfronts and staff uniforms – are not considered trademarks within the meaning of the Trademarks Act. Instead, such signs may be protected under section 22 of the Marketing Practice Act. By virtue of section 22 of the Marketing Practice Act, traders must not use business identifiers and similar devices that do not belong to them, nor use their own business identifiers in a manner that is likely to cause confusion with those of others.

366. Trade dress and get-up are protectable subject matter under the Trademarks Act, cf. section 2 paragraph 1. When this kind of subject matter was introduced into the Act in 1936, an important issue was how to delimit trademark protection in relation to protection under design rights and patent rights. Trademark protection cannot be extended to the technical or functional elements of the goods. Such protection is only available under patent law and utility model law. Trademark protection of trade dress and get-up does not exclude protection under the Designs Act; however, significant differences exist as to the conditions of protection and the scope of protection under the Trademarks Act and the Designs Act respectively.[674] If a specific trade dress does not satisfy the conditions of protection under the Designs Act, the industrial design comprised in the trade dress is not protectable as such under the Trademarks Act; trademark protection only relates to the part of the trade dress that constitutes a distinctive business mark.[675]

674. Cf. Report No. 199, *En ny dansk lov om varemærker* (Copenhagen, 1958), 105 ff.
675. *See* J. Schovsbo, 'Varemærkeretlig beskyttelse af industrielt design?', *Nordiskt Immateriellt Rättsskydd* (1996): 53–68.

Chapter 5. Trade Names

§1. Sources – Legislation

367. Trade names are governed by various provisions of the Acts related to company law in addition to section 22 of the Marketing Practice Act.[676] The former Acts comprise the Companies Act,[677] the Act on Undertakings Carrying on Business for Profit[678] and the Act on Commercial Foundations.[679]

§2. The Protection of Trade Names

I. Public Companies, Private Companies and Commercial Foundations

368. The name of a public-limited company carrying on business for profit subject to the Companies Act (*aktieselskab*; contracted to A/S) shall be registered in the central register administered by the Danish Business Authority (*Erhvervsstyrelsen*). The same applies to the name of a private company carrying on business for profit (*anpartsselskab*; contracted to ApS), and the name of a commercial foundation. Where an application for registration of a trademark is filed, the Patent and Trademark Office searches the register of company names. However, the Danish Business Authority does not search the Trademark Register prior to registration of a company name.[680] Accordingly, the validity of a registered company name is uncertain. If the Danish Business Authority refuses to register a company name, the decision may be appealed to the Company Appeals Board (*Erhvervsankenævnet*). The owner of an earlier company name cannot file oppositions with the Danish Business Authority. If anyone believes that a registration is detrimental to him/her, the question of deleting such registration shall be decided by the courts of law. Actions to this effect shall be instituted against the company not later than six months after the announcement of the registration in the database system of the Authority. The court shall send a transcript to the Danish Business Authority.[681] Presumably, the six-month time limit only applies to claims based on the Companies Act and the Act on Commercial Foundations.[682]

676. Consolidated Act No. 866 of 15 Jun. 2022.
677. Consolidated Act No. 168 of 1 Sep. 2023.
678. Consolidated Act No. 249 of 1 Feb. 2021.
679. Consolidated Act No. 984 of 20 Sep. 2019.
680. *See Ugeskrift for Retsvæsen* 1990.544 SH.
681. Cf. s. 20 paras 1 and 2 of the Companies Act. A similar provision is contained in s. 21 paras 1 and 2 of the Act on Commercial Foundations.
682. Cf. M. Koktvedgaard, *Lærebog i konkurrenceret*, 3rd edn (Copenhagen: Jurist- og Økonomforbundets Forlag, 1997), 312.

369. A company name shall consist of words or word combinations, and hence, device marks cannot be registered according to the Companies Act and the Act on Commercial Foundations. All company names are eligible for protection under the Trademarks Act.[683]

370. Public-limited companies are under an obligation to and have an exclusive right to use the word '*aktieselskab*' or any contractions derived therefrom, and private companies are under an obligation to and have an exclusive right to use the word '*anpartsselskab*' or the contraction 'ApS' in their name.[684] Commercial foundations are under an obligation to use the word '*fond*' (foundation) in their name but do not have an exclusive right hereto.[685]

371. By virtue of section 2 paragraph 2 of the Companies Act, the names of companies shall differ clearly from each other. The name must not include surnames, names of firms, specific names of real property, trademarks, distinctive business marks, etc., that do not belong to the company or anything that may be confused therewith. A similar provision is contained in section 5 paragraph 3 of the Act on Commercial Foundations. Case law related to these provisions to a certain extent parallels case law dealing with trademark infringement, for example, by emphasizing the distinctive character of the names and the likelihood of confusion. Accordingly, a coined and fanciful company name with a high degree of distinctiveness is granted relatively strong protection compared to a descriptive or suggestive name. In the case reported in *Ugeskrift for Retsvæsen* 1952.1133 SH, a company had registered the trademark 'Boco' for agricultural machinery and agricultural implements. A subsequent registration of the company name 'A/S Boco Plastic' for a public company producing various plastic items primarily toys and buttons was found to violate the pertinent provision of the Companies Act due to the plaintiff's trademark. The court argued that 'Boco' was a word without semantic content, and combined with the predominant significance of the word in the defendant's company name, the public may perceive the defendant's company as being related to the plaintiff who had used the trademark extensively and thereby enhanced the distinctive character of the mark. In *Ugeskrift for Retsvæsen* 1994.128 V, a public company named 'Euro Plast A/S' claimed that the name of the defendant public company 'Europlast Vinduer og Døre A/S' infringed the right of the plaintiff by virtue of section 2 paragraph 2 of the Companies Act. The court found that the plaintiff's name was protected under section 2 paragraph 2; however, the name was a combination of two common words and therefore did not have a high degree of distinctiveness. Furthermore, since the two companies did not produce the same kinds of products (plastic bags and doors/windows, respectively) and, consequently, did not share the same customers, the court held that there was no likelihood of confusion between the two company names and the plaintiff's claim was dismissed.

683. Cf. s. 2 para. 1 of the Trademarks Act.
684. Cf. s. 2 para. 1 of the Companies Act.
685. Cf. s. 5 para. 1 of the Act on Commercial Foundations.

372. The protection of company names applies to the territory of the State and is not limited to smaller geographical regions even if the company is a small local company unknown in large parts of the country. In principle, the protection of company names extends to company names used in other lines of business. However, case law is ambiguous on this point. In *Ugeskrift for Retsvæsen* 1991.216 Ø, 'Neotek' was the distinctive part of the plaintiff's company name,[686] but nevertheless, protection against the defendant's identical company name 'Neotek' was refused on the grounds that the two companies were effective within different lines of business, and being different in respect of the kinds of goods produced (film processing machines and plastic items for office use), clientele and marketing. Consequently, the court found that the two company names were not likely to be confused. The Supreme Court decision reported in *Ugeskrift for Retsvæsen* 1999.1406 H created uncertainty as to whether similarity of the industries is a significant element in assessing likelihood of confusion in respect of two company names. In that case, the plaintiff, an undertaking named 'Multi Choice', was protected against another company's use of the name 'Multi-choice Danmark A/S' in spite of the two companies belonging to two separated industries. Subsequent case law from the Supreme Court[687] indicates that similarity of the industries still is a significant element in assessing likelihood of confusion in respect of two company names, and the reason for the decision in *Ugeskrift for Retsvæsen* 1999.1406 H was that the plaintiff demonstrated a substantial number of cases of actual confusion.

373. The name of a company must not be likely to mislead. It must not include any specification of undertakings that have no connection with the objects of the company. If the name describes a specific activity, it must not be maintained in that form if the nature of the activities changes significantly, cf. section 2 paragraph 3 of the Companies Act. A prohibition of misleading names is included into section 5 paragraph 3 of the Act on Commercial Foundations. Where a company name includes the name of a city or another specific place, the activities of the company shall be related to that place. However, if the relation to the specific place ceases and the company name has been used extensively, it can be maintained. The use of plurals in the company name as a prefix or suffix, for example, 'united', requires that two or more companies actually have been united or merged. Company names in the form of foreign language words are not deemed as names of foreign companies and thus are not likely to mislead.

In respect of branches of foreign companies, the branch name shall include the company name with the addition of the word '*filial*' (branch) as well as a clear indication of the nationality of the company.[688]

---

686. The entire name was 'Maskinfabrikken Neotek, Ringsted ApS'. 'Maskinfabrikken" means 'the engine works' and 'Ringsted' is the name of a town.
687. *Ugeskrift for Retsvæsen* 2003.107 H.
688. Cf. s. 347 para. 1 of the Companies Act.

II. Undertakings Carrying on Business for Profit

374. The Act on Undertakings Carrying on Business for Profit[689] applies to all commercial companies that are not subject to the Acts of company law mentioned *supra*. According to section 1 paragraph 2 of the Act, for the purpose of the Act, undertakings means sole traders, partnerships, limited partnerships, cooperatives (cooperative societies) and other limited liability businesses and societies to which the Companies Act or the Act on Commercial Foundations does not apply. Branches of similar foreign undertakings are also governed by the Act on Undertakings Carrying on Business for Profit.

375. For the purpose of the Act on Undertakings Carrying on Business for Profit, the name of an undertaking means the name under which the undertaking exercises its business or any part of such business and which is applied when signing for the undertaking.[690] The name of a limited liability undertaking[691] shall be registered in the central register administered by the Danish Business Authority.[692] The name of an undertaking that is not a limited liability undertaking – that is, sole traders, partnerships and limited partnerships[693] – shall not and cannot be registered according to the Act on Undertakings Carrying on Business for Profit.

376. A provision similar to section 2 paragraph 2 of the Companies Act stating that names of undertakings shall differ clearly from each other is contained in section 6 paragraph 2 of the Act on Undertakings Carrying on Business for Profit. Similar to company names protected under company law, protection of registered names of undertakings applies to the territory of the State. In the preparatory works of the Act, it is said that the requirement in section 6 paragraph 2, according to which the names of undertakings shall differ clearly from each other, has to be construed more narrowly in relation to unregistered names of undertakings since the practical needs in relation to protection of unregistered names of undertakings imply that it is sufficiently for an unregistered name of an undertaking to differ clearly from names used within the local area.

377. Section 6 paragraph 3 of the Act prohibits misleading names of undertakings on the same lines as section 2 paragraph 3 of the Companies Act. By virtue of section 6 paragraph 4, partnerships, limited partnerships and cooperatives (cooperative societies) may use those designations, or abbreviations thereof, in their names. None others may use these designations, or designations that may be confused therewith.

---

689. Consolidated Act No. 249 of 1 Feb. 2021.
690. Cf. s. 6 para. 1 of the Act.
691. A limited liability undertaking means an undertaking in which none of the members are personally and jointly and severally liable without limitation, cf. s. 3 of the Act.
692. Cf. s. 8 of the Act.
693. A limited partnership means an undertaking in which one or more members, the general partners, are personally and jointly and severally liable, without limitation, for the debts and obligations of the undertaking, whereas one or more members, the limited partners, have limited liability for the debts and obligations of the undertaking, cf. s. 2 para. 2 of the Act.

Where anyone retires as a liable member of an undertaking, his/her name may be retained in the name of the undertaking if permission from the person concerned or his/her heirs has been obtained.[694] The name of a limited liability undertaking shall contain information about the limitation of liability. The only abbreviation permitted for limited liability cooperatives is 'A.M.B.A'.[695] A branch of a foreign undertaking shall include the word '*filial*' (branch) and clearly indicate the nationality of the undertaking.[696]

378. Oppositions against the registration of the name of an undertaking cannot be filed with the Danish Business Authority, and the decision of the Danish Business Authority cannot be appealed to a higher administrative authority. Where anyone believes that a registration is detrimental to him/her, the question of deleting such registration shall be decided by the courts of law. Actions to this effect shall be instituted against the undertaking within six months of the publication of the registration.[697] The same principle applies under the Companies Act.

III. Section 22 of the Marketing Practice Act

379. The general rule on protection of distinctive business marks dates back to 1912 and is now found in section 22 of the Marketing Practice Act. By virtue of section 22 of the Marketing Practice Act, traders must not use business identifiers and similar devices that do not belong to them, nor use their own business identifiers in a manner that is likely to cause confusion with those of others.

380. The first part of section 22 prohibits the commercial use of marks to which the user is not legally entitled. Legal entitlement to a mark can be obtained by the registration of a company name, the name of an undertaking, a trademark, or the law of personal names. The second part of section 22 concerns marks to which a person is legally entitled and the person's own coined marks. Such marks can be used commercially as long as they are not likely to be confused with other marks.

381. Protection of names of companies and undertakings under the pertinent Acts does not preclude protection under section 22 of the Marketing Practice Act. One may question whether there is a practical need of section 22 considering the various provisions mentioned *supra* in addition to the protection provided by the Trademarks Act. Section 22 differs in one important respect from the other provisions related to trademarks, trade names and company names since protection under section 22 may be confined to a local area as opposed to countrywide protection. Wide geographical protection may be found to be too comprehensive in matters of only local interest, and in such matters, the law provides adequate protection by means of section 22. Usually, claims related to infringement of company names and

694. Cf. s. 6 para. 5 of the Act.
695. Cf. s. 6 para. 6 of the Act.
696. Cf. s. 6 para. 8 of the Act.
697. Cf. s. 17 paras 1 and 2 of the Act.

trade names are based on the specific provisions on company names and trade names in addition to the general rule in section 22 of the Marketing Practice Act. Furthermore, one should note that where a person claims that a registered company name shall be deleted, court actions to that effect shall be instituted not later than six months after the announcement of the registration; the six-month time limit does not apply to a similar claim based on section 22 of the Marketing Practice Act.

Chapter 6. Industrial Designs

§1. Sources – Legislation

382. The first Danish Act on Industrial Designs was adopted in 1905.[698] Comprehensive cooperation between the Nordic countries regarding design rights took place in the 1960s and resulted in the Danish Designs Act of 1970. The contents of the 1970 Act were similar to the corresponding acts of the other Nordic countries. The valid Designs Act is at present consolidated Act No. 89 of 29 October 2019.[699]

The Directive 98/71/EC of the European Parliament and of the Council of 13 October 1998 on the legal protection of designs was implemented by the 2000 Act, which resulted in significant amendments compared to the previous Designs Act.

383. Denmark is a party to the Paris Convention for the Protection of Industrial Property since 1894 and has acceded to the Locarno Agreement Establishing an International Classification for Industrial Designs Signed at Locarno on 8 October 1968. Denmark has not acceded to the Hague Agreement Concerning the International Deposit of Industrial Designs of 6 November 1925.

384. At the beginning of the century, substantial protection of various forms of creations of applied arts was not available. The first Act on Industrial Designs was adopted in response to a practical need for legal protection of such creations. The extension of copyrightable subject matter to works of applied art has to a significant extent in many areas reduced the practical needs for protection by design rights.

§2. Subject Matter of Protection

385. Protectable subject matter under the Act are 'designs'. A design within the meaning of the Act is defined in section 2 paragraph (i) of the Act as the appearance of a product or part of a product resultant from the features of, in particular, the lines, contours, colour, shape, texture or material of the product and its ornamentation. A 'product' shall in the Designs Act mean any industrial or handicraft item, including parts intended to be assembled into a complex product, packaging, get-up, graphic symbols and typographic typefaces, however, excluding computer programs.[700] A 'complex product' shall mean a product composed of multiple components that can be replaced, permitting disassembly and reassembly of the product.[701]

---

698. Act No. 107 of 1 Apr. 1905.

699. Under the provisions of the Act a number of orders have been issued: Order No. 1099 of 20 Nov. 2008 on the Application and Registration of Industrial Designs; Order No. 1079 of 17 Nov. 2008 on the Coming into Force of Ch. 10 of the Designs Act; Order No. 12 of 12 Jan. 2012 on the remuneration of the Patent and Trademark Office for the performance of tasks, specific transactions and transcripts, etc. and Order No. 1578 of 14 Dec. 2016 on a special unit in the Patent and Trademark Office on enforcement and piracy.

700. Section 2 para. (ii) of the Act.

701. Section 2 para. (iii) of the Act.

The definition of a design comprises two-dimensional as well as three-dimensional designs. Semi-manufacturers and parts of larger products are protectable subject matter under the Act, provided such articles are offered for sale independently of the larger product. Hence, for example, spare parts for automobiles are eligible for protection.[702]

Similar to copyright, protection by design rights is related to the appearance of an article; however, designs are not presupposed to have an aesthetical or ornamental element or intention. Consequently, protectable subject matter under the Designs Act extends to various industrial goods. In practice, most applications for design protection concern household articles, tools, hardware, packaging, building units, spare parts, etc., which normally are not eligible for copyright protection.

386. Whether the specific appearance of a design is dictated by aesthetic or functional considerations is not relevant in determining the protectable subject matter, but the exclusive rights granted under the Act do not protect the technical function of the design – only the appearance of the design. Thus, it is a fundamental principle of design law that it grants no protection of the functionality of the design.[703] The idea of a design is not protectable; only the specific expression of the design qualifies for protection. Older case law was rigorous in enforcing this principle and numerous design rights were held to be invalid because they had functional features. Using the present more lenient assessment, many of these designs would probably be held to be protectable under the Act. Nevertheless, the Industrial Property Board of Appeal (*Ankenævnet for Industriel Ejendomsret*) has rejected an application for design protection of a wine bottle with a measuring scale on the ground that protection would apply to the idea of integrating a measuring scale into a wine bottle irrespective that the idea may have been new.[704] In the case reported in *Ugeskrift for Retsvæsen* 1990.334 SH, the Maritime and Commercial Court decided that the basic form of a T-diaper (i.e., a diaper shaped in the form of a T) was not eligible for protection under the Designs Act. In reaching its decision, the court emphasized that the shape of a T-diaper can only be varied in a limited number of ways due to technical and economic considerations related to the production. However, the specific form of the diaper was eligible for protection under the Act. In the case reported in *Nordiskt Immateriellt Rättsskydd* 1985.322, the design for a garage door was found to be protectable under the Act, contrary to three elements that could be included in the garage door construction, among them a design for a garage door window. The Eastern Court of Appeal held that the three elements viewed as creations did not constitute designs within the meaning of the Act. According to the court, these elements were merely figures specifying the precise form of the protectable garage door.

702. On design protection of automobile spare parts *see* J. Schovsbo & N.H. Svendsen. *Designret*. 2nd edn (Copenhagen: Jurist-og Økonomforbundet Forlag, 2013) 112 f and 151 ff., *See also* the special provision in s. 23, para. 2 on the term of protection for certain designs.
703. Cf. s. 8 para. 1 subpara. (1) of the Act.
704. Decision of 19 Jan. 1990 (Case M 7/88).

387. By virtue of section 1 of the Act, the creator of a design or his/her successor in title may acquire by registration in accordance with the Act the exclusive right to the design. Accordingly, a design within the meaning of the Act has to be created by humans, and phenomena existing in nature, such as flowers and animals, are not protectable subject matter. However, depictions of such phenomena are eligible for protection under the Act.

388. In delimiting protectable subject matter under the Designs Act, one should note that a design right comes into existence by registration. Apart from the unregistered design right of the Design Regulation (6/2002/EC), unregistered design rights do not exist in Danish law.

By virtue of section 7 paragraph 1 subparagraph (i) of the Act, a design right shall not subsist where the design conflicts with public policy or accepted principles of morality. The provision is very seldom used. Additionally, pursuant to section 7 paragraph 1 subparagraph (ii), a design right shall not subsist where the design conflicts with a prior design that has been made available to the public after the filing date of the application or, if priority is claimed, the date of priority provided the application date of the prior design precedes the application date of the design in question. The provision of section 7 paragraph 1 subparagraph (ii) supplements the requirement of novelty stipulated in section 3 of the Act. Finally, according to section 7 paragraph 1 subparagraph (iii), a design right shall not subsist where the design (a) constitutes use of any of the items listed in Article 6c of the Paris Convention for the Protection of Industrial Property or other badges, emblems and escutcheons not covered by Article 6c of the said Convention, which are of particular public interest, (b) includes a trademark, trade name or distinctive sign of real property of another person, (c) constitutes use of a work protected by copyright laws and (d) contains a prior design.

§3. Conditions of Protection

389. The conditions of protection are stated in section 3 of the Act. Accordingly, a design right can only be obtained where the design is new and has individual character. In respect of the requirement of novelty, a design shall be deemed new if no identical design has been available to the public before the filing date of the application for registration or, if priority is claimed, the date of priority. Designs shall be deemed to be identical where their features differ only in immaterial details.[705] In respect of the requirement of individual character, a design shall be deemed to have individual character where the overall impression it produces on the informed user differs from the overall impression produced on such user by any design that has been available to the public before the filing date of the application or, if priority is claimed, the date of priority. In assessing the individual character of a design, the degree of freedom of the designer in developing the design shall be taken into consideration.[706]

705. Section 3 para. 2 of the Act.
706. Section 3 para. 3 of the Act.

A design of a component in a complex product shall only be deemed to be new and have an individual character where: (i) the component upon being incorporated into the complex product remains visible during normal use of the product and (ii) the visible features of the component comply with the requirements as to novelty and individual character.[707] 'Normal use' shall mean use of the complex product by the end-user, excluding maintenance, servicing or repair work.[708]

The concept of 'public availability', which is crucial in determining whether the conditions of protection are satisfied, is further specified in section 5 of the Act; thus, a design shall be deemed to have been made available to the public where it has been published following a registration or otherwise made public, or has been displayed, exploited commercially or otherwise disclosed.[709] A design shall not, however, be deemed to have been made available to the public where: (i) the circumstances stated in section 5 paragraph 1 could not reasonably have become known in the normal course of business to the circles specialized in the sector concerned, operating within the Community, before the filing date of the application or, if priority is claimed, the date of priority or (ii) the design has been disclosed to a third party under explicit or implicit conditions of confidentiality.[710]

390. By the 2000 Act, a grace period was introduced in Danish design law. A design shall not be deemed to have been made available to the public where it has been published during the twelve-month period preceding the filing date of the application or, if priority is claimed, the date of priority: (i) by the designer, his/her successor in title or a third party as a result of information provided or steps taken by the designer, or his/her successor in title, or (ii) as a consequence of abuse in relation to the designer or his/her successor in title.[711]

391. In respect of the requirements of novelty and individual character in section 3, a design may nevertheless be registered where an application for registration is filed in Denmark within six months after the design has been displayed for the first time at an official or officially recognized international exhibition, the application shall on request of the applicant obtain priority from this date. The exhibitions referred to be such exhibitions as defined in the Convention on International Exhibitions, signed in Paris on 22 November 1928, subsequently revised on 30 November 1972.[712]

392. Section 16 of the Act implements the obligations arising under Article 4 of the Paris Convention regarding right of priority. According to section 16 paragraph 1, where a design is contained in an application for registration of a design or for protection of a utility model in another State that is party to the Paris Convention of 20 March 1883 for the Protection of Industrial Property, or that is a member of the

707. Section 4 para. 1 of the Act.
708. Section 4 para. 2 of the Act.
709. Section 5 para. 1 of the Act.
710. Section 5 para. 2 of the Act.
711. Section 6 of the Act.
712. Section 16 para. 4 of the Act. The provision also applies to the conditions in s. 7 para. 1 subparas (ii) and (iii) of the Act.

WTO, and the design registration is applied for in this State within six months of the date of filing in this other State, the application shall, pursuant to sections 3 and 7(1)(ii) and (iii) of the Act, on request of the applicant be considered filed simultaneously with the application in this other State. A similar right of priority is granted in relation to applications filed in countries that have not acceded to the Paris Convention or is a member of the WTO, provided a similar right of priority applies to Danish applications under the laws of the respective countries and the laws of those countries in the main correspond to the Paris Convention.[713] Thus, a principle of reciprocity applies in this respect. Additionally, a similar right of priority applies to designs included in applications for utility model rights or design rights filed in Denmark.[714]

393. The Designs Act stipulates no requirement for industrial application.

§4. Formalities

394. According to section 1 of the Act, exclusive right to a design may be obtained through registration. Thus, the rights granted under the Act are conditioned on registration; unregistered design rights do not exist in Danish law (apart from the unregistered design right of the Design Regulation (6/2002/EC)). Provisions on the application and registration procedure are contained in Chapter II of the Act and Order No. 1099 of 20 November 2008 on the Application and Registration of Industrial Designs (the Order).

I. The Design Application

395. Applications for registration of designs shall be filed with the Patent and Trademark Office.[715] No formal requirements apply to the application; however, application forms may be requested from the Patent and Trademark Office free of charge.[716] The application shall state the name or company name of the applicant and contain a reproduction of the design.[717] The application may moreover contain a model. Where a model is filed, the model shall constitute the base for the registration of the design.[718] Where the applicant chooses to disclose the design by depositing a model, the model shall be in a small scale within the dimensional limitations specified in section 4 paragraph 3 of the Order. The application shall mention the creator of the design;[719] where the applicant is not the creator of the design, the applicant or the creator may request that the creator of the design be specified in the design register. Where the design is the result of collaboration between more

713. Section 16 para. 2 of the Act.
714. Section 16 para. 3 of the Act.
715. Cf. s. 13 para. 1 of the Act.
716. Cf. s. 1 of the Order.
717. Cf. s. 13 para. 2 of the Act.
718. Cf. s. 13 para. 3 of the Act.
719. Cf. s. 2 para. 2 of the Order.

than one designer, a specification of the group of designers in question may replace a specification of the individual designers.[720] The prescribed fees shall accompany the application.[721]

396. The Design Register is divided into classes in accordance with the Locarno Agreement and the application shall indicate to which classes the design belongs.[722]

397. The applicant may apply for multiple registration (*depôt multiple*). An application may comprise more than one design, provided the products for which the designs are to be applied are related, cf. The Locarno arrangement.[723] The provision is aimed at certain groups of articles that are closely related. When an application for multiple registration is filed, the applicant may claim right of priority in relation to one or more of the designs. Such a right of priority may be claimed on the basis of several applications, even if these applications are filed in different countries. If right of priority is claimed on the basis of several applications, the priority date of the first application applies.[724]

398. An application may not be altered so as to relate to a design other than the design stated in the application.[725] The provision precludes the applicant from subsequently extending the scope of the application; however, it does not prevent the applicant from reducing the scope of the application.

An applicant may divide an application that concerns several designs into several individual applications. These individual applications are deemed to be filed at the same date as the original application.[726]

II. Examination

399. The Patent and Trademark Office shall ensure that the application relates to a design, cf. section 2 paragraph (i) of the Act. Furthermore, the Office examines that the provision of section 7 paragraph 1 subparagraph (i) (conflicts with public policy or accepted principles of morality) does not obstruct registration and, furthermore, that the application only contains one design.[727] In addition, the applicant may request the Patent and Trademark Office to examine other matters of significance for the design right to the knowledge of the Office. The applicant shall for the request pay the prescribed fee.[728] Where the applicant has requested such a supplementary examination, the Patent and Trademark Office searches all valid Danish design registrations and pending applications for designs, in addition to the Danish

720. Cf. s. 13 para. 4 of the Act.
721. Cf. s. 13 para. 5 of the Act.
722. Cf. ss 2 para. 1 subpara. 4 and 17–18 of the Order.
723. Cf. s. 15 of the Act.
724. Cf. s. 8 of the Order.
725. Cf. s. 14 para. 2 of the Act.
726. Cf. ss 22 and 23 of the Order.
727. Cf. s. 17 para. 1 of the Act. *See* however s. 15 of the Act.
728. Cf. s. 17 para. 2 of the Act.

design registrations that have been deleted within the last five years.[729] On the basis of the supplementary examination, the Patent and Trademark Office creates a search report that is sent to the applicant.[730]

The mandatory examination is limited to establish whether the formal requirements have been met. The supplementary examination and the search report provide guidelines for the applicant and cannot in itself result in the rejection of registration.[731] Consequently, the applicant has no certainty as to the validity of the subsequent registration.

400. Where the application complies with the rules and regulations and no objection has been found to registration, the design shall be registered. The registration is published by the Patent and Trademark Office. Publication may be deferred for up to six months counted from the filing date or, if priority is claimed, the date of priority provided the applicant so requests in his/her application.[732]

Where the applicant has not observed the rules and regulations laid down for the application, or the Patent and Trademark Office otherwise finds objections to the registration of the application, the Patent and Trademark Office shall notify the applicant accordingly and invite him/her to file his/her observations or to take steps to correct his/her application within a fixed time limit.[733] Where the applicant fails within expiry of the time limit to file his/her observations or to take steps to correct the application, the application shall be shelved.[734] The examination of the application may be re-established on request of the applicant, provided he/she files his/her observations or takes steps to correct the application within two months after expiry of the fixed time limit and, within the same time limit, pays the prescribed re-establishment fee. Re-establishment may be granted only once.[735] Where the Patent and Trademark Office finds any objection to granting registration after the applicant has had an opportunity to file his/her observations on the objection, the application shall be rejected unless the Patent and Trademark Office finds grounds for renewing the request pursuant to section 19 paragraph 1.[736]

III. Oppositions

401. Where the application is in the prescribed form and no objection has been found to registration, the application is published in order to give the public an opportunity to enter oppositions. From the date when the application is laid open to public inspection, the application documents shall be available to everyone.[737]

729. Cf. s. 11 para. 1 of the Order.
730. Cf. s. 12 para. 1 of the Order.
731. Cf. s. 12 para. 2 of the Order.
732. Cf. s. 18 of the Act.
733. Cf. s. 19 para. 1 of the Act.
734. Cf. s. 19 para. 2 of the Act.
735. Cf. s. 19 para. 3 of the Act.
736. Cf. s. 19 para. 4 of the Act.
737. Cf. s. 21 para. 1 of the Act.

Any person may, when a design has been registered with the Patent and Trademark Office, file a request for complete or partial cancellation of the registration. The request may exclusively be reasoned by: (i) the registration not complying with sections 1–8, (ii) the application being amended contrary to section 14 paragraph 2, (iii) the provisions of section 15 not being complied with, and (iv) the registration being maintained for more than fifteen years, contrary to section 23 paragraph 2.[738] The opposition shall be reasoned and accompanied by documentation.[739] Where another person other than the registered owner of the design registration has filed the request, the registered owner shall be informed of the submitted material and invited to file his/her observations.[740]

Where an objection exists to the maintenance of a design registration in accordance with a decision pursuant to the provisions referred to *supra*, the registration shall be cancelled by the Patent and Trademark Office. The Office shall moreover cancel the registration where the registered owner of the design renounces his/her right.[741] Where the Patent and Trademark Office based on a request finds no grounds for complete or partial cancellation of the registration, the request is dismissed and the registration is maintained.[742]

IV. Appeals

402. The applicant may file appeals with the Patent and Trademark Board of Appeal against the final decision of the Patent and Trademark Office regarding a design application. The same applies for the registered owner of the design where a design registration is completely or partially cancelled. Where the design registration is maintained in an amended or original form, the decision may be appealed against by the person having filed the request for complete or partial cancellation of the design registration. Where the latter withdraws his/her appeal, the appeal may nevertheless be examined, provided there exist special grounds for such action.[743] Appeals are filed with the Patent and Trademark Board of Appeal within two months after the Patent and Trademark Office has notified the party in question of the decision. The prescribed fee for appeal shall be paid within the same time limit. Failure to do so shall result in dismissal of the appeal. Filing an appeal with the Patent and Trademark Board of Appeal has a suspensive effect.[744] The decisions of the Patent and Trademark Board of Appeal may not be brought before another administrative authority.[745] Decisions of the Patent and Trademark Office, which may be brought before the Patent and Trademark Board of Appeal, may not be brought before the courts before the decision of the Patent and Trademark Board of

738. Cf. s. 25 para. 1 of the Act.
739. Cf. s. 26 para. 1 of the Act and s. 19 of the Order.
740. Cf. s. 26 para. 2 of the Act.
741. Cf. s. 32 para. 1 of the Act.
742. Cf. s. 32 para. 2 of the Act.
743. Cf. s. 34 of the Act.
744. Cf. s. 35 para. 1 of the Act.
745. Cf. s. 35 para. 2 of the Act.

Appeal is available. Where a party wants to bring a decision of the Patent and Trademark Board of Appeal before the courts, the proceedings shall be instituted within two months of the day the party in question was notified of the decision. The proceedings shall have a suspensive effect.[746]

403. Registrations, renewals and terminations are published in the *Design Gazette* (*Dansk Designtidende*), which is published by the Patent and Trademark Office.[747]

§5. Ownership and Transfer

404. The right to apply for design protection originates in the creator of the design. This fundamental feature is reflected in section 13 paragraph 3 of the Act, according to which the creator may request that the creator of the design be specified in the design register. By virtue of section 1, the creator of a design, or his/her successor in title, may acquire by registration the exclusive right to use the design in the course of trade. Hence, the right to apply for design protection is assignable.

405. The special situation, where another than the applicant claims that he/she and not the applicant is entitled to the design, is dealt with by the provisions of sections 29 and 30 of the Act. Where any person claims to be entitled to a design registered or applied for, the Patent and Trademark Office may, finding the claim doubtful, invite him/her to institute proceedings within a fixed time limit. Where the invitation is not complied with, the claim may be disregarded. Notification to this effect shall be given in the request.[748] Where proceedings have been instituted as to the title to a design, the Patent and Trademarks Office shall suspend the examination of the application, pending the final settlement of the proceedings.[749] Where anyone proves before the Patent and Trademark Office that he/she and not the applicant or the registered owner of the design is entitled to a design comprised in a design registered or applied for, the Patent and Trademark Office shall transfer the application or registration to him/her if he/she so requests. The transferee shall pay the prescribed fee.[750] Where transfer of application or registration is requested, the application may not be amended, shelved, rejected or accepted and the registration may not be amended or cancelled, completely or partially, before the request for transfer has been finally considered.[751]

746. Cf. s. 35 para. 2 of the Act.
747. Cf. s. 16 para. 1 of the Order.
748. Cf. s. 29 para. 1 of the Act.
749. Cf. s. 29 para. 2 of the Act.
750. Cf. s. 30 para. 1 of the Act.
751. Cf. s. 30 para. 2 of the Act.

I. Transfer and Licence

406. A registered design right may be transferred in full or in part. The Designs Act does not stipulate any formal requirements in relation to transfers and licences. Consequently, oral agreements to that effect are valid. In the case of a design having been passed to another where a licence has been granted, a design has been mortgaged, execution has been levied on the design or the registered owner of the design is subject to insolvency proceedings, this shall on request be entered into the design register.[752] This notification is voluntary and not a condition of validity; however, it may have evidentiary value in specific situations.

407. Apart from the provisions in section 51 of the Act on notification in the Register, the Act does not contain provision on transfers and licences; therefore, the issue is governed by the general legal principles applying to intellectual property licences.

II. Designs Made in the Course of Employment

408. Probably most designs are made in the course of employment. Nevertheless, such designs are not subject to specific provisions of the Act. The issue was discussed in Report No. 417 Copenhagen 1966 *'En ny dansk lov om mønstre'* (pp. 85–87). The Committee that wrote the report concluded that it was inexpedient to govern the rights to designs created by employees by provisions of the Designs Act. According to the Committee, those issues should be dealt with in employment contracts or by way of special agreements.

As the main rule, it is assumed that rights to designs made in the course of employment are transferred to the employer even in the absence of an agreement to that effect. Where a registered design is protected under the Copyright Act as well, the transfer of rights is entirely governed by copyright law.[753]

§6. Scope of Exclusive Rights

409. The design right implies that no other person may exploit the design without explicit consent from the registered owner. The aforementioned exploitation includes, in particular, the making, offering, marketing, importing, exporting or use of a product to which the design is applied, or stocking such a product for those purposes.[754] The design right includes any design that does not produce on the informed user a different overall impression. In assessing the scope of the design right, the degree of freedom of the designer in developing his/her design shall be taken into consideration.[755]

752. Cf. s. 51 para. 1 of the Act.
753. Cf. Schovsbo, Rosenmeier & Petersen (2024), 483.
754. Cf. s. 9 para. 1 of the Act.
755. Cf. s. 9 para. 2 of the Act.

Normally, mere alterations in the dimensions of a design do not produce on the informed user a different overall impression. Hence, a toy car may produce the same overall impression as an ordinary car and thus infringe the design right to the ordinary car. Similarly, a change in the material in which a design-protected article is made may not produce a different overall impression.

410. The Designs Act does not grant any form of moral rights.

§7. Limitations of the Scope of Protection

411. The rights conferred by a design right do not extend to: (i) acts done for non-commercial purposes; (ii) acts done for experimental purposes;[756] or (iii) acts of reproduction for the purpose of making citations[757] or of teaching, provided that such acts are compatible with fair trade practice and do not unduly prejudice normal exploitation of the design, and reference is made to the source.[758]

412. Various provisions of the Act relate to the much-debated issue of design protection of automobile spare parts. As noted above, spare parts are protectable subject matter; however, according to section 8 paragraph 1 subparagraph (ii), a design right shall not subsist in features of the appearance of a product that must be reproduced in its exact form and dimensions in order to permit the product to which the design is applied to be mechanically connected to or placed in, on, around or against another product, to enable either product to perform its function (must fit). Section 8 paragraph 1 subparagraph (ii) is modified by section 8 paragraph 2, according to which a design right nevertheless may subsist in a design that is new and has individual character pursuant to section 3, provided the design allows for multiple assembly or connection of products within a modular system, consisting of mutually interchangeable parts. Spare parts protected under the Designs Act are subject to the provision of section 23 paragraph 2 of the Act, according to which a design registration is to be valid only for a maximum of fifteen years for a design of a component that is used in the repairs of a complex product, providing the product with its original appearance.

I. Spare Parts and Accessories for Aircraft

413. The rights conferred by a design right do not extend to: (i) equipment on ships and aircraft registered in another State when these temporarily enter the

756. The provision resembles s. 3 para. 3 subpara. (iii) of the Patents Act but is not likely to have the same practical significance as the corresponding provision of the Patents Act.
757. The provision resembles s. 22 of the Copyright Act.
758. Cf. s. 10 para. 1 of the Act.

territory of this State, and (ii) the importation to this State of spare parts and accessories for the purpose of repairing such craft and the execution of repairs on such craft.[759]

II. Exhaustion

414. The rights conferred by a design right does not extend to acts relating to a product containing a protected design when the product has been marketed in the EEA by the registered owner of the design right or with his/her consent, cf. section 12 of the Act. The provision conforms to the general principle of regional exhaustion of intellectual property rights in the EU; thus, a design right is not exhausted when a product containing a protected design is marketed in a country outside the EEA.

§8. Duration of Protection

415. A design registration is valid for the period or periods of five years, as filed for in the application, from the filing date of the application. Registration may, on request, be renewed for further periods to a total of twenty years. Each period runs from the expiry of the preceding period.[760] Application for renewal of a design registration shall be filed by paying to the Patent and Trademark Office the prescribed renewal fee not earlier than three months before and not later than six months after expiry of the registration period. Where the fee is paid after expiry of the period, an augmented fee shall be paid.[761] The Patent and Trademark Office collects the prescribed renewal fee from the registered owner of the design or his/her agent but shall not be held responsible for any loss of right as a consequence of non-collection.[762] Where the prescribed renewal fee has not been paid within six months after expiry of the registration period, the registration shall be cancelled.[763] Renewal of the registration shall be published.[764]

In conformity with section 72 of the Patents Act, section 48 of the Designs Act provides for the restoration of design registrations that have lapsed by reason of non-observance of a time limit vis-à-vis the Patent and Trademark Authority prescribed by or provided for in the Act – including time limits for payment of renewal fees. Restoration requires that the design applicant has taken all due care reasonably required. The request shall be filed with the Patent and Trademark Office within two months from the removal of the obstacle causing non-observance of the time limit but no later than one year after expiry of the time limit. The omitted action

759. Cf. s. 11 of the Act. The provision resembles s. 5 para. 2 of the Patents Act *mutatis mutandis*.
760. Cf. s. 23 para. 1 of the Act. In respect of a design of a component, which is used in the repairs of a complex product providing the product with its original appearance, the term of protection is limited to a maximum of fifteen years, cf. s. 23 para. 2 of the Act.
761. Cf. s. 24 para. 1 of the Act.
762. Cf. s. 24 para. 2 of the Act.
763. Cf. s. 24 para. 3 of the Act.
764. Cf. s. 24 para. 4 of the Act.

shall be performed, and the fee prescribed for re-establishment shall be paid within the same time limits.[765] In addition, where a registered owner of a design has failed to pay the renewal fee within the time limit as laid down in section 24 paragraph 1, the request for restoration shall be filed, and the renewal fee shall be paid not later than six months after expiry of the time limit.[766]

I. Revocation

416. A design registration may be declared completely or partially invalid by a judgment where the registration did not comply with: (i) sections 1–8 of the Act, (ii) the application was amended contrary to section 14 paragraph 2 of the Act, (iii) the provisions of section 15 have not been complied with or (iv) the registration has been maintained for more than fifteen years, contrary to section 23 paragraph 2.[767] Court proceedings shall be instituted within a year subsequent to the person in question having acquired knowledge of the registration and of other factors, on which the proceedings are based. Where the registered owner of the design acted in good faith when the design was registered or when the design right passed to him/her, the proceedings may not be instituted later than three years after the registration of the design.[768] A design may be declared invalid after the design right has been terminated or the registered owner of the design renounces his/her right.[769]

417. In certain cases, a design registration may be transferred to another person instead of being revoked. Where a design has been registered in the name of a person who is not the rightful owner as defined in section 1, the Court shall, where a claim is filed by the rightful owner, transfer the design right to him/her. Where another person is entitled to the design right, the Patent and Trademark Office shall transfer the registration to the entitled person, cf. section 31 paragraph 1 of the Act. The person who has been refused a design registration pursuant to section 31 paragraph 1 has a relatively narrow possibility of continued use of the design under conditions that resemble a compulsory licence. Accordingly, where a person disqualified from design registration in good faith has exploited the design in Denmark or has taken substantial steps for that purpose, he/she may, against payment of reasonable compensation and on fulfilment of other reasonable terms, continue commenced or commence intended exploitation, provided the general character is maintained. In similar circumstances, licensees shall enjoy the same right, cf. section 31 paragraph 2 of the Act. The rights pursuant to section 31 paragraph 2 may only pass to others with the business in which the design is exploited or in which exploitation of the design was intended.[770]

765. Cf. s. 48 para. 1 of the Act.
766. Cf. s. 48 para. 2 of the Act.
767. Cf. s. 27 para. 1 of the Act.
768. Cf. s. 27 para. 3 of the Act.
769. Cf. s. 27 para. 4 of the Act.
770. Cf. s. 31 para. 3 of the Act.

§9. INFRINGEMENT AND REMEDIES

418. The scope of protection of a registered design is determined by the specification of the design in the registration and the articles for which the design is registered. Articles that are alleged to infringe a registered design shall be compared with the registration. That is, a registered design is infringed if the alleged infringing article produces on the informed user the same overall impression as the registered design.

I. Jurisdiction

419. Civil proceedings, on the outcome of which the application of the Designs Act has considerable significance, may be brought before The Maritime and Commercial Court of Copenhagen, unless the parties agree otherwise.[771] Furthermore, The Maritime and Commercial Court of Copenhagen is the Community design Court of First Instance and the Danish Supreme Court and the two Court of Appeals are the Community design court of second instance pursuant to the Community design regulation.

II. Remedies

420. The competence of the specific unit established by the Patents and Trademark Office for the enforcement of patent rights and the combating of piracy is extended to design rights pursuant to section 41b of the Designs Act (*see supra* paragraph 235).

421. Like the other intellectual property Acts, the Designs Act does not contain provisions for injunctions. In case of infringement, interim injunctions may be rescinded according to the provisions of the Act on Civil Proceedings (*see supra* paragraphs 134 f and 236 f).

422. Section 37 of the Act on damages is identical to the corresponding provisions of the other intellectual property Acts (*see supra* paragraphs 136 f and 238 f.).

Where anyone unauthorized exploits a design sought registered after the application documents have been made available to the public, and the application results in a design registration, the provisions as to design infringement shall apply *mutatis mutandis*. However, this does not apply to the provision of section 38 (destruction, seizure and recall, etc.). Any person who commits design infringement before the application documents were made available to the public is liable to pay compensation and damages where and to the extent this is found reasonable, however, not exceeding the profit he/she is assumed to have made by the design infringement.[772]

771. Cf. s. 42 para. 1 of the Act.
772. Cf. s. 39 para. 1 of the Act. The provision is similar to s. 60 of the Patents Act.

Thus, the remedies available to an applicant who benefits from provisional protection pursuant to section 39 of the Act are restricted in certain respects. Claims for damages under section 39 shall not come to an end before one year after the registration.[773]

423. Section 36 of the Act on penalties is identical to section 57 of the Patents Act (*see supra* paragraph 243).

424. Section 38 of the Act on destruction, seizure and recall is identical to section 59 of the Patents Act (*see supra* paragraph 240).

425. Section 39a of the Act on the publication of judgments is identical to the corresponding provisions of the other intellectual property Acts (*see supra* paragraphs 142 and 244).

426. The provisions of the Act on Civil Proceedings on search and right of information (*see supra* paragraphs 139-140 and 241-242 apply to design rights.

§10. Overlapping and Relation to Other Intellectual Property Laws

427. Although design law is based on patent law principles, crucial differences exist between the two areas of intellectual property law, most notably as regards protectable subject matter. Protection by design rights should be perceived as a supplement to patent protection rather than a substitute. Protection under design law and patent law respectively is cumulative, which is quite obvious when it is taken into consideration that design law protects an article's appearance while patent law protects functional features.

428. By virtue of section 10 paragraph 1 of the Copyright Act, protection under the Designs Act does not preclude copyright. For example, in *Ugeskrift for Retsvæsen* 1978.337 H, the specific form of a wood casing of a transformer substation qualified for protection under the Designs Act as well as under the Copyright Act. Contrary to patent law, cumulative design and copyright protection relate to the same phenomenon, and that is the appearance of an article or a work.

429. Section 3 of the Marketing Practice Act, which prohibits acts that are contrary to good marketing practice, overlaps significantly with the scope of the Designs Act. Slavish copying of a product on the market may be deemed contrary to good marketing practice within the meaning of section 3 of the Marketing Practice Act and consequently unlawful. This also applies to products that are not protected under intellectual property law. Protection under section 3 of the Marketing Practice Act is not based on formalities or contingent on rigorous conditions of protection; however, it is a prerequisite that the original product has market value. More specifically, relief under section 3 of the Marketing Practice Act requires that the

773. Cf. s. 39 para. 2 of the Act.

two creations are related in the marketplace, which, for example, is the case for actual competing products and, furthermore, that the competitor has acted unfairly by his/her production, marketing or distribution activities. In cases where the scope of protection under the Designs Act and section 3 of the Marketing Practice Act overlaps, from a practical point of view, the registered design primarily has evidentiary value. According to unreported case law, it is less onerous to have an interim injunction rescinded if the design is registered. Hence, to a certain extent, the registration of a design facilitates the enforcement of rights rather than creating new rights.

Nevertheless, in other cases, section 3 of the Marketing Practice Act may provide supplementary protection for a registered design. The case reported in *Ugeskrift for Retsvæsen* 1980.578 SH concerned a registered design for a bottle. The fact that the plaintiff's registered design was not directly infringed by the defendant's bottle did not preclude that the defendant's act of marketing the same product in his own bottles was decided on the basis of section 3 of the Marketing Practice Act.

Chapter 7. Plant Variety Protection

§1. SOURCES – LEGISLATION

430. The first Danish Plant Variety Protection Act was passed in 1962. The Act was based on the principles of the International Union for the Protection of New Varieties of Plants (UPOV) Convention.[774] The Convention came into force for Denmark in 1968, which led to various amendments of the Act. Subsequently, Denmark has ratified the 1978 text of UPOV Convention and the Act was amended accordingly. A general revision of the Act took place in 1995 in order to clear the ground for the future Danish ratification of the 1991 text of the UPOV Convention. The consolidated Act is at present Act No. 1131 of 3 July 2020.[775] The Act is administered by the Danish Agricultural Agency Plant Directorate (*Landbrugsstyrelsen*).[776]

431. The Council Regulation 2100/94/EC of 27 July 1994 on Community plant variety rights has no direct implications on the Danish Plant Variety Protection Act and a person is free to choose whether to apply for plant variety right under the Council Regulation or under the Danish Act. However, the Council Regulation precludes protection of the same variety under the Council Regulation as well as under national law. By virtue of Article 107 of the Council Regulation, Member States shall take all appropriate measures to ensure that the same provisions are made applicable to penalize infringements of community plant variety rights as applied in the matter of infringements of corresponding national rights. In order to meet this obligation, Act No. 301 of 10 May 1995 on the applicability of The EC Regulation on Community Plant Variety Rights has been adopted conferring on the Minister of Food, Agriculture and Fisheries the powers to issue regulations to that effect. The Minister has used his powers to issue Order No. 630 of 20 July 1995.

§2. SUBJECT MATTER OF PROTECTION

432. New, uniform and stable plant varieties may, on application filed with the Board for Plant Novelties (*Plantenyhedsnævnet*), be granted protection under the Act. According to section 1 paragraph 1 of the Act, varieties of species and genera

---

774. Union internationale pour la protection des obtentions végétales. However, it was disputed whether the Act was in conformity with the Convention, *see* M. Plesner, 'Retslig beskyttelse af biologiske produkter – her: Planter', *Nordiskt Immateriellt Rättsskyd* (1978): 89.

775. Under the provisions of the Act various orders have been issued. The most important are Order No. 76 of 29 Jan. 2020 on Propagation of Plant Novelties for Professional Use on a Person's Own Holding; Order No. 1010 of 26 Jun. 2020 1690 on Payment for Tasks related to Inclusion on the List of Plant Varieties etc.; Order No. 1095 of 1 Jun. 2021 on Plant Variety Denominations; and Order No. 1013 of 26 Jun. 2020 on the Board for Plant Novelties.

776. In general on plant variety protection, *see* Lars Karnøe (ed.), *Immaterialret. Indhold – værdiansættelse – skat* (Copenhagen: Thomson Reuters, 2008), 111–162.

of plantsw may be protected as plant novelties, provided the conditions of protection are satisfied. Varieties made by improvement as well as varieties found in nature are eligible for protection.

§3. Conditions of Protection

433. The conditions of protection are specified in section 1 paragraph 1 of the Act. Accordingly, varieties may be protected as plant novelties if at the time of granting the protection they are: (i) independent, by which is meant that they are distinguishable by one or more characteristics, or by a combination of characteristics, from any other variety known at the time when protection is applied for; (ii) sufficiently uniform; (iii) stable in their specific characteristics (main characteristics) when propagated in accordance with the method specified by the breeder; and (iv) new, by which is meant that the propagating material or harvested material of the variety has not prior to the application been offered for sale, sold or in any other manner transferred with the consent of the owner of the variety and with a view to commercial utilization: (a) in this country for more than one year, or (b) in a foreign country for more than four years or, in the case of grape wines, trees and their rootstocks, for more than six years.[777]

434. Various specific exemptions to the novelty requirement of section 1 paragraph 1 subparagraph (iv) of the Act are contained in section 1 paragraph 2. Accordingly, notwithstanding section 1 paragraph 1 subparagraph (iv), a variety is considered a novelty: (1) even though material of the variety has been sold or transferred: (a) to an official institution for legal purposes; (b) to others in accordance with a contract or other legally binding arrangement with a view solely to propagation or treatment and storage for the purpose of propagation, provided that the recipient did not hold a right of disposal over the material of the variety; or (c) by one company to another company, if one of the companies is owned by the other, or if both companies are owned by a third company, provided that none of the companies is cooperative societies; and (2) even though propagation material or harvested material of the variety produced from plants that have been cultivated for the purpose of experiments or breeding has been offered for sale, sold or transferred to others, provided that this has happened without reference to the variety. By virtue of section 1 paragraph 3, section 1 paragraph 2 does not apply to varieties used for the production of a hybrid variety if repeated use of the variety is necessary for the production and if material of the hybrid variety has been sold or transferred to others.[778] The Minister of Food, Agriculture and Fisheries may, as an exception,

777. Section 1 para. 1 subpara. (iv)(a) and (b) is similar to Art. 10 para. 1 of the Council Regulation 2100/94/EC and Art. 6 para. 1 of the UPOV Convention.
778. Section 1 paras 2 and 3 are similar to the Art. 10 paras 2 and 3 of the Council Regulation 2100/94/EC.

approve the protection of a variety that does not satisfy the novelty requirement as laid down in section 1 paragraph 1 subparagraph (iv), if it is considered to be of economic interest to agriculture.[779]

§4. Formalities

435. An application for entry of a variety in the Register of Plant Novelties shall be submitted to the Board for Plant Novelties (*Plantenyhedsnævnet*) by the holder of the variety.[780] If the holder is not resident in or does not have his/her registered office in a Member State of the EU, such application shall be made by an agent, appointed by the applicant, who is resident in or has his/her registered office in Denmark.[781] The Board may demand that the applicant furnish all such information as is deemed necessary to try the application and may fix a time limit for this. The Board may further demand that material to be used for examination, cf. section 9, be submitted within a specified period.[782] At the time of the filing of the application, an application fee shall be paid.[783] The application is entered in the journal kept by the Board for Plant Novelties immediately after receipt, and a copy of the application provided with the Board for Plant Novelties' note as to the date of entry in the journal is returned immediately to the applicant. Notice of the application is published by the Board for Plant Novelties.[784] The journal is accessible to the public. However, this is not the case as regards information concerning the genealogical components of hybrid varieties and descriptions hereof if the applicant has requested that the information be treated as confidential.[785] The Board for Plant Novelties may delete an entry from the journal if the applicant does not furnish the information or testing material required by the Board pursuant to section 3 paragraph 3 of the Act within the time limit fixed by the Board.[786]

436. From the date of filing of the application, the applicant enjoys a right of priority to protection of the variety if any other person subsequently submits an application for protection of the same variety.[787] At the request of the applicant, the Board for Plant Novelties may establish priority for the application from the date of the first application for protection of the variety in any Member State of the UPOV if the first application was filed within twelve months. The request shall be made at

779. Cf. s. 2 of the Act.
780. The Board for Plant Novelties is a board set up by the Minister of Food, Agriculture and Fisheries, pursuant to s. 22 of the Act, to administer the provisions of Chs 2 and 3 (ss 3–15) of the Act.
781. Cf. s. 3 para. 1 of the Act.
782. Cf. s. 3 para. 3 of the Act.
783. Cf. s. 3 para. 4 of the Act.
784. Cf. s. 4 para. 1 of the Act.
785. Cf. s. 4 para. 2 of the Act. The provision is in conformity with ss 7 para. 1 and 30 para. 2 of Freedom of Information Act; Act No. 145 of 24 Feb. 2020 with later amendment.
786. Cf. s. 5 of the Act.
787. Cf. s. 6 para. 1 of the Act.

the time of the filing of the application in Denmark and shall be accompanied by documentation of the receipt of the first application.[788]

I. Examination

437. As soon as possible after entry of the application in the journal, the Board for Plant Novelties makes a provisional examination to establish whether the variety may be considered to fulfil the conditions of protection. If, based upon such examinations, the Board finds that the conditions of protection are fulfilled, the Board publishes a notice of the application together with an invitation to all concerned to make known within a specified time limit any objections to the registration of the variety.[789] Pursuant to section 9 of the Act, the Board decides whether additional examination of the variety applied for is necessary in order to obtain protection. Accordingly, it is stated in section 9 paragraph 1 that before a variety for which an application has been filed can obtain protection, the Board for Plant Novelties shall establish whether the variety can be considered to fulfil the conditions for protection, including whether it has the special characteristics mentioned in the application. To this end, the Board shall arrange for an examination of the variety to the necessary extent. The examination of whether a variety satisfies the condition of protection shall be conducted by a private legal person appointed in accordance with section 5 a paragraph in the Act on Plants and Plant Health.[790] The Board may decide that the presented examination results are sufficient to establish that the conditions of protection are satisfied without conducting its own examination.

438. If the variety is considered to satisfy the conditions of protection, the Board for Plant Novelties enters the variety in the Register of Plant Novelties under a variety denomination that has been approved in accordance with provisions laid down by the Minister of Food, Agriculture and Fisheries.[791] The Board for Plant Novelties may refuse registration of a variety if the holder of the variety does not, within three months, comply with the Board's request to propose a denomination for the variety or fails to propose a new denomination, where the Board has found that the denomination proposed does not satisfy the conditions for approval.[792] The variety denomination shall be suitable as a generic designation for the variety and as a means of identification of the variety, and furthermore, the denomination shall satisfy the conditions of Council Regulation 2100/94/EC Article 63 paragraphs 3 and 4 and the Commission Regulation (EU) 2021/384, cf. sections 5 paragraph 1 and 8 paragraph 2 of Order No. 1095 of 1 June 2021. In particular, it implies that a denomination will not be approved if:

---

788. Cf. s. 6 para. 2 of the Act.
789. Cf. s. 7 of the Act.
790. Cf. s. 9, para. 2 of the Act.
791. Cf. s. 10 para. 1 of the Act.
792. Cf. s. 10 para. 2 of the Act.

- an earlier right belonging to a third party prevents the use of the variety name in Denmark, in a Member State of the EU or in another Member State of UPOV,
- it may be difficult for users in general to recognize or reproduce,
- it is identical or may be confused with a variety name under which another variety of the same species or of a closely related species is registered in an official register of varieties or under which material of another variety has been marketed in Denmark in a Member State of the EU or in another Member State of UPOV, unless the other variety no longer exists and its variety name has not acquired greater importance,
- it is identical or may be confused with other variety names which are commonly used in the marketing of goods or which, according to other legal provisions, may not be used as denominations,
- it is likely to be offensive or contrary to public order in Denmark, in a member state of the EU or in another Member State of UPOV,
- it is likely to be misleading or cause confusion as to the characteristics, value or identity of the variety or the identity of the breeder or any other party involved in the matter.[793]

The Board for Plant Novelties may carry out post-control to ensure that the plant novelty is maintained satisfactorily by the holder of the variety.[794] The holder of the variety shall, within the time limits fixed by the Board, make the necessary plant material available for the post-control to be performed by the Board for Plant Novelties.[795]

II. Variety Denomination

439. The plant novelty shall be designated by the approved variety denomination. This applies even after expiry of the period of protection.[796] The provision is further specified in section 11 of Order No. 1095 of 1 June 2021. Accordingly, the variety denomination shall be used at any sale, any act of advertising and any mention of the variety even after expiry of the period of protection. When sold, the variety name must be clearly and legibly stated.[797] It is permitted to use an additional denomination for the variety in connection with the variety denomination.[798] According to administrative practice, an additional denomination may be a trademark, a personal name, a company name, a place name or a specific name of real property. If a trademark, trade name or the like is used as an additional denomination, the variety denomination shall be presented in a way that makes it easily recognizable as the variety denomination. The additional denomination shall be

793. Cf. s. 5 para. 3 of Order No. 1095 of 1 Jun. 2021.
794. Cf. s. 13 para. 1 of the Act.
795. Cf. s. 13 para. 2 of the Act.
796. Cf. s. 11 para. 1 of the Act.
797. Cf. s. 11 para. 1 of Order No. 1095 of 1 Jun. 2021.
798. Cf. s. 11 para. 2 of the Act.

notified to the Board for Plant Novelties.[799] At the request of the holder of the variety, the Board for Plant Novelties may, in special cases, permit that the plant novelty be given another denomination than the one originally approved.[800] The Minister of Environment and Food lays down provisions on the denomination of plant novelties.[801]

III. Certificate of Protection

440. Simultaneously with the publication of the registration, the Board for Plant Novelties issues a certificate of protection, which is delivered to the applicant against payment of a registration fee.[802]

§5. Ownership and Transfer

441. The person who bred, or discovered and developed the variety, or his/her successor in title, is entitled to apply for plant variety protection.[803] The applicant shall before the Board for Plant Novelties produce evidence of his/her right to apply for entry of the variety in the Register. If the application is made by an agent on behalf of the holder of the variety, the agent shall produce documentation of his/her authority to represent the owner in all matters relating to the application and registration.[804] The Board for Plant Novelties refers any objections to the applicant's right to apply for protection of the variety to the ordinary courts of law. When the Board is informed of such legal proceedings, it furnishes the application with a note to that effect.[805] Where legal proceedings are pending, a note to this effect is made in the Register of Plant Novelties.[806]

442. The Act does not contain any provisions on the transfer of plant variety rights. Nevertheless, similar to other intellectual property rights, plant variety rights may freely be transferred to other persons and the transfer is not contingent on formalities.

§6. Scope of Exclusive Rights

443. Living plants and plant material derived from a plant novelty are protectable subject matter under the Act. However, the scope of the exclusive right is confined to the use of such living plants and plant material for propagation of the plant

799. Cf. s. 11 para. 2 of Order No. 1095 of 1 Jun. 2021.
800. Cf. s. 11 para. 3 of the Act.
801. Cf. s. 11 para. 4 of the Act .
802. Cf. s. 12 para. 1 1st clause of the Act.
803. Cf. Art. 1 of the UPOV Convention.
804. Cf. s. 3 para. 2 of the Act.
805. Cf. s. 8 para. 1 of the Act.
806. Cf. s. 10 para. 3 of the Act.

novelty. Consequently, the Act does not confer on the holder of a plant novelty the right to stipulate terms on the sale of the final product such as the use of a particular trademark, a particular packing, etc. By virtue of section 16 paragraph 1 of the Act, material of a plant novelty may only: (i) be used for commercial production, propagation or treatment and storage with a view to propagation subject to permission by the holder of the variety and only on the terms and conditions, including payment of an appropriate royalty, specified by the holder; and (ii) be offered for sale, sold, transferred or stored with a view to sale or transfer subject to permission by the holder of the variety and only on the terms and conditions, including payment of an appropriate royalty, specified by the holder.

444. The Minister of Food, Agriculture and Fisheries may lay down provisions to the effect that any person propagating plant novelties of specified species for professional use on his own holding shall pay a royalty to the holder of the variety (farmers' privilege).[807] The Minister has used his powers to issue Order No. 76 of 29 January 2020, which extends the variety holder's right in this respect. The right of remuneration of Order No. 76 is confined to certain specific forms of use regarding various varieties mentioned in the annex to the Order. These varieties include the varieties enumerated in Article 15(2) of the UPOV Convention and Article 14(2) of the Council Regulation. The holder of the variety determines the royalty that shall be reasonable.[808]

445. To facilitate the holder of a variety in enforcing his/her exclusive right, section 16 paragraph 3 of the Act states that any person who propagates a plant novelty or sells propagating material of the plant novelty shall provide the holder of the variety with the information necessary for calculation and collection of royalty.

446. Section 16 paragraph 4 of the Act enables the variety holder, on certain conditions, to exercise his/her right to propagation material from a protected variety also in relation to any harvested material obtained from the plant novelty (subparagraph (i)) and to varieties essentially derived from a protected variety (subparagraph (ii)). Accordingly, the provisions of section 16 paragraphs 1–3 of the Act mentioned *supra* apply correspondingly: (i) to harvested material obtained from the use of propagation material of a plant novelty if the holder of the variety: (a) has not permitted such use of the material and (b) has not had the possibility of exercising his/her rights to the material in accordance with section 16 paragraph 1 of the Act; (ii) to varieties that: (a) are essentially derived from a plant novelty if this is not itself essentially a derived variety, or (b) are not independent in relation to the plant novelty, cf. section 1 paragraph 1 of the Act, or (c) can be produced only by

807. Cf. s. 16 para. 2 of the Act.
808. Cf. s. 1 para. 3 of Order No. 701 of 22 Jun. 1996.

repeated use of the plant novelty.[809] The Minister of Food, Agriculture and Fisheries may decide that on the conditions laid down in section 16 paragraph 4 subparagraph (i), section 16 paragraphs 1–3 shall also apply to products produced from propagation material of a plant novelty or any harvested material obtained therefrom.[810]

447. The holder of a variety is not entitled to demand a fee for the use of an additional variety denomination registered as a trademark, in pursuance of section 11 paragraph 2 of the Act, until after the expiration of a period of twenty-five (thirty respectively) years pursuant to section 12 paragraph 3 of the Act, calculated from the date of issue of the certificate of protection for the plant novelty irrespective of whether the registration is maintained throughout the period.[811] The purpose of the provision is to prevent a holder of a variety from using the plant variety protection to work up an additional denomination protected under the Trademarks Act and subsequently request the Patent and Trademark Office to delete the registration of the variety but continue to demand a royalty for the use of the trademark-protected additional denomination.

448. The conditions specified by the holder of the variety pursuant to section 16 paragraph 1 of the Act may only concern the use and offer for sale as stated in section 16 paragraph 1 subparagraphs 1 and 2 and royalties. The terms and conditions shall be reasonable and identical for all producers, cf. section 16 paragraph 6 of the Act. Conditions stipulated by the holder of the variety for the use of the plant novelty are not considered reasonable if they concern rights that are not conferred on the holder of the variety by the Act.

§7. Limitations of the Scope of Protection

449. By virtue of section 17 of the Act, plant novelties may be used freely for research and breeding activities.[812] The purpose of section 17 is to allow breeding activities aiming at the creation of a new variety eligible for protection under the Act, and such activities shall be distinguished from commercial propagation of a plant novelty.

450. Section 20 paragraph 1 of the Act contains a provision on compulsory exploitation right. If the Minister of Food, Agriculture and Fisheries considers it necessary to ensure distribution of a plant novelty or to prevent substantial deterioration of the conditions for a branch of industry, he/she may order the holder of the

809. The provision is similar to Art. 14(3) of the UPOV Convention and Art. 13 of the Council Regulation.
810. Cf. s. 16 para. 5 of the Act. The provision is similar to Art. 14(4) of the UPOV Convention and Art. 13(3) of the Council Regulation.
811. Cf. s. 19 para. 1 of the Act. However, this provision does not apply to propagating material of a variety protected in Denmark if the propagating material originates from a State which has not protected the variety, cf. s. 19 para. 2 of the Act.
812. The provision is similar to Art. 15(b) and (c) of the Council Regulation.

variety to give one or more persons permission for the commercial propagation and sale of propagation material of a plant novelty and to fulfil, or cause others to fulfil orders for suitable propagating material within a reasonable time limit. The provisions of section 16 apply correspondingly.[813]

Where the holder of a patent concerning a biotechnological invention cannot exploit the invention without infringing a prior plant variety right, he/she may apply for a compulsory licence for non-exclusive use of the plant variety protected by that right, subject to payment of an appropriate royalty. Such a compulsory licence will be granted only if the patent holder demonstrates that he/she has addressed the holder of the variety and has not been able to obtain a voluntary licence agreement and in addition demonstrates that the invention makes up an essential technical progress of substantial economic importance compared to the plant variety.[814] Where the holder of a variety has been granted compulsory licence pursuant to the Patents Act in respect of a protected invention, the patent holder will be entitled to a cross-licence on reasonable terms to use the plant variety.[815]

§8. Duration of Protection

451. The term of protection of a variety is connected to the date of registration of the variety and the certificate of protection issued by the Board for Plant Novelties on the same date. The certificate of protection is valid for a period of one year, and the period of validity may be extended by one year at a time for up to twenty-five years or, for varieties of potatoes, up to thirty years, calculated from the date of issue of the certificate of protection, cf. however, section 21 paragraph 1.[816] The validity of the certificate of protection is extended against payment of an annual registration fee to the Board for Plant Novelties.[817] Irrespective of these provisions, the Minister of Food, Agriculture and Fisheries may lay down provisions to the effect that the validity of the certificate of protection for varieties of further specified species and genera can be extended for a period of up to thirty years.[818]

452. By virtue of section 21, the variety is protected from the date of filing of the application irrespective that the twenty-five years term of protection starts from the date of the final registration. Accordingly, the terms and conditions referred to in section 16 paragraph 1 of the Act (on the exclusive right) may be applied by the holder of the variety in the period from acceptance of the application for protection of a variety until its entry into the Register of Plant Novelties (the period of application), provided that the applicant notifies the Board for Plant Novelties thereof. The protection period stated in section 12 shall in this case be calculated from the

---

813. The provision is in conformity with Art. 17(1) of the UPOV Convention and Art. 29(1) of the Council Regulation.
814. Cf. s. 20 para. 2 of the Act.
815. Cf. s. 20 para. 3 of the Act.
816. Cf. s. 12 para. 1 2nd clause of the Act.
817. Cf. s. 12 para. 2 of the Act.
818. Cf. s. 12 para. 3 of the Act. The provision corresponds to Art. 19(2) of the UPOV Convention and Art. 19(2) of the Council Regulation.

date of entry of the notice in the journal kept by the Board for Plant Novelties. The provisions of sections 11 and 20 apply correspondingly during the period of application.[819] Any royalties during the period of application shall be deposited by the producer on a blocked account in a financial institution in favour of the holder of the variety. The amount shall be released if the variety is entered in the Register of Plant Novelties. Otherwise, the deposited amount, inclusive of any interest accrued, shall be repaid to the producer.[820] If the application for protection of a variety is withdrawn, or if the entry of the variety in the Register of Plant Novelties is refused, the variety may be used freely for propagation. A producer, who during the period of application has used the variety for propagation, shall be in the same position as if an unprotected variety had been used.[821]

I. Revocation

453. The Board for Plant Novelties deletes a plant novelty from the Register of Plant Novelties if: (i) it is established that at the time of registration, the plant novelty did not satisfy the conditions for entry laid down in section 1 of the Act; (ii) at the post-control, the Board finds that the plant novelty has not been maintained satisfactorily; (iii) the Board receives a written request from the holder of the variety to this effect; or (iv) the annual registration fee has not been paid.[822] The Board for Plant Novelties may further delete a plant novelty from the Register of Plant Novelties if the holder of the variety does not within the time limit fixed by the Board comply with the Board's request: (i) to make available to the Board the material needed for post-control or (ii) to propose a new name for the variety in cases where the Board has subsequently found that the approved name does not satisfy the provisions laid down by the Minister of Environment and Food.[823] The plant novelty is deleted from the Register two months after the holder of the variety has been notified of the decision of the Board for Plant Novelties unless, before expiry, the case has been brought before the courts of law by the holder of the variety.[824]

If a plant novelty has been deleted from the Register of Plant Novelties, it cannot be re-entered in the Register. The Board for Plant Novelties publishes a notice of the deletion and the reason for it.[825] An unprotected variety may be used freely for propagation.

819. Cf. s. 21 para. 1 of the Act.
820. Cf. s. 21 para. 2 of the Act.
821. Cf. s. 21 para. 3 of the Act.
822. Cf. s. 14 para. 1 of the Act.
823. Cf. s. 14 para. 2 of the Act.
824. Cf. s. 14 para. 3 of the Act.
825. Cf. s. 15 of the Act.

§9. Infringement and Remedies

454. The Act does not contain any provisions on injunctions. Similar to the other Acts on intellectual property, the legal basis for injunctions is the general rules in Chapter 40 of the Act on Civil Proceedings (*see supra* paragraphs 134 f and 236 f.).

455. Section 26a of the Damages Liability Act is identical to the corresponding provisions of the other intellectual property Acts (*see supra* paragraphs 136 f and 238 f.).

456. Any person who contravenes section 16 paragraphs 1, 3 or 4 (on the exclusive right) is liable to a fine. Contravention of the said provision is subject to private prosecution.[826] Any person who contravenes section 11 paragraph 1 (on designating the variety with the approved variety denomination) and section 20 (regarding compulsory exploitation rights) is likewise punished by a fine.[827] In addition, the powers of the Minister of Food, Agriculture and Fisheries to issue regulations under section 11 paragraphs 4 and 16 paragraphs 2 and 5 includes the power to adopt provisions for the punishment by a fine for contravention of the regulations.[828]

Where a contravention has been committed by companies, private companies, or cooperative societies, that is, the punishment by a fine may be imposed on the company as such.[829]

457. Section 26b of the Act on destruction, seizure and recall is identical to section 59 of the Patents Act (*see supra* paragraph 240).

458. Section 26c of the Act on the publication of judgments is identical to the corresponding provisions of the other intellectual property Acts (*see supra* paragraphs 142 and 244.

459. The provisions of the Act on Civil Proceedings on search and right of information (*see supra* paragraphs 139-140 and 241-242) apply to plant variety rights.

§10. Overlapping and Relation to Other Intellectual Property Laws

460. The Act complies with the 1991 text of the UPOV Convention, and hence, protected plant novelties are not precluded from protection under the Patents Act. However, one should note section 1 paragraph 4 (1st clause) of the Patents Act, which excludes species of plants from patentable subject matter.

826. Cf. s. 26 para. 1 of the Act.
827. Cf. s. 26 para. 2 of the Act.
828. Cf. s. 26 para. 3 of the Act.
829. Cf. s. 26 para. 4 of the Act.

461. It is disputed whether section 3 of the Marketing Practice Act may provide protection for plant varieties. As the main rule, this is not the case. However, under specific and aggravating circumstances, presumably, section 3 of the Marketing Practice Act is applicable.[830]

830. *See* M. Plesner (1978), 91; and P.H. Schmidt, *Teknologi og immaterialret* (Copenhagen: G.E.C. Gad, 1989), 114 ff.

Chapter 8. Chip Protection

§1. Sources – Legislation

462. The Act on Protection of Topographies of Semiconductor Products[831] was adopted in December 1987 in order to implement the Council Directive 87/54/EEC of 16 December 1986 on the legal protection of topographies of semiconductor products[832] and came into force on 10 December 1987. The Act instituted a new sui generis right in Danish intellectual property law.

§2. Subject Matter of Protection

463. The protected subject matter is topographies of semiconductor products.[833] The definitions of 'semiconductor product' and of the 'topography' of a semiconductor product are copied from Article 1(1) (a) and Article 1(1) (b) of the Council Directive into section 1 of the Act. Thus, a 'semiconductor product' shall mean the final or intermediate form of any product consisting of a body of material that includes a layer of semiconducting material; and having one or more other layers composed of conducting, insulating or semiconducting material, the layers being arranged in accordance with a predetermined three-dimensional pattern; and intended to perform, exclusively or together with other functions, an electronic function.[834] The 'topography' of a semiconductor product shall mean a series of related images, however, fixed or encoded and representing the three-dimensional pattern of the layers of which a semiconductor product is composed and in which series each image has the pattern or part of the pattern of a surface of the semiconductor product at any stage of its manufacture.[835]

464. The Act does not protect semiconductor products as such; only topographies of semiconductor products represent a three-dimensional pattern. Owing to

831. Consolidated Act No. 92 of 29 Jan. 2019 on Protection of Topographies of Semiconductor Products. The preparatory works are referred to in FT 1987–1988, F, col. 899, 912, 2939, 3210, FT 1987–1988, A, col. 579, FT 1987–1988, B, col. 55, FT 1987–1988, C, col. 78. Interpreting the Act, one should further consult the Report No. 1064 Copenhagen 1986 '*Ophavsret og edb*', 70–83, drawn up by the Committee on a Revision of the Copyright Act. Under the provisions of the Act several orders have been issued concerning the scope of the Act, exhaustion of the rights and the practical administration of the rights: Order No. 482 of 10 Jun. 2003 on Applications for Protection of Topographies of Semiconductors; Order No. 892 of 19 Feb. 2009 on the Patent and Trademark Board of Appeal (*Ankenævnet for patenter og varemærker*); Order No. 238 of 30 Mar. 1994 on Amendments of the Rules on Exhaustion of the Patents Act, the Trademarks Act and the Act on Protection of Topographies of Semiconductor Products; Order No. 1274 of 18 Dec. 1996 on Extending the Scope of the Act on the Protection of Topographies of Semiconductor Products to Persons from Certain Countries and Territories; and Order No. 12 of 12 Jan. 2012 on the remuneration of the Patent and Trademark Office for the performance of tasks, specific transactions and transcripts, etc.
832. O.J. 1987 L 24/36.
833. Cf. s. 2 para. 1.
834. Section 1 para. 1.
835. Section 1 para. 2.

the Council Directive, the scope of protection under the Danish Act is broader than the scope of protection under the US Semiconductor Chip Protection Act 1984 (SCPA). Contrary to the Danish Act, first, the SCPA only protects three-dimensional patterns manufactured by means of masks or templates, not by means of other techniques, and second, the SCPA only protects the final three-dimensional mask work, not parts of the pattern of a surface of the semiconductor product at any stage of its manufacture.[836]

465. According to section 7 of the Act, the protection does not extend to any concept, process, system, technique or encoded information embodied in the topography other than the topography itself;[837] that is, the technical function of the semiconductor product is not protectable. Such protection is only available under patent law.

§3. Conditions of Protection

466. Not all topographies of semiconductor products are protected by the Act. In order to qualify for protection, a topography of a semiconductor product shall be the result of its creator's own intellectual effort, and, furthermore, the topography must not be commonplace in the semiconductor industry.[838] Consequently, two conditions must be satisfied in order to qualify for protection. The creator's own intellectual effort requires some degree of subjective originality in creating the topography.[839] The condition resembles the originality requirement within copyright law. Even when the condition is satisfied, additionally, the topography shall satisfy the condition of not being commonplace in the semiconductor industry. This condition is not similar to the requirement of objective novelty under patent law. The latter condition should be construed in such a way that a topography copied from an existing topography does not qualify for protection just because the topography is not a literal copy. In the preparatory works of the Act, it is stated that a topography copied from an existing topography usually does not require significant effort or investments and, consequently, does not qualify for protection.[840] Whether a specific topography satisfies the conditions of protection should probably be assessed in light of the prerequisite effort and investments.

As a practical rule, the conditions of protection must be assumed to be satisfied if a prospective creator of another topography performing the same functions is unlikely to create a topography manifested in an identical three-dimensional pattern.[841]

836. Cf. P.H. Schmidt, *Teknologi og immaterialret – Et studie i patent-og ophavsretten særligt med henblik på retsbeskyttelsen af edb-programmer og micro-chips* (Copenhagen: Gad, 1989), 323–326.
837. Cf. Art. 8 of the Council Directive.
838. Section 2 para. 2. The wording is identical to Art. 2(2) of the Council Directive.
839. Cf. FT 1987–1988, A, col. 592.
840. Cf. FT 1987–1988, A, col. 592.
841. Cf. Riis (2001) 181.

Where the topography consists of elements that are commonplace in the semiconductor industry, it shall be protected only if the combination of such elements, taken as a whole, fulfils the conditions of protection.[842]

467. Specific parts of the topography are protected by the sui generis right if these parts satisfy the conditions of protection. In this respect, it does not matter whether other parts of the topography qualify for protection.

§4. Formalities

468. Article 4 of the Council Directive gives the Member States the possibility of establishing a registration system implying registration of a topography as a condition for the exclusive right to come into existence. Protection of topographies of semiconductor products under the Danish Act is based on such a registration system. Exclusive rights under the Act only come into existence when an application for registration of a topography has been filed with the Patent and Trademark Office (*Patent-og Varemærkestyrelsen*) no later than two years after the day when the topography was exploited commercially for the first time.[843] By 'commercial exploitation of a topography' means supply, sale, rental, leasing or any other method of commercial distribution of a topography or a semiconductor product embodying the topography.[844] Though not expressly stated in the Act, an offer for these purposes is also considered 'commercial exploitation'.[845] Often, the production of a semiconductor product takes place in a specific company specialized in production of semiconductor products, and the semiconductor product is only used in the production function of another company. In that case, and if the semiconductor product is used under conditions of confidentiality in a way that no further distribution to third parties occurs, the use is not considered commercial exploitation within the meaning of the Act.[846]

469. The rules of the registration process are laid down in an order issued by the Minister of Industry, Business and Financial Affairs.[847] The application for registration consists of an application form, which is requested from the Patent and Trademark Office, and annexes. Application and annexes have to be in Danish.[848] Among other things, the application shall include information on the commercial exploitation of the topography if the topography has been exploited commercially before the

842. Section 2 para. 2 last sentence. Cf. Art. 2(2) of the Council Directive. The provision conforms to a general principle in intellectual property law; the compilation of well-known elements may constitute a new and original product of the mind eligible for protection by intellectual property rights.
843. Section 5 para. 1 of the Act.
844. Section 3 para. 1 of the Act.
845. The provision implements Art. 1(1)(c) of the Council Directive.
846. Section 3 para. 2. Cf. Art. 1(1)(c) last sentence of the Council Directive.
847. Order No. 482 of 10 Jun. 2003 (the Order).
848. Material for the identification and description of the topography may include technical terms in English.

date of application.[849] Annexes including material for the identification and description of the topography shall be enclosed with the application.[850] Material for the identification and description of the topography shall include drawings or photographies of: (i) the layouts for the production of the semiconductor product; (ii) masks or mask parts for the production of the semiconductor product; or (iii) the layers of the semiconductor product.[851]

The material for the identification and description of the topography can be kept secret from the public if it is declared a trade secret by the applicant. However, no more than half the number of layers can be declared trade secrets.[852] The Patent and Trademark Office keeps a journal of received applications for registration and ensures public access to the journal.[853] A fee shall be enclosed with the application.[854]

470. After receiving an application, the Patent and Trademark Office conducts a formal examination of the application in order to ensure that the application and annexes conform to the requirements regarding the form and contents of the application and the annexes.[855] The Patent and Trademark Office does not examine whether the substantive conditions of protection are satisfied; that is, whether the topography is a result of the creator's own intellectual effort and whether the topography is not commonplace in the semiconductor industry. If the Patent and Trademark Office finds that the application and annexes comply with the requirements, the topography is registered and is allotted a registration number. Notice on registration and registration number is published in the gazette of the Patent and Trademark Office (*Dansk Patenttidende*).[856] After notification in *Dansk Patenttidende*, the documents of the case shall be available for the public, except for documents that are considered trade secrets, according to sections 8 and 9 of the Order.[857] According to section 19, a register of registered topographies shall be kept. In practice, the Register is administered by the Patent and Trademark Office.

471. The process of registration creates a practical need for competitors in the industry to monitor the registrations in order to ensure that the conditions of protection are satisfied. If a competitor or others are able to establish that the conditions of protection are not satisfied, the Patent and Trademark Office shall revoke the registration of the topography.[858] Decisions made by the Patent and Trademark Office based on the Act may be brought before the Patent and Trademark Board of

849. Section 2 para. 2(4) of the Order.
850. Section 2 para. 2 of the Order.
851. Section 6 para. 1 of the Order.
852. Section 8 of the Order.
853. Section 12 of the Order.
854. Section 8 of the Act and s. 2 para. 3 of the Order.
855. Section 13 of the Order.
856. Section 15 of the Order.
857. Section 16 of the Order.
858. Section 10 of the Act.

Appeal (*Ankenævnet for patenter og varemærker*).[859] A decision by the Patent and Trademark Board of Appeal is a precondition for bringing the case before a court.[860]

472. The possibility in Article 4 of the Council Directive of making protection of topographies contingent on deposition has not been adopted in the Danish Act. Nor does the Act require that semiconductor products manufactured using protected topographies shall carry any form of indication.[861]

473. The protective system in Denmark concerning semiconductor products has not proved a great success. Since the Act was adopted, only a few topographies of semiconductor products have been registered each year. Accordingly, the protective system cannot be said to have had any significant influence on industry practice.

§5. Ownership and Transfer

474. In conformity with Article 3(1) of the Directive, the right to protection shall apply to the creator of a topography of a semiconductor product or to persons to whom the right has been conferred.[862] The right to protection is granted to natural persons who are nationals of a Member State or who have their habitual residence on the territory of a Member State.[863]

475. Normally, the process of developing topographies of semiconductor products is very complex and involves significant economic resources. In order to protect the investments of companies that undertake the development of topographies of semiconductor products, section 4 paragraph 1 subparagraph (ii) of the Act stipulates that the right to protection of a topography created in the course of employment or a topography created on commission shall apply in favour of the employer or the party by whom the topography has been commissioned, unless the terms of employment or the terms of the contract provide, or must be assumed to provide, that the right shall apply in favour of the creator.[864] The provision is based on a notion that the development of a topography of a semiconductor product is initiated at the request of the employer and at the expense of the employer. Thus, it appears reasonable to ensure the employer the right to exploit the topography commercially.[865] Section 4 paragraph 1 subparagraph (ii) of the Act makes it possible for

859. The rules governing *Ankenævnet for patenter og varemærker* are laid down in Order No. 892 of 21 Sep. 2009.
860. Section 17 of the Act.
861. Cf. Art. 9 of the Council Directive.
862. Section 1 para. 1 of the Act.
863. Section 4 para. 1 subpara. 1 of the Act. Cf. Art. 3(3)(a) of the Directive.
864. Section 4 para. 1 subpara. 2 of the Act. Cf. Art. 3(3)(a) and (b) of the Directive.
865. The provision conferring the right from the employee to the employer is similar to the provision in s. 59 of the Copyright Act regarding copyright to computer programs created in the course of employment.

companies and other legal persons to be conferred the right of protection of topographies created in the course of employment or on commission. Natural persons acquiring rights to protection of topographies under section 4 paragraph 1 subparagraph (ii) of the Act have to be nationals of a Member State or have their habitual residence on the territory of a Member State; and legal persons acquiring rights under section 4 paragraph 1 subparagraph (ii) of the Act must have a real and effective establishment on the territory of a Member State.

476. Additionally, the right to protection shall apply in favour of a natural or a legal person in cases where the topography is created by another person and where the topography is not created in the course of employment or created on commission, when the respective natural or legal person has been exclusively authorized to exploit commercially the topography throughout the Community by the person entitled to dispose of it and when the first commercial exploitation of the topography takes place in a Member State.[866] The provision emphasizes the attachment to the EU as a decisive element in order to be eligible for protection. The purpose of the provision is for example to grant protection of topographies created by a Danish subsidiary situated outside the EU in cases where the topography is to be exploited commercially by the Danish parent company.[867]

477. Section 4 paragraph 1 subparagraph (iv) expressly states that the rights conferred by the Act are alienable since the right to protection applies to the successors in title of the persons mentioned in section 4 paragraph 1 subparagraphs (i–iii) of the Act.[868] Where the right of protection of a topography is assigned to another person or where a licence is granted, including compulsory licence, on request, these acts have to be entered into the Register against a fee.[869] The notification of these Acts in the Register has no binding legal effect.

478. Under the provision of section 4 paragraph 2 of the Act, the protection of topographies granted by the Act is extended to persons, companies and legal entities from certain other countries and territories by virtue of Order No. 1274 of 18 December 1996, which implements the Council Decision of 9 October 1990[870] and the Council Decision of 22 December 1994.[871] Pursuant to section 1 of the Order, the right of protection applies to the following natural persons, legal persons and other legal entities irrespective of the conditions laid down in section 4 paragraph 1 of the Act: (i) natural persons who are nationals of or are domiciled in the territory of a Member of the WTO Agreement; (ii) legal entities that have or natural persons who have a real and effective establishment for the creation of topographies or the

866. Section 4 para. 1 subpara. 3 of the Act. Cf. Art. 3(4) of the Directive.
867. Cf. FT 1987–1988, A, col. 595.
868. Cf. Art. 3(5) of the Directive.
869. Section 9 of the Act. *See also* s. 19 of Order No. 482 of 10 Jun. 2003.
870. Council Decision of 9 Oct. 1990 on the extension of the legal protection of topographies of semiconductor products to persons from certain countries and territories (90/510/EEC), O.J. 1990 L 285/29.
871. Council Decision of 22 Dec. 1994 on the extension of the legal protection of topographies of semiconductor products to persons from a Member of the WTO (94/824/EC), O.J. 1994 L 349/201.

production of integrated circuits in the territory of a Member of the WTO Agreement; (iii) natural persons who are nationals of a country or have their habitual residence on the territory of a country listed in the annex to the Order; and (iv) legal persons of a country or territory listed in the annex to the Order that have a real and effective industrial or commercial establishment in such a country or territory.

§6. Scope of Exclusive Rights

479. The owner of a right of protection of a topography obtains the exclusive right to: (i) reproduce the topography; (ii) exploit the topography commercially; and (iii) import the topography or a semiconductor product manufactured by using the topography for the purpose of commercial exploitation.[872]

It is pointed out in the Act that the right of reproduction includes manufacture of a semiconductor product by using the protected topography.[873] The exclusive right of reproduction is limited to copies of the protected topography, and hence, independent development of a topography does not infringe the right of protection of a pre-existing protected topography. The reproduction right has to be interpreted in the light of the permitted act of reverse engineering by virtue of section 6 paragraph 2 subparagraphs (ii) and (iii) of the Act.[874] According to the preparatory works, the reproduction right only protects against 'pure copies'. It is not quite clear what is meant by this. On the one hand, it must imply that the scope of protection is narrower than the scope of copyright protection. On the other hand, the scope of protection must, presumably, be sufficiently broad to protect against more than just perfectly identical copies.[875]

480. The exclusive right to commercial exploitation includes the right to prohibit or authorize the supply, sale, rental, leasing or any other method of commercial distribution of a topography or a semiconductor product embodying the topography or an offer for these purposes.[876] The owner of the right of protection can prohibit the commercial exploitation of the topography even if the topography is used under conditions of confidentiality, irrespective of the definition of 'commercial exploitation' in section 3 of the Act. Exploitation of a protected topography for non-commercial purposes, including reproduction of the topography, is permitted.[877]

The exclusive right to prohibit or authorize import of a topography applies to importation for the purpose of commercial exploitation. Consequently, the right does not include importation for the purpose of private use.

872. Section 6 para. 1 subparas 1–3 of the Act.
873. Section 6 para. 1 of the Act.
874. Cf. FT 1987–1988, A, col. 598.
875. Cf. Schmidt (1989), 328 ff; *see also* Report No. 1064 Copenhagen 1986, '*Ophavsret og edb*', 81 ff.
876. Cf. s. 3 para. 1. *See* §4.
877. Cf. Art. 5 (2) of the Directive.

§7. LIMITATIONS OF THE SCOPE OF PROTECTION

481. The exclusive right to prohibit or authorize commercial exploitation or the importation for that purpose is confined by the principle of exhaustion, which is included in section 6 paragraph 2 subparagraph (i) of the Act.[878] The principle states that the exclusive rights to prohibit or authorize commercial exploitation or the importation for that purpose shall not apply to any such act committed after the topography or a semiconductor product manufactured by using the topography has been put on the market in a Member State by the person entitled to authorize its marketing or with his/her consent. By virtue of section 3 of Order No. 238 of 30 March 1994, the principle of exhaustion also applies when the topography has been put on the market in a country that has ratified or acceded to the EEA Agreement.[879]

482. The marketing of a protected topography or a semiconductor product manufactured by using this topography outside the EEA does not confine the scope of protection by exhaustion of the rights. However, this kind of marketing may have other legal consequences within the EEA. Marketing of a topography in a country that is not part of the EEA is considered 'commercial exploitation' in the sense of section 3 of the Act, for example, implying that the two-year period stated in section 5 paragraph 1 of the Act starts running when the topography has been put on the market in a country outside the EEA.[880]

483. By virtue of section 6 paragraph 2 subparagraph (ii), it is permitted to reverse engineer a protected topography. The section states that the reproduction for the purpose of analysing, evaluating or teaching in the topography itself or the concepts, processes, systems or techniques embodied in the topography is exempted from the right of protection.[881] In continuation of section 6 paragraph 2 subparagraph (ii), the following subparagraph (iii) stipulates that any such act in relation to the creation of a topography meeting the requirements of section 2 paragraph 2 and created on the basis of an analysis and evaluation of another topography shall be exempted from the exclusive right of protection.[882] This means that a competitor is permitted to analyse and evaluate a protected topography and use the results of these acts to create a new topography. It is a prerequisite that the new topography in its own right satisfies the conditions of protection, that is, being the result of the creator's own intellectual effort and not being commonplace in the semiconductor industry. Only the 'pure copy' infringes the right in the pre-existing topography. The burden of proof that the new topography is not a 'pure copy' is put on the creator of the new topography.[883]

The provisions in section 6 paragraph 2 subparagraphs (ii) and (iii) emphasize the delicate balance between protecting the investments of the producers of topographies and ensuring workable competition between these producers. Overly strong

878. Cf. Art. 5(5) of the Directive.
879. The EEA.
880. Cf. FT 1987–1988, A, col. 599.
881. Cf. Art. 5(3) of the Directive.
882. Cf. Art. 5(4) of the Directive.
883. Cf. FT 1987–1988, A, col. 599.

protection of topographies may create monopolies and stifle the technological development in the semiconductor industry to the detriment of society at large.

484. The possibility in Article 6 of the Directive of adopting a compulsory licence in respect of the right of protection of topographies has been used in the Danish Act. According to section 13 paragraph 1 of the Act, the Maritime and Commercial Court may grant compulsory licence if a semiconductor product has not been supplied in a reasonable number by the right owner. It is a further condition for the Court to grant licence that the right owner has been offered reasonable remuneration for expanding the supply of the semiconductor product. The practical need for compulsory licence can be questioned since the possibility of reverse engineering appears to solve most of the potential conflicts that are subject to section 13 of the Act. However, situations may occur where reverse engineering and the development of a new topography do not satisfy the conditions of protection in section 2 paragraph 2 of the Act; thus, compulsory licence is the only way to ensure the legal use of a topography performing functions essential to the society. The compulsory licence in section 13 of the Act aims at certain semiconductor products performing functions essential to the society where the interest of the right owner in prohibiting the use of the protected topography is insignificant compared to the consequences for society at large of prohibiting the use of the topography. Examples of this kind of semiconductor products mentioned in the preparatory works are semiconductor products used in telecommunication, in satellites or in military installations where a specific function under the existing technology can only be performed by a particular semiconductor product. Another example mentioned involves a large multinational company, which, due to competitive strategic reasons, prohibits a Danish company from using a protected topography that in the foreseeable future cannot be substituted by another topography.

Complying with the conditions in Article 6 of the Directive, compulsory licences shall not be granted automatically and by operation of law. The Maritime and Commercial Court decides on the terms of the licence including the size of remuneration. If the actual circumstances have changed substantially at the request of each of the parties, the Court may revoke the licence or decide on new terms of the licence.[884]

485. According to section 6 paragraph 3 of the Act a person who, when he/she acquires a semiconductor product, does not know, or has no reasonable grounds to believe, that the product is embodying a protected topography is permitted to continue to commercially exploit that product on reasonable terms, which are agreed upon between the parties.[885] The provision aims at situations where, for example, a bona fide product has been bought in a foreign country and the product is placed in that foreign country at the time when the buyer realizes that importation of the product infringes a valid right. Reasonable terms on the commercial exploitation and the importation for that purpose taking place after the time where the buyer realizes or ought to realize the existence of a right of protection shall be agreed upon between

884. Section 13 para. 2 of the Act. The provision is similar to s. 50 of the Patents Act.
885. Cf. Art. 5(6) of the Directive.

the parties. A reasonable remuneration may constitute the reasonable terms on the commercial exploitation and the importation for that purpose, and the size of reasonable remuneration could correspond to a normal licence fee in the semiconductor industry. In case the parties cannot agree upon reasonable terms on the commercial exploitation, the issue may be decided by the courts.[886]

486. If a person has obtained registration of a topography and another person subsequently proves to be entitled to the registration, the registration may be transferred to the entitled person by court decision.[887] In that case, the former person, who has been deprived of the registration, has exploited the topography commercially in Denmark in good faith or has made substantial preparations for the commercial exploitation of the topography in Denmark, is permitted to continue the initiated or planned exploitation against reasonable remuneration to the right owner and on reasonable terms, in addition, to maintain the general character of the initiated or planned exploitation. Under similar conditions, the same applies in favour of registered licensees.[888] Rights conferred on the basis of section 11 paragraph 4 of the Act can only be transferred to other parties as an integrated part of the company in which the rights are exploited or in which the rights are planned to be exploited.[889]

§8. Duration of Protection

487. The period of protection starts running from the day where the topography is commercially exploited for the first time or from the day where an application for registration of the topography is filed with the Patent and Trademark Office in due form.[890] The earlier of the two days shall apply. In certain cases, it is considered convenient for the producer of a topography to be able to test the topography in a commercial context before filing an application for registration, and that is the reason for granting protection at a date earlier than the day when the application has been filed. Protection from the day where the topography for the first time is commercially exploited requires that an application is filed with the Patent and Trademark Office at the latest two years after the first day of commercial exploitation and that the application results in a registration of the topography. In the period of time between the first day of commercial exploitation and the day where the application is filed with the Patent and Trademark Office, the topography is protected by the provisions in section 23 of the Marketing Practices Act and the provisions on protection of trade secrets in the Trade Secrets Act and in the Civil Penal Code.[891]

488. The duration of protection of topographies is ten years from the end of the calendar year in which the topography is first commercially exploited anywhere in

886. Cf. FT 1987–1988, A, col. 599–600.
887. Cf. s. 11 para. 2 of the Act.
888. Cf. s. 11 para. 4 of the Act. The provision is similar to s. 53 para. 2 of the Patents Act.
889. Section 11 para. 5. The provision is similar to s. 53 para. 3 of the Patents Act.
890. Section 5 para. 2 subparas 1 and 2 of the Act.
891. Cf. FT 1987–1988, A, col. 597.

the world or in which an application for registration is filed with the Patent and Trademark Office.[892] The right of protection expires after ten years from the end of the calendar year, implying that in certain cases almost eleven years of protection is available. Compared to other intellectual property rights, the duration of protection of topographies is relatively short. In the preparatory works,[893] it is argued that ten years of protection should meet the practical needs of the industry in consideration of the rapid technological progress in the semiconductor industry and the interest of the general public in appropriating the new technology.

489. The possibility of obtaining a registration of a topography is forfeited if the topography is not commercially exploited within a specific period of time. Thus, according to section 5 paragraph 4 of the Act, where an application for registration of the topography has not been filed with the Patent and Trademark Office or where the topography has not been commercially exploited within a period of fifteen years from its first fixation or encoding, any exclusive rights can no longer come into existence.[894]

§9. Infringement and Remedies

I. Infringement

490. In a prospective legal dispute, the practical value of a registration is confined to establishing the right owner's claim in respect of time and scope on the condition that the registration is not revoked. Since the registration is not contingent on a substantial examination of the conditions of protection, thus, the Patent and Trademark Office does not conduct a search of pre-existing topographies, the registration de facto constitutes a presumption of the existence of the right and the owner of the right.

491. Where an application for registration of a topography has been filed, and a person other than the applicant proves to be entitled to the registration, by request, the Patent and Trademark Office shall transfer the application to the entitled person.[895] Where a person has obtained a registration and another person proves to be entitled to the registration, the registration may be transferred to the entitled person by court decision.[896] The entitled person who requests a transfer of an application or a registration shall personally satisfy the conditions stipulated in the Act.[897] Thus, the entitled person cannot obtain a registration if it is excluded due to the time limits in section 5 paragraphs 1 and 4 of the Act.[898]

892. Section 5 para. 3 of the Act. Cf. Art. 7(3) of the Directive.
893. Cf. FT 1987–1988, A, col. 598.
894. Cf. Art. 7(4) of the Directive.
895. Section 11 para. 1 of the Act.
896. *Ibid.*
897. *Ibid.*, para. 3 of the Act.
898. The provisions of s. 11 of the Act are based on Art. 4(6) of the Directive.

II. Remedies

492. Like the other intellectual property Acts, the Act on topographies does not contain provisions on injunctions. In case of infringement, interim injunctions may be rescinded according to the provisions of the Act on Civil Proceedings (*see supra* paragraphs 134 f. and 236 f.

493. Section 14 of the Act on liability is identical to the corresponding provisions of the other intellectual property Acts (*see supra* paragraphs 136 f. and 238 f.).

494. By virtue of section 16 of the Act, infringement of the right may be sanctioned by liability to punishment. Section 16 was included into the Act with special reference to piracy concerning products protected by intellectual property rights. Intentional violations of section 6 paragraph 1 of the Act, which states the scope of the exclusive rights, are punished with a fine. Additionally, a person who advances erroneous or misleading statements or suppresses information of importance to the case in connection with an application for registration is punished with a fine. The latter form of liability to punishment has to be seen in the light of the fact that the applicant decides which information is enclosed with the application, and the Patent and Trademark Office only conducts a formal examination of the application. Where the violation is committed by a company or another legal person, the company as such is liable to a fine. In aggravating circumstances, the infringer may be liable to imprisonment.

495. Section 15 of the Act on destruction, seizure and recall is identical to section 59 of the Patents Act (*see supra* paragraph 240).

496. Section 15a of the Act on the publication of judgments is identical to the corresponding provisions of the other intellectual property Acts (*see supra* paragraphs 142 and 244).

497. The provisions of the Act on Civil Proceedings on search and right of information (*see supra* paragraphs 139-140 and 241-242 apply to rights of protection of topographies.

§10. Overlapping and Relation to Other Intellectual Property Laws

498. The sui generis right under the Act is partially cumulative; thus, it does not exclude protection of semiconductor products under patent law and design law. According to section 10 paragraph 2 of the Copyright Act, topographies of semiconductor products are excluded from copyright protection. However, a semiconductor product may include a computer program protected by copyright. This may create a rather obscure situation concerning the proper regime of protection. The topography is only protected under the Act on Protection of Topographies of Semiconductor Products, but where the topography embodies a computer program, the computer program as such is copyright protected if it satisfies the conditions of copyright protection.[899] The exclusion of topographies from copyright protection indicates a relatively close connection between the Act on Protection of Topographies of Semiconductor Products and the principles of protection in copyright law.

499. In principle, topographies of semiconductor products may be patented, but in most cases, topographies do not manifest a sufficiently inventive step to qualify for patent protection. Protection under the Act on Protection of Topographies of Semiconductor Products aims at acts of forming and elaborating specific topographies, which, normally, is a process falling outside the scope of patent protection.[900]

500. Though it cannot be excluded, it is questionable whether topographies of semiconductor products may be protected by design rights. Protection under the Designs Act aims at the external appearance of a product including ornamentations. Additionally, the protection of an industrial design requires novelty on the day of submission of the application for registration of an industrial design right, which is a more rigorous condition than 'not being commonplace in the industry'.[901]

501. Protection of topographies may to a certain extent be sought under the law of unfair competition. Section 3 of the Marketing Practice Act establishes a general norm for the exercise of business activities and prohibits any activity that is contrary to 'good marketing practice'. 'Marketing' in the sense of the Act is a very broad concept including any market-related business activity. *Inter alia,* section 3 provides protection against imitations of products. All product imitations are not in violation of section 3; violation implies that the imitation has to be marketed in an unfair way, and furthermore, it must have adverse implications on the market for the original product. Slavish imitation of a competitor's product will in many cases be unfair if the former product is put on the market; thus, a literal copy of a competitor's topography may be in violation of section 3 where the original topography does not satisfy the conditions of protection under the Act on Protection of Topographies of Semiconductor Products.[902]

502. The provisions on trade secrets may also prove an important means of de facto protection of topographies of semiconductor products.

899. *See* Schmidt (1989), 334 ff.
900. Cf. *ibid.*, 336.
901. Cf. Report No. 1064 Copenhagen 1986, '*Ophavsret og edb*', 75 ff.
902. In case the imitated topography is integrated in a complex product, for example, electric appliances, it is more uncertain whether protection is available under s. 1; *see* Report No. 1064 Copenhagen 1986, '*Ophavsret og edb*', 78 ff.

Chapter 9. Trade Secrets/Confidential Information

§1. Sources – Legislation

503. Directive (EU) 2016/943 on the protection of undisclosed know-how and business information (trade secrets) against their unlawful acquisition, use and disclosure was implemented in Denmark in 2018.[903] Before the coming into force of the Act, the most important means to protect trade secrets was section 23 of the Marketing Practice Act. Section 23 of the Marketing Practice Act is now revoked but case law decided under section 23 is to a certain extent considered to have precedential value. It is thus stated in the preparatory works to the Act that the concept of a trade secret that developed in case law under section 23 corresponds to the definition of a trade secret in the Trade Secrets Directive.[904]

Supplementary protection of trade secrets is provided by the provisions of sections 263 and 264 of the Civil Penal Code[905] on industrial espionage.

§2. The Protection of Trade Secrets/Confidential Information

I. Subject Matter of Protection and Conditions of Protection

504. A trade secret is defined in section 2 of the Act as information that:

(a) is secret in the sense that it is not, in its entirety or in its precise form or composition, generally known among or readily accessible to persons in the circles that normally deal with that type of information;
(b) has commercial value because it is secret; and
(c) has, in the circumstances, been subject to reasonable measures of secrecy by the person lawfully in control of the information.

The definition comprises information of a technical as well as a commercial nature; for example, drawings, descriptions, recipes, formulas, customer lists, customer records and price calculations.

The Act also defines the concept of 'infringing goods' which means goods whose design, characteristics, function, production process or marketing substantially ben efit from trade secrets that have been illegally acquired, used or disclosed.[906]

The Act does not include any stipulations on what kind of information is not protected under the Act. However, the Trade Secrets Directive states that:

> The definition of trade secret excludes trivial information and the experience and skills gained by employees in the normal course of their employment, and

903. Act No. 309 of 25 Apr. 2018.
904. T. Riis & J. Schovsbo, *Lov om forretningshemmeligheder – med kommentarer* (Copenhagen: Ex Tuto, 2019), 92 f.
905. Consolidated Act No. 434 of 25 Apr. 2024 with later amendments.
906. Cf. s. 2 para. (iv) of the Act.

> also excludes information which is generally known among, or is readily accessible to, persons within the circles that normally deal with the kind of information in question.[907]

It also follows from the Directive that the protection of trade secrets shall not be understood to offer any ground for restricting the mobility of employees. In particular, in relation to the exercise of such mobility, protection shall not offer any ground for: (a) limiting employees' use of information that does not constitute a trade secret; (b) limiting employees' use of experience and skills honestly acquired in the normal course of their employment; (c) imposing any additional restrictions on employees in their employment contracts other than restrictions imposed in accordance with Union law or national law.[908]

505. A trade secret presupposes that the underlying information is significant to the enterprise and that the information has been revealed only to a limited number of the enterprise's employees. If the information is known to a larger part of the relevant branch of trade, no trade secret exists. Accordingly, to a certain extent, the enterprise may influence which information is to be considered a trade secret protectable under the Act.

506. A 'trade secret holder' is any natural or legal person who legally controls a trade secret.[909]

II. Scope of Exclusive Rights and Limitations on the Scope of Protection

A. *Scope of Exclusive Rights*

507. The scope of the exclusive rights is stipulated in section 4 of the Act. Section 4 is structured in four paragraphs. Paragraph 1 concerns the *acquisition* of a trade secret without the consent of the trade secret holder; paragraph 2 concerns the *use or disclosure* of a trade secret without the consent of the trade secret holder; paragraph 3 concerns the *acquisition, use or disclosure* of a trade secret; whereas paragraph 4 concerns acts relating to *infringing goods.*

Acquiring a trade secret without the consent of the trade secret holder is considered an illegal act if the trade secret is acquired by:

(1) unauthorized access to, appropriation or copying of documents, objects, materials, substances or electronic files lawfully controlled by the trade secret holder that contain a trade secret or from which a trade secret can be derived; or

---

907. Recital 14.
908. Cf. s. 1 para. 3 of the Act.
909. Cf. s. 2 para. (ii) of the Act.

(2) any other behaviour that, under the circumstances, is considered contrary to honest business practice.[910]

508. Trade secrets may be acquired by copying or reproducing the information by other technical means, as well as by memorizing the information. If trade secrets have been acquired by removing drawings, models and the like, it may in the specific circumstances be considered theft within the meaning of the Civil Penal Code.

The use or disclosure of a trade secret without the consent of the trade secret holder is considered an illegal act if the trade secret is used or disclosed by a person who has:

(1) acquired the trade secret unlawfully;
(2) breached a confidentiality agreement or any other obligation not to disclose the trade secret; or
(3) breached a contractual obligation or any other obligation to restrict the use of the trade secret.[911]

The acquisition, use or disclosure of a trade secret is also considered an unlawful act if, at the time of the acquisition, use or disclosure, a person knew or under the circumstances should have known that the trade secret had been acquired directly or indirectly from another person who used or disclosed the trade secret unlawfully, in accordance to section 4 paragraph 2.[912] Compared to section 4 paragraphs 1 and 2, section 4 paragraph 3 extends the number of persons who can be liable under the Act. It is comparable to the criminal concept of possession of stolen goods and, hence, it requires that the person knew or under the circumstances should have known that the information infringed rights in trade secrets. The production, offering for sale or marketing of infringing goods or the import, export or storage of infringing goods for that purpose shall also be considered unlawful use of a trade secret if the person carrying out these activities knew or, under the circumstances, should have known that the trade secret had been used unlawfully, in accordance to subsection 2.[913]

509. Sections 6 and 7 of the Act contain provisions on the protection of trade secrets during litigation. The rationale behind these provisions is that a trade secret holder should not abstain from enforcing the rights before the courts out of fear that the trade secrets in question are revealed. To this effect, some of the ordinary rules of civil procedure are modified to the benefit of the trade secret holder. However, is not clear that the specific rules in the Trade Secrets Act on the protection of trade secrets during litigation should be very effective.[914]

910. Cf. s. 4 para. 1 of the Act.
911. Cf. s. 4 para. 2 of the Act.
912. Cf. s. 4 para. 3 of the Act.
913. Cf. s. 4 para. 4 of the Act.
914. *See* T. Riis & J. Schovsbo, 2019, 164 f.

B. Limitations on the Scope of Protection

510. Section 3 of the Act stipulates a number of limitations on the scope of protection. First, the acquisition of a trade secret is considered a lawful act if the trade secret is acquired by independent discovery or creation.[915] One can argue that formally, this provision is not a limitation on the scope of protection but rather a delimitation of protectable subject matter under the Act. A similar principle of excluding independent discovery or creation from the scope of protection is also applicable in copyright law.

511. Second, the acquisition of a trade secret is considered a lawful act if the trade secret is acquired by observation, examination, disassembly or testing of a product or object to which the public has access or which the person acquiring the information lawfully possesses and where that person is not bound by any legally valid obligation to restrict the acquisition of the trade secret.[916] The possibility of reverse engineering is also relevant in relation to the conditions of protection. If it is very easy to extract claimed trade secrets from a marketed product by reverse engineering, arguably, the information has not been subject to reasonable measures of secrecy by the person lawfully in control of the information and, thus, the conditions of protection as a trade secret are not satisfied. Hence, the reverse engineering limitation in section 3 paragraph (ii) has only practical significance in cases where it requires a certain amount of effort and skills to reverse engineer successfully.

512. Third, the acquisition of a trade secret is considered a lawful act if the trade secret is acquired by the exercise of information and consultation rights of employees or employees' representatives in accordance with EU law and national law or practice.[917]

513. Fourth, the acquisition of a trade secret is considered a lawful act if the trade secret is acquired by any other practice which, in the circumstances, is consistent with honest business practice.[918]

514. Furthermore, section 5 of the Act stipulates that the rights of trade secrets cannot be enforced in the following situations:

(1) the acquisition, use or disclosure is made to exercise the right to freedom of information and expression, including respect for media freedom and media pluralism;
(2) the acquisition, use or disclosure is made to uncover wrongdoing, irregularities or illegal activities, and the defendant acted to protect the general public interest (whistleblowing);

915. Cf. s. 3 para. 1 subpara. (i) of the Act.
916. Cf. s. 3 para. 1 subpara. (ii) of the Act.
917. Cf. s. 3 para. 1 subpara. (iii) of the Act.
918. Cf. s. 3 para. 1 subpara. (iv) of the Act.

(3) the trade secret is disclosed by employees to their representatives in the course of the legitimate performance of their duties by those representatives in accordance with Union or national law, where the disclosure is necessary for the performance of those duties.

III. Remedies

515. Rights in trade secrets are not covered by the scope of the Enforcement Directive.[919] Member states may in their national legislation decide to make the provisions of the Enforcement Directive applicable to rights in trade secrets, and a few Member States have done so.[920] But there is no obligation to extend the scope of the Enforcement Directive in this way. Accordingly, there was a need to include enforcement provisions in the Trades Secrets Directive if the enforcement of rights in trade secrets also should be harmonized. Obviously, the easy and simple solution would have been to extend the scope of application of the Enforcement Directive to trade secrets by copying the provisions of the Enforcement Directive into the Trade Secrets Directive. But the EU legislator did not opt for that solution. Some provisions of the Enforcement Directive were copied into the Trade Secrets Directive; others were copied in a modified form, while still others were left out, and a few new enforcement provisions were introduced.[921]

516. Partly, as a consequence of the EU approach to the harmonization of enforcement of rights in trade secrets, the specific provisions on search for the purpose of preserving evidence are not available in trade secrets cases. The same applies to the right of information, which is only available in intellectual property cases.

517. The Danish Act on Trade Secrets contains provisions on interim injunctions (section 8); handing over infringing goods to the trade secret holder (section 9); assistance in maintaining a prohibition or injunction (section 10); damages for unwarranted interim injunctions (section 11); judgments on prohibition or injunction (section 12–13); laches (section 14); damages (section 15); default fines (section 16); publication of judgments (section 17); penalties (section 18).

518. The provisions in section 8 on interim injunctions are to a large extent inspired by the similar provision in the Act on Civil Proceedings with some notable differences. In general, the conditions for being granted an interim injunction have been eased in the Trade Secrets Act compared to the Act on Civil Proceedings. First, one of the five conditions for being granted an interim injunction in the Act on Civil

919. Statement by the Commission concerning Art. 2 of Directive 2004/48/EC of the European Parliament and of the Council on the enforcement of intellectual property rights (2005/295/EC), OJ L 94, 13.4.2005, p. 37.

920. Italy, Portugal, Slovak Republic and to a certain extent in Romania.

921. *See* T. Riis. *Enforcement of rights in trade secrets*, in J. Schovsbo, T. Minssen & T. Riis (eds). *The Harmonization and Protection of Trade Secrets in the EU. An Appraisal of the EU Directive* (Edward Elgar, 2020).

Proceedings is not required under the Trade Secrets Act, and that is the condition that the ability of the claimant to enforce her/his right will be lost if the party has to await a full trial. Second, section 8 paragraph 3 enumerates eight circumstances that shall be taken into consideration in assessing the proportionality of granting an interim injunction.[922] Arguably, the court is precluded from taking into account other circumstances. The proportionality principle in the Act on Civil Proceedings is 'open' and thus not limited to 8 specific circumstances. Consequently, it must be assumed that the proportionality principle in the Act on Civil Proceedings is more effective and potentially can prevent more injunctions from being granted compared to the Trade Secrets Act.

519. Section 8 is supplemented by section 9 and 15.[923] If the court grants an interim injunction or order pursuant to section 8, the court may, at the request of the trade secret holder, at the same time decide on the handing over to the trade secret holder the allegedly infringing goods if there are specific reasons to assume that they will be used to infringe the injunction or order, cf. section 9. According to section 15, the bailiff's Court may, in the event of non-compliance with an interim injunction or order at the request of the trade secret holder, impose a penalty fine on the party against whom the prohibition, order or measure is directed.

520. According to the penalty provision of section 18 of the Act, violation of section 4 of the Act is punishable by a fine or imprisonment for up to one year and six months, unless a higher penalty is prescribed under section 299 a of the Civil Penal Code, if the person concerned:

(1) is in an employment or cooperative relationship with the trade secret holder or performs a task for the trade secret holder;
(2) has lawful access to the trade secret holder's business; or
(3) has been entrusted with technical drawings, descriptions, recipes, models, etc., in connection with the performance of work.

521. As regards the legal content, section 15 of the Act on damages appears identical to the corresponding damages provisions in the intellectual property acts.

§3. Industrial Espionage

522. Intruders upon the enterprise's premises who acquire trade secrets are considered industrial espionage, which is governed by the pertinent provisions of the Civil Penal Code. The provisions of the Civil Penal Code on industrial espionage are applicable to the intrusion by others than employees and cooperative partners

922. Section 17 para. 3 of the Act on publication of judgments contains a proportionality principle that also enumerates a number of circumstances that shall be taken into consideration in assessing proportionality in relation to a decision on publication of judgments. However, s. 17 only enumerates five circumstances and not eight as in s. 8.
923. Section 10 of the Act is also a supplement to s. 8.

upon the enterprise's business premises. By virtue of section 263 paragraph 3, cf. section 263 paragraphs 1 and 2, any unauthorized person who intentionally opens or withdraws from somebody a letter, a telegram or another sealed message, and avails himself/herself of the content, with the purpose of appropriating an enterprise's trade secrets, or in other particularly aggravating circumstances, is liable to a fine or imprisonment for a term not exceeding six years. The same applies to any unauthorized person who intentionally gains access to the secret compartments of others, and persons who by using a device to secretly listen or record statements made in private, telephone conversations, or other conversations or negotiations taking place in closed rooms in which such a person does not participate or to which such a person has gained unauthorized access.

523. According to the general rule of section 264 paragraph 1 of the Civil Penal Code, any unauthorized person who gains access to the house of another or to some other private place is liable to a fine or imprisonment for a term not exceeding six months. If the acts referred to in section 264 paragraph 1 are committed with the purpose of appropriating trade secrets of an enterprise or in other aggravating circumstances, the offence may carry a more severe penalty of imprisonment for a term not exceeding six years. Particularly aggravating circumstances include cases where the offence is committed under such circumstances that it causes significant harm to others or involves a particular risk thereof.[924]

524. The penalty provisions of sections 263 and 264 of the Civil Penal Code are also applicable to a person who has not committed an offence mentioned in sections 263 and 264 but nevertheless has made unauthorized use of or has availed himself/herself of information that has been furnished by such an offence.[925]

924. Cf. s. 264 para. 2 of the Civil Penal Code.
925. Cf. s. 264c of the Civil Penal Code.

Selected Bibliography

Andersen, M.B. & M. Koktvedgaard. *Bioteknologi og patentret*. Copenhagen: Forskningsdirektoratet, 1990.

Andersen, M.B. *Lov om arbejdstageres opfindelser*. Copenhagen: Akademikernes Centralorganisation, 1995.

Andersen, N.M., A. Carlquist & A. Rubinstein. *Retshåndhævelse af immaterialrettigheder*. Copenhagen: Jurist-og Økonomforbundets Forlag, 2006.

Bender, H. *Edb-rettigheder*. Copenhagen: Jurist-og Økonomforbundets Forlag, 1998.

Blomqvist, J. *Overdragelse af ophavsrettigheder*. Copenhagen: Jurist-og Økonomforbundets Forlag, 1986.

Blume, P. *Databaseret*. Copenhagen: Forlaget FSR, 1996.

Brinck-Jensen, J, M. Rosenmeier, J. Schovsbo & T. Sommer. *Ansattes immaterialle rettigheder*. Copenhagen: Jurist-og Økonomforbundets Forlag, 2013.

Carlsen, R. *Varemærker – Registreringspraksis*. Copenhagen: Direktoratet for Patent-og varemærkevæsenet, 1980.

Deichmann, H.K. *Programkoncepter. Ophavsret til tv-formater*. Copenhagen: Forlaget Thomson GadJura, 2002.

Dybdahl, L. *Europæisk patent*. 2nd edn. Copenhagen: Forlaget Thomson. GadJura, 2004.

Frøbert, K.A. *Retten til tekst, lyd og billeder*. 2nd edn. Akademisk Forlag, 1996.

Jakobsen, T.H. & A.L. Schelin. *Ophavsretten i medierne*. Copenhagen: Christian Ejlers Forlag, 1997.

Karnøe, L. (ed.). *Immaterialret. Indhold – værdiansættelse – skat*. Copenhagen: Thomson Reuters, 2008.

Koktvedgaard, M. & L. Østerborg. *Patentloven*. 2nd edn. Copenhagen: Juristforbundets Forlag, 1979.

Koktvedgaard, M. *Immaterialretspositioner*. Copenhagen: Jurist-og Økonomforbundets Forlag, 1965.

Lindgreen, N., J. Schovsbo, T. Sommer & J. Thorsen, *Patentloven med kommentarer*. Copenhagen: Jurist-og Økonomforbundets Forlag, 2024.

Lund, T. *Ophavsretsloven og fotografiloven*. Copenhagen: GEC Gads Forlag, 1961.

Madsen, P.B. *Markedsret – Del 3*. 8th edn. Copenhagen: Jurist-og Økonomforbundets Forlag, 2023.

Pedersen, M.D. *Bogen om ophavsretten*. Copenhagen: oplagEditio, 1998.

Petersen, C.S. *Immaterialrettigheder og foreløbige forbud*. Copenhagen: Jurist-og Økonomforbundets Forlag, 2008.

Petersen, C.S., P.M. Hansen & T. Riis. *Judicielle forbud/påbud og immaterialretsproces*. Copenhagen: 2015.
Riis, T. *Enerettigheder og vederlagsrettigheder. Håndhævelse af immaterialrettigheder i økonomisk perspektiv*. Copenhagen: Jurist-og Økonomforbundets Forlag, 2005.
Riis, T. *Immaterialret & IT*. Copenhagen: Jurist-og Økonomforbundets Forlag, 2001.
Riis, T. & Schovsbo, J. *Lov om forretningshemmeligheder – med kommentarer* (Copenhagen: Ex Tuto, 2019).
Rosenmeier, M. *Ophavsret for begyndere. En bog til ikke-jurister*. 4th edn. Copenhagen: UBVA, Jurist-og Økonomforbundets Forlag, 2018 (https://ubva.dk/wp-content/uploads/2020/01/ophavsret-for-begyndere-4udgave.pdf).
Rosenmeier, M. *Ophavsretlig beskyttelse af musikværker*. Copenhagen: Jurist-og Økonomforbundets Forlag, 1996.
Rosenmeier, M. *Værkslæren i ophavsretten*. Copenhagen: Jurist-og Økonomforbundets Forlag, 2001.
Rothe, B. *Ophavsrettens stedbørn*. Copenhagen: Jurist-og Økonomforbundets Forlag, 1987.
Ryberg, B. *Beskyttelsesomfanget i dansk patentret*. Copenhagen: Gjellerup, 2002.
Schlüter, J., J. Bay & J.P. Mathiasen. *Musikaftaler*. Paradigma, Copenhagen: Forlaget Thomson, 2006.
Schmidt, P.H. *Retsbeskyttelse af edb-programmer*. Copenhagen: GadJura, 1998.
Schmidt, P.H. *Teknologi og immaterialret*. Copenhagen: GEC Gad, 1989.
Schønning, P. & J. Blomqvist. *International ophavsret*. Copenhagen: Jurist-og Økonomforbundets Forlag, 2011.
Schønning, P. *Ophavsretsloven med kommentarer*. 8th edn. Copenhagen: Karnov Group, 2024.
Schønning, P., et al. *Grundlæggende immaterialret*. 2nd edn. Copenhagen: Gjellerup, 2009.
Schovsbo, J. & M. Rosenmeier & Clement Salung Petersen. *Immaterialret*. 7th edn. Copenhagen: Jurist-og Økonomforbundets Forlag, 2024.
Schovsbo, J. & N.H. Svendsen. *Designret*. 2nd edn. Copenhagen: Jurist-og Økonomforbundet Forlag, 2013.
Schovsbo, J. *Grænsefladespørgsmål mellem immaterialretten og konkurrenceretten*. Copenhagen: Jurist-og Økonomforbundets Forlag, 1996. (On the interface between intellectual property law and competition law).
Schovsbo, J. *Immaterialretsaftaler – fra kontrakt til status i kontraktsretten*. Copenhagen: Jurist-og Økonomforbundets Forlag, 2001. (On the interface between intellectual property law and contract law).
Schovsbo, J. *Lov om opfindelser ved offentlige forskningsinstitutioner*. Copenhagen: Jurist-og Økonomforbundets Forlag, 2001.
Skovbo, E.A. *Erstatning for ophavsretlige krænkelser*. Copenhagen: Forlaget Thomasson GadJura, 2005.
Stoltze, L. *Internetret*. Copenhagen: Nyt Juridisk Forlag, 2001.
Trzaskowski, J. (ed.) *Internetretten*. 4th edn. Copenhagen: Ex Tuto Publishing, 2024.
Udsen, H. *IT-retten*. 5th edn. Copenhagen: Ex Tuto, 2021.

Wallberg, K. & M.F. Ravn. *Varemærkeloven*. Copenhagen: Jurist-og Økonomforbundets Forlag, 2021.

Wiborg, O., O.M. Nielsen & B. Ryberg. *Opfindelser Patenter Licenser*. Copenhagen: Thomson Forlaget FSR, 2000.

Selected Bibliography

Index

The numbers here refer to paragraph numbers.

Index

Index

www.ingramcontent.com/pod-product-compliance
Ingram Content Group UK Ltd.
Pitfield, Milton Keynes, MK11 3LW, UK
UKHW020138290926
15471UKWH00003B/560

9 789403 518992